# GLOBALISATION BETWEEN GLOOM AND PROSPERITY

# GLOBALISATION BETWEEN GLOOM AND PROSPERITY

Arvind Singh

KALPAZ

Globalisation Between Gloom and Prosperity



ISBN-978-81-7835-959-5



Published in 2013 in India by
Kalpaz Publications,
C-30 Satyawati Nagar
Delhi-110 052.

E-mail: Kalpaz@hotmail.com

*Laser Typesetting* : Awadhesh Computers, Delhi

*Printed at:* G. Print Process Delhi

"Dedicates"

*Asha, Aditya, and Apoorva*

# Contents

# List of Figures and Tables

# Preface

The writing of this book has been pure pleasure–not withstanding personal diversions. The major objective of this study is an appraisal of the dynamics of globalisation, with its attendant ramifications, and underpinnings that have bearing on nation state, communities and people. The stark polarisation evident in economic realms, with its cycles of shocks, and recessions, underneath has seemingly transformed the character of life, visions and dreams. The transition to quick gains, no-holds-barred profiteering by multinationals, institutions and responsibility deficit palpable in public bodies all over the world is an agonizing pointer to the phenomenon of globalisation.

As it stands, this is an analytical and exploratory work. The literature on globalisation resonates with the specialized strands of economists, sociologists and development theorists, who cast their indelible imprint of their disciplines. I have attempted to weave through the diverse disciplines under one shade, in a lucid style to reach the lay readers and the academia. Myriad questions pertaining to globalisation are answered by combining an overarching analytical approach and a multilevel empirical enquiry. My main goal is not theory building rather to purely account for the causative factors, dynamics and patterns as they impinge upon plethora of issues affecting human conditions.

*Arvind Singh*

# Acknowledgements

I am deeply grateful to the several institutions and many people who have been generous in helping me during the years I worked on the globalisation theme. Foremost among these is the Indian Institute of Advance Studies Shimla, which provided me with admirable support and a lively intellectual home for over three years. Here the inputs of Professor Peter Dsouza, director IIAS, Professor Naim, Chicago University, Professor Madhurendra Kumar, Kumaun University Nainital, Professor Harbans Mukhia, JNU Delhi prooved vital in shaping my thoughts on issues. Professor Gail Omvedts searching criticisms helped me in reviewing my empirical datas. During the course of my work I am personally indebted to Pranay Krishna Srivastav, Allahabad University, Professor APS Chauhan Jiwaji University Gwalior, Professor Ronki Ram, Panjab University Chandigarh, who helped me in fetching datas on various issues. At personal level my gratitude extends to my friends Dr Niranjan Kumar Singh and VP Mall who accopmpanied me on my visits across India, to show that a bigger part of humanity is still outside the network society, growling under the burden of abysmal poverty.

My gratitude also extends to my Publisher Kalpaz Publications, for having done a commendable work in editing and coming out with the issue in the necessary time frame.

# Abbreviations

| | | |
|---|---|---|
| AOA | — | Agreement on Agriculture |
| APEC | — | Asia Pacific Economic Cooperation |
| ASEAN | — | Association of South-East Asian Nations |
| CARICOM | — | Caribbean Community |
| CATW | — | Coalition Against Trafficking in Woman |
| CSD | — | Commission for Sustainable Development |
| DAN | — | Direct Action Network |
| ECOWAS | — | Economic Community of West African States |
| EFF | — | Extended Fund Facility |
| ESAF | — | Enhanced Structural Adjustment Facility |
| EU | — | European Union |
| FDI | — | Foreign Direct Investment |
| GATT | — | General Agreement on Tariff and Trade |
| GCC | — | The Gulf Cooperation Council |
| GDI | — | Gender related Development Index |
| GEF | — | Global Environment Facility |
| GEM | — | Gender Empowerment Measure |
| GLASOD | — | Global Assessment of Soil Degradation |
| GM | — | Genetically Modified |
| HDI | — | Human Development Index |

| | | |
|---|---|---|
| HDR | — | Human Development Report |
| HLABSD | — | High Level Advisory Board on Sustainable Development |
| HNI | - | High Networth Individuals |
| ILO | — | International Labour Organisation |
| ISRIC | — | International Soil Reference and Information Centre. |
| LAIA | — | Latin American Integration Association |
| MNC | — | Multinational Corporations |
| NAFTA | — | North American Free Trade Agreement |
| OECD | — | Organisation of Economic Community and Development |
| PGA | — | People's Global Action |
| PTA | — | Preferential Trade area for Eastern and Southern African States |
| RTI | — | Right to Information |
| SAARC | — | The South Asian Association for Regional Cooperation |
| SADCC | — | Southern African Development Coordination Conference |
| SAF | — | Structural Adjustment Facility |
| TPPI | — | Technological Production Process Innovations |
| UNCED | — | United Nation's Conference on Environment and Development |
| UNDP | — | United Nation's Development Programme |
| UNEP | — | United Nation's Environment Programme |

| | | |
|---|---|---|
| UNFCC | – | United Nation's Framework Convention on Climate Change |
| UNICEF | – | United Nation's Children's Fund |
| WSF | – | World Social Forum |
| WTO | – | World Trade Organisation |

# 1

# Introduction

## Conceptualising Globalisation

Globalisation as a process defies clear definition, it possesses different meanings for different groups, having a variety of agendas. Globalisation as a term became fashionable about the mid 1980s, when it began to replace terms like 'internationalisation' and 'transnationalisation' as a better concept for describing the ever intensifying networks of cross-border human interaction. Much of the exercise is expanded on the current debate, on globalisation centers, on the nature of the process, whether it is merely another stage in the inexorable march of capitalism, or it is a distinct and new experience which locates capitalist expansion within a broader: political, environmental, social and cultural superstructure, more so than earlier global excursions of capital. Much of the confusion pertaining to definition of globalisation arises from the wrong notions, i.e internationalisation (as in the increasing interwovenness of national economies through international trade) and trasnationalisation (as in the increasing organisation of production on a cross-border basis by multinational organisations). Thus, for example, economic globalisation is often perceived as a process in which distinct national economies, and therefore domestic strategies of national economics management are increasingly irrelevant.

The world has internationalised in its basic dynamics, it is dominated by uncontrollable market forces, and it has as its principal economic actors and major agents of change truly transnational corporations that owe allegiance to no nation-state and locate wherever in the global market advantage lies.[1]

Strong globalisationists, who are of the argument that the current globalisation is a distinctly new phenomenon, opine that previous periods of capitalist expansion, into the Third world lacked the speed, technological sophistication, economic integration and ideological commitment to functionalism, which are the hallmarks of globalisation in the twenty first century (e.f. OHMAE, 1990; 1995; Bryan and Farrell, 1996; Matheus, 1997). Strong globalisationists also underline the efficacy of the market over the state and take the neo-liberal position that globalisation has universally benign economic spinoffs. The proponents of this school adhere to the opinion that it is the multinational companies (MNCs) and not states that are the most effective providers of economic prosperity. The following key factors are stressed by theorists, supporting this thesis.[2]

1. The development and wide availability of low cost communication technology such as fibre optics cables, computers, internet, fax machines, digital transmissions and satellites, which has meant that the populations of states are increasingly becoming subjected to a 'global culture' that is beyond the power of individual governments to control;
2. The emergence of MNCs with predominant resources and power can rival with many states, but unlike states

are not rooted in geography and are easily able to relocate their plants according to shifting demand and the availability of local advantages such as cheap wage cost, low business taxes and weak trade unions;

3. The increasingly global nature of trade, has rendered states power ineffective. States have to respond to factors beyond their control such as imperatives of MNCs and the fluctuations of the world's financial markets overall, it is claimed that world markets and MNCs are more powerful forces in international affairs than states and that these new forces of globalisation cannot be effectively governed. Ohmae (1995) defines global change in terms of what he calls the four 'i's: investment, industry, information technology and individual consumers. He opines that investment via financial markets has grown rapidly in recent years, as technology has greatly increased the opportunity for speculators to bypass national government controls. Opportunities for investment are provided by globalised corporations, which unlike the old geographically bound firms are also to move swiftly into developing markets such as India and china. Global firms singular loyalty remains to their shareholders, rather than the particular country.

Soft or weak globalizations, on the other hand describe current global processes, simply as another stage in capitalist expansion (see, for example, *Sassen, 1998; Kennedy, 1993; Sjolander, 1996*). They insist that technology merely makes the process more efficient, not different from earlier phases in fundamental characteristics and objectives. Weak globalisationists contend further that the current globalisation is merely a hicup in western hegemony or, at best, the remodification of the structures that underpin that hegemony. The phenomenon is not new, it has merely been recent in the scintillating hues of high-tech. The internet may have replaced ocean vessels, but the basic operations of accumulating resources at the core remain essential to the process. The immediate post-second world war era may have required the formalisation of economic strategies through the Bretton Wood institutions, but the very structure of IMF and World Bank, still perpetuates the hegemonic economic order by the OECD nations (*Hirst and Thompson, 1996; Kapstein, 1991/92*).

In their book, 'Globalisation in question', Paul Hirst and Grahame Thompson, review the historical evidence of world trade and capital flows in relation to output, degrees of financial and monetary integration and the character of governance in the international economy. They give a surprising figure that the level of integration, interdependence and openness of national economies in the present era is not unprecedented. If one measures integration, by the amount of goods and services that are produced world wide, then it was the year 1913 when the percentage (the export ratio of production) reached 33 percent, compared to today which is 31 percent.[3] As far as the relative dominance of transnational corporations in world production and trade is concerned, there is a remarkable constancy, and not of a dramatic change in the long historical period. First in relation to total world output, the percentage share of world production subject to transnational corporate control has remained relatively stable. Similarly Paul Hirst and Grahame Thompson point out, as far as the leading OECD economies are concerned, international businesses are still largely confined to their home territory in terms of their overall business activity, that is in terms of location of sales, affiliates, declared profits, and research and finance.

While many globalists agree with Ohmae's neo-liberal interpretation, there are others who vehemently contradict him apart from the soft globalisationists. Noticeable among these is David Korten who in his book "When Corporations

Rule the World", stresses the global nature of world problems. Thus Korten notes the disintegrative effects of the ecologically unsustainable quest for continued economic growth, and the extremes of inequality between the world's rich and poor. In the face of these pressures traditional forms of governance seem incapable of resisting the process of economic globalisation that is shifting power away from government towards a handful of corporations and financial institutions (1995:12). Far from being beneficial as Ohmae argues, these developments and underpinnings are a modern form of the imperial phenomenon, whereby the undemocratic and short term drive for profit, at the expense of people, is the principle force guiding globalisation (*Korten; 1995:28*). For Korten, corporations are not a mere economic entities but rather they are 'dominant governance institutions'. Therefore they are barriers to, rather champions of, free markets and genuine competitions.

Similarly we must not confuse globalisation with the integration of real territorial economies worldwide. While globalisation has proceeded in the last few decades, the geographical reach of the world capitalism has actually receded. Thus, if we take as an indicator of global reach the percentage share of all five continents in world trade, then we find that the percentage share of two continents, Latin America and Africa in world trade has actually declined.[4] Likewise the global reach of foreign capital flows has declined by a wide margin since the colonial period.

## Globalisation and Third World

The scholarly exercise of differentiating between weak and strong globalisation may not be that relevant in the case of the third world where the major concern is with the effects of the process on the poor. Whether weak or strong, as in earlier historical episodes, the encounter between Western capital and the third world has not been a meeting of minds. To the contrary, the process has always been a specific drama orchestrated by strong hegemonic forces to solidify the interests of global capital. Towards this rules of admission, formalisation, engagement are constantly maneuvred, in order to co-opt selected sectors and classes into the global system and the majority of the people and the regions are increasingly marginalised. Globalisation project's most potent engine has been the neo-liberal position characterised by the unwarranted focus on roll back of state responsibility and faith in the market. Unfortunately, this position does not make clear how widespread privatisation of education, health, electricity, water supply and other basic services will improve standards of living in the third world.[5] An important task in the third world countries is the poverty-alleviation programme. The governments have to ensure that there is a broader mass participation in the consumption of critical goods and services. Given this condition, one may argue that even though state involvement may not be a sufficient condition for poverty alleviation, it is certainly a necessary one. The third world state has its well known shortcomings, which include corruption, mismanagement and unemployment. Yet, even with these problems, the state is still a necessary mechanism for distributing wealth in economies with nascent market structures. Although private enterprise may be more efficient and streamlined, it panders directly to the interests of the powerful by subordinating the concerns of the poor. In fact, the efficiency of the market derives directly from its ability to differentiate between need and wants, and to exclude the needy (those without purchasing power) from the consumption of many commodities. The uncharitableness of global market is exemplified by two recent events. first, the treaty on Multilateral Agreement on Investments (MAI) negotiated by twenty nine advanced countries aimed at denying the states the authority to give preferences to domestic or local capital over foreign capital. Second, the IMF's attempt to negotiate an amendment of its Articles of Agreement in order to obtain the authority to require member countries to commit to more complete liberalisation and restricting the powers of government to regulate the flow of currency. One can certainly ascribe these actions as unfriendly to poor people's need. These policies in fact give the market more power to subsume the state authority and to undermine the state authority of facilitating social welfare and poverty alleviation, over macro economic restructuring to liberalise trade.[6]

Few observers would deny that although many of the progressive economic, social and political changes that have occurred in Asia over the past quarter of a century can be attributed to globalisation, increasing international integration and interdependence have not benefited all Asian countries equally and some groups of people especially the poorest, have benefitted less or not at all. Walden Bello, a leading critic, contends that globalisation is a process controlled by the richer countries in North America and Western Europe to the world's poorer countries. He attributes much of the poverty and economic disparity in Asia to the damage caused by the financial crisis of the late 1990s and by foreign capital-intensive, low-wage export oriented economic development strategies adopted by Asian governments over the past thirty years. Pointing to regional, urban-rural, and income and class inequalities in many countries in the region, he argues that continued participation in a global trade and investment system dominated by Western countries will bring Asia more, rather than less economic and political instability. He contends along with other critics, that globally oriented economic development policies have relegated many Asian countries to the control of Western based transnational corporations and that growth driven by globalisation is resulting in economic, social and ecological devastation in the region.[7]

## Nature of Globalisation

Most books on the global economy define globalisation as a process in which there has been an unprecedented acceleration in the movement of information, commodities and people (*Anderson, Cavanagh and Lee, 2000:4-25*). However in order to classify how globalisation is implicated in the social constructions of scarcity, it is necessary to locate it at the center of a nexus of relations: technical, social, cultural and so on. Globalisation demands a set of policies that ironically create the social conditions that are said to result from the inevitable logic of global capital. It can be argued that processes of globalisation are promoted more by neo-liberal political ideology than economics.

Economic globalisation was made possible by new and revolutionary development in communication technology, which allowed the rapid transmission of numeric, textual and graphic information. It is this capacity to design structures in one place and realise them in tangible forms in another far removed place which allows companies like Nike, Gap and GM to organise tightly their far flung global networks. One result of this spatial organisation of the world economy is that a third of all international trade is not between countries but between branches of the same company. Intra-company transactions allow a firm to avoid taxes by setting prices to minimise earnings in countries with low tax rates, an accounting practice known as transfer pricing.[8] Similarly information technology has also given unprecedented mobility to capital, where billons of dollars move across national boundaries at lightening speed with little or no regulation. Thus foreign institutional investors and domestic institutional investors entry and exit on the stock market of developing countries, rides the waves, and makes headlines in the newspapers.

Robertson a sociologist has formulated interesting comparisons, on the process of globalisation. Earlier he held the view that processes of globalisation were being hindered by cultural and functional cleavages. He opines that there were earlier three cleavages: religious (between fundamental Islam and Christianity); Legal diplomatic between democracies and absolutist states (the West versus East divide); and industrial between cultures that emphasise norms consistent with industry (rationality, individualisation, impersonal authority and others) like (North-South divide). The potential for these cleavages is greatly enhanced these days as a result of space "compression" of the world, and global consciousness compression of the world is the real experience of the way that interdependencies are being created in the economies of the world to such an extent, that today the way we live our lives on this side of the globe has immediate consequences for people on the other side of the globe. If there is any shift in the preferences of consumption in Europe and America, then it may deeply affect jobs in the Far East and India. Industrial processes, and mode of production and growth could inevitably have environmental and ecological repercussions in the immediate neighbourhood. Big dam projects in India may cause flooding in Pakistan or Bangladesh. An earthquake in Japan, or a tsunami could cause a fall in the value of dollar. The forest burning practice in Saharan Africa or Brazil may cause holes in the Ozone layer. This is what is meant by "compression" in the world.

World compression is not an altogether a new idea, what makes it unique is that Robertson argues that "world compression" intensifies "global consciousness". Global consciousness is manifested in the way we, people all over the world, in a discourse unified through mass communication speak of military Political issues in terms of 'world order' or of economic issues as in international recession. We speak of 'world peace' and 'human rights' while issues of pollution and purification are talked about in terms of 'saving the planet'. Thus, although in Robertson's view, globalisation has been going on for a very long time, pre-dating even the rise of capitalism and modernity, it has accelerated only in the last decade or so, because it has moved to the level of consciousness.[9]

The emergence of corporate globalism has widely altered the relation between capital and labour. The bargaining power of the labour has been considerably weakened by capitals ability to shift production from one place to another, to threaten closing of branch plants and pull out and persuade third world governments to regulate and control labour on behalf of global firms. Thus in the last two decades the preferred choice of capital has been China, where the government's coercive tactics of disciplining labour has brought huge dividends to the corporations. Secondly, labour has also been weakened from the view point of consumption *(Barnet and Cavanagh, 1994: 283-209)*. Traditionally capital has drawn on labour not only for its productive power, but also on labour's capacity to consume products of firms. Henry Ford employed the thinking of paying labour to spur demand by $5 per day because of this rationale. Today corporate globalism has weakened the alliance between capital and labour because corporations do not depend on national markets alone (*Luttwalk, 1998: 91-99*). Thus even though India is a very poor country of over 125 million people for global firms, it represents a market of at least a 100 million class consumers.

An important theme that appears in the literature on globalisation and culture is the rapid homogenisations of culture. The larger cultural theme under globalisation is the intensified pressure to modernise, a matter that has received much attention in the work of the Swedish philosopher Helena

Norberg-Hodge (1991). The cultural pressure to modernise has ramifications in production, consumption and identity formation.[10] In the production's sphere, Western style schools isolate children from their culture and local environment, leaving them unable to use local resources. Politically the forces of economic globalisation have weakened the ability of national governments and undermined sovereignty and self-determination. Internationalisation of capital markets and the free management of money across borders have eroded the power of governments to regulate the economy through traditional Keynesian fiscal and monetary policy. Global firms relative independence to move in and out of borders has made government's job of regulating the economies quiet difficult. They turn out to be mute spectators in the casino game of capital. Third world governments are further weakened by their inability to pay mounting debts, which has brought them to the heels of the international monetary regulator such as IMF, World Bank and WTO (Ohmae, 1991; 1996; Lechner and Bali; 2000; 195-235).

Greatest fears in the Globalisation Discourse have been in the ecological sustainability. Production requires matter and energy as inputs. Globalisation has given global firms far more access to resources across borders than was possible under colonialism. While during colonialism, the corporations did not possess the hegemony of technology, today they are replete with it. Multinational companies like United fruit, Unilever and Nestle are involved in vast portions of international production and trade. In fact, transnationals directly or indirectly command 80 per cent of the land around the world that is cultivated for export crops such as bananas, tobacco and cotton (*Karliner* 1997:17); *Millions* of acres that once fed poor families in poor countries, are getting lost to corporate take over. The deforestation has intensified and firms like Georgia-pacific, and Sumitomo among many are the principal culprits. Economic globalisation has magnified, intensified and exported the scope of transforming our life support systems into repositories of waste leading to the globalisation of the ecological crisis.[11]

The evidence of this comes from global warming, acid rain, air pollution, deforestation, accelerated soil erosion and salinisation of irrigated land, water pollution from agricultural runoff and pesticides in food sources. Under economic globalisation third world countries have come to play a central role as repositories of hazardous waste. Nations such as Thailand, Indonesia and Mexico invite global firms with package deals of cheap non-union labour and almost non-existent environmental laws. Another aspect of this is the rapid rise of an export industry in toxic waste, chemical and nuclear, to be buried in land fills of poor countries (*Karliner, 1997*).

The supremacy of global finance and its tendency to appropriate profit has added high incidence of instability in the financial system. Floating exchange rates and reduced tariff barriers have made financial markets inherently instable. Fitzgerald outlines five aspects to this instability. First, financial markets are in permanent disequilibrium because demand always exceeds supply at the clearing rate of interest, because risk can never be fully reflected in this rate. Second, there is built-in disjuncture between the cost and time of interpreting information, especially information on the solvency of states (especially from 'emerging markets' in developing countries) on the one hand, and the intense speed of the necessary reactions on the other. Third, financial markets increasingly deal in future expectations which are by their nature uncertain. Fourth, existing regulative institutions can intensify the very flows they were intended to remedy.

The failures of rating agencies can lead to information-induced triggers of 'herd behaviour' (exacerbated by the polarised structure of financial markets) in which there are cascades of private assets deflation when private commercial debt is suddenly redeemed. Private debt is then bailed out by states. IMF solutions have exacerbated the most recent crisis by giving a green light to liberalisation and short term private portfolio investment, precipitating crises, and by imposing uniform austerity packages in their wake, making recovery more difficult. And fifth, financial investment gets to be biased in favour of the kind of assets which can be sold fast. Exit and diversification rather than information and direct control are used to contain risk. Small developing countries are most vulnerable to the instability of the financial markets.[12]

Wolfgang Sach's argument is straight forward and devastating. The main distinction between nineteenth century globalisation and the current era is that the earth can no longer be free ridden. It is a finite resource. The technology driven globalisation are creating a global tragedy of the commons under the aegis of private property rights. Furthermore, the entire system is driven by a manipulated apetite for consumption on which there is no foreseeable brake. Gains in the environmental efficiency of global capital have so far been made disproportionately at the expense of natural resources endowment of the developing world.

## Stages of Globalisation

The year 1980 marks an unprecedented economic integration. Integration has taken place earlier also, but not of this scale, in terms of quantity and volume. Fig. 1.1 tracks these flows. World trade is measured relatively to world income. Capital flows are proxied by the stock of foreign capital in developing countries relative to their GDP. Migration is proxied by the number of immigrants to the United States. Historically, before about 1870, none of these flows were sufficiently large to warrant the term globalisation.

For about 142 years, starting around 1870, all these flows rapidly became substantial driven by falling costs. The disparate national economies started to integrate, the economies began to globalise. However, globalisation is not an inevitable process, this first wave was reversed by a retreat to nationalism. Between 1914 and 1945 transport cost continued to fall, but trade barriers rose as countries followed begger-thy-neighbour policies. By the end of that period trade had collapsed back to around its 1870 level. After 1945, efforts were undertaken to stablise the international economic order by creating the Brettonwood institutions, i.e., IMF and World Bank. These institutions along with GATT reigned the governments to reduce protectionism. As trade barriers came down, and transport cost continued to fall, trade revived.[13] This second wave of globalisation, which lasted around 1980, was approximately a return to the pattern of the first wave, with a difference, that global economy was to work under the regulation of IMF and World Bank. Since 1980, scenario has undergone rapid transformation, as new "globalisers" from the developing countries have also made their presence felt by appropriating the world share of markets in manufactured goods and services.

There has been a dramatic rise in the share of manufacture in the exports of developing countries from about 25 per cent in 1980 to more than 80 per cent today.[14] FDI investments have also increased in these countries. This has brought an important change: low income countries are now competing head-on with high income countries while previously they specialised in primary commodities. During this new wave of globalisation, world trade has grown massively.

## The First wave of Globalisation: 1870-1914

The first wave of globalisation, from 1870 to 1914, preceding the first world war was a result of combination of factors which included falling transportation cost, due to shift from sail to steamships, reduction in tariff barriers, pioneered by an Anglo-French agreement. The opening of the Suez canal linking the Mediterranean ocean and the Indian ocean brought the transportation cost to low levels. Similarly the opening up of railways speeded up the import of primary commodities at cheaper cost, thereby giving stimulus to the textile industry. Cheaper transport and the lifting of man-made barriers opened up the possibility of using abundant land. New technologies created huge opportunities for land intensive commodity exports. The concomitant pattern of trade was that land intensive primary commodities were exchanged for manufactures. Exports as a share of world income nearly doubled to about 8 percent (*Maddison.* 2001).

The production of primary commodities required people. Sixty million migrated from Europe to North America and Australia to work on newly available land. South-South labour flows were also extensive. Lindert and Williamson (2001 b) speculate that the flows from the densely populated China and India to less densely populated SriLanka, Burma, Thailand, the Phillipines and Vietnam were of the same order of magnitude as the movements from the Europe to the Americas.

That would make the total labour flows during the first wave of globalisation nearly 10 per cent of the world's population. Here it is pertinent to note that most of the labour migration from developing countries was forced, an offshoot of colonialism.

The production of primary commodities for export required not just labour but large amounts of capital. As of 1870 the foreign capital stock in developing countries was only about 9 per cent of their income (Fig. 1.1).

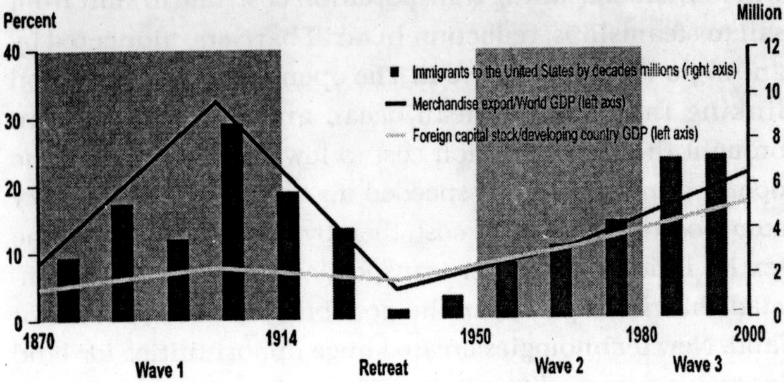


Fig. 1.1. Three waves of globalisation

***Source*** : Foreign Capital stock/developing country GDDP: Madison (2001), table 3.3; Merchandise exports world GDP: Madison (2001), table F-5: Migration : Immigration and naturalization service (1998)

However institutions needed for financial markets were copied. These institutions, combined with the improvements in information permitted by the telegraph, enabled governments in developing countries to tap into the major capital markets. Indeed, during this period around half of all British savings were channeled abroad. By 1914 the foreign capital stock of developing countries had risen to 32 per cent[15] of their income (World Bank Report, Oxford Univ. Press pp. 24-25). Globally growth accelerated sharply per capita incomes which had risen by 0.5 per cent per year in the previous 50 years, rose by an annual average of 1.3 per cent. The countries that participated in it often took off economically, both the exporters of manufacturers, people and capital and the importers. The global horizon witnesses the advent of new countries such as Argentina, Australia, New Zealand, and the United States, who became rich, by exporting primary commodities while importing people, institutions and capital. All these countries left the rest of the world behind.

Between the globalising countries themselves there was convergence. Mass migration was a major force equalizing incomes between them. "Emigration is estimated to have raised Irish wages by 32 percent, Italian by 28 percent and Norwegian by 10 percent. Immigration is estimated to have lowered Argentina wages by 22 per cent, Australia by 15 percent, Canada by 16 percent and America by 8 per cent. Indeed, during this phase, migration was probably more important than either trade or capital movements" (*Lindert and Williamson,* 2001).

The impact of globalisation on inequality within this period varied according to location specific land right patterns. Since exports from the developing countries were largely land based, hence the trade related benefits percolated largely to the land owning class in the developing world. since most were colonies, land ownership itself was subject to the power imbalance inherent in the colonial relationship. Where land ownership was concentrated, as in Latin America, increased trade could be associated with increased inequality. Where land was more equally owned, as in west Africa, the benefits of trade were spread more widely: conversely, in Europe the region importing land intensive goods, globalisation ruined landowners. For example, Cannadine (1990) describes the spectacular economic collapse of the English aristocracy between 1880 and 1914. In Europe the first wave of globalisation also coincided with the establishment for the first time in history of the great legislative pillars of social protection-free mass education, worker insurance, and pensions (Gray 1998).

Ever since 1820-50 years before globalisation world income inequality as measured by the mean lag deviation had started to increase drastically (Figure 1.2). This continued during the first wave of globalisation. Despite widening world inequality, the unprecedented increase in growth, reduced poverty as never before. In the 50 years before 1870, the incidence of poverty had been virtually constant, falling at the rate of just 0.3 percent per year. During the wave of globalisation the rate of decline more than doubled to 0.8 percent. Even this was insufficient to offset the increase in population growth, so that the absolute number of poor people increased.[16]

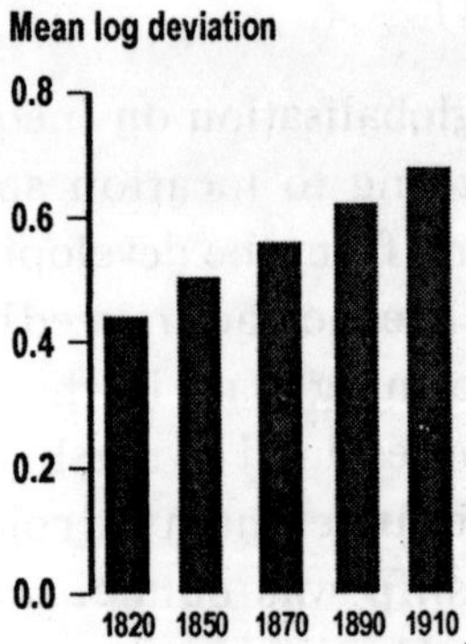


**Fig. 1.2. Worldwide household inequality (1820–1910).**

Source: Bourguignon and Morrisson (2001)

## The Retreat into Nationalism : 1914-15

Technology continued to reduce transport cost, however trade policy during this period went into reversal. Sea freight cost fell by a third, as Mundell (2000) Puts it: "The twentieth century began with a highly efficient international monetary system, which got destroyed in World War-I, and its bungled recreation in the inter-war period brought on the great depression". The governments responded to depression by protectionism. The United States led the way into the abyss: the Smoot-Hawley tariff, which led to retaliation abroad, was the first, between 1929 and 1933. US imports fell by 30 per cent and, the exports fell even more, by 40 per cent.

The tendency of raising protection nation wide, drove the trade to low levels. By 1950 exports as a share of world income were down to around 5 per cent—roughly back to where it had been in 1870. Protectionism had undone 80 years of technical progress in transport.[17]

The retreat towards nationalism had its ominous impact on the capital markets. Many high income countries imposed controls preventing the export of capital, and many developing countries defaulted on their liabilities. By 1950 the foreign capital stock of developing countries was reduced to just 4 per cent of income — far below even the modest level of 1870.

The retreat into nationalism produced anti-immigrant sentiment and governments imposed drastic restrictions on new comers. Immigration in the United States declined from 15 million during 1870-1914 to 6 million between 1914 and 1950.

The massive retreat from globalisation did not reverse the trend to greater world inequality. By 1950 the world was for less equal than it had been in 1914 (figure 1.3).

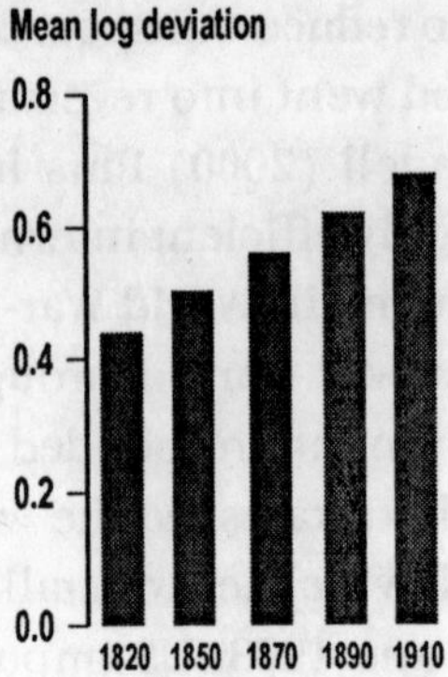


**Fig. 1.3. Worldwide household inequality (1820–1910).**

*Source:* Bourguignon and Morrisson (2001).

Average incomes were, however, substantially lower than the latter, previous trend been maintained, the world rate of growth fell by about third. The world's experiment with reversing globalisation showed that it was entirely possible but not attractive. The economic historian Angus Maddison summarises it thus: "Between 1913 and 1950 the world economy grew much more slowly than in 1870-1913, world trade grew much less than world income, and the degree of inequality between regions increased substantially" (*Maddison*, 2001, p. 22).

## The second wave of Globalisation: 1945-80

The jolt given to the economic growth, as a result of retreat to protectionism, paved the way for harmonising the economic waywardness after the second world war. The institutionalisation of the Brettonwood Institutions, for restoring international economic stability, was pioneered.

These institutions along with the GATT persuaded the nations to reduce trade barriers to reasonable limits, so as not to stifle the exchange of merchandise and goods. It was imperative that if the war torn world was to see the light of economic restoration, then all nations will have to strive to reduce the tariff duties. Here, however, trade liberalisation was selective both in terms of which countries participated and which products were included. Broadly, by 1980 trade between developed countries in manufactured goods had been substantially freed of barriers, but barriers facing developing countries had been substantially removed only for those primary commodities that did not compete with agriculture in the developed countries. For Agriculture and manufactures, developing countries faced severe barriers. Further, most developing countries erected barriers against each other and against developed countries.

The partial reduction in trade barriers was reinforced by continued reduction in the transport cost: between 1950 and late 1970. Sea freight charges again fell by a third (World Development Report). Overall, trade doubled relative to world income, approximately recovering the level it had reached during the first wave of globalisation. Howevers, the resulting liberalisation was very lopsided. For developing countries the components of trade remained skewed as the South remained exporter of primary commodities and low value added goods while North exported manufactures and services. The management of capital was confined among the nations of North.

By contrast, for rich countries the second wave of globalisation was spectacular. The lifting of barriers between them greatly expanded the exchange of manufactures. For the first time international specialisation within manufacturing became important, allowing scale of economies to be realised. This helped to drive up the incomes of the rich countries relative to the west.

During the second globalisation wave most developing countries did not participate in the growth of global manufacturing and services trade. The combination of persistent trade barriers in developed countries, and poor investment climates and anti-trade policies in developing countries, confined them to dependence on primary commodities. Even by 1980 only 25 per cent of the merchandise exports of developing countries were manufactured goods.[18] During globalisation's second wave there were effectively two trading systems: The old North-South systems and the new Intra-North systems. The intra-North systems was quiters powerfully equalising. Lower income industrial countries caught up with higher income ones.

Second waves globalisation coincided with the growth of policies for redistribution and social protection within developed societies–not only did inequalities reduce between countries–probably an effect of globalisation–but inequality was reduced within countries, probably as a result of these programmes. The second wave of globalisation was thus spectacularly successful in reducing poverty within the OECD countries. Rapid growth coincided with greater equity. Second wave of globalisation was not conducive for developing countries. Although per capita income growth recovered from the inter-war slowdown, it was substantially slower than the rich economies. The number of poor people continued to rise. Non-income dimensions of poverty improved–notably rising life expectancy and rising school enrolments. In terms of equity, within developing countries in aggregate there was little change either between countries or within them.

## The New Wave of Globalisation

The new wave of globalisation that began in 1980 is distinctive and remarkable, due to its sheer scale, speed and reach in terms of international migration, capital movements, economic volatility and reduction in tariff barriers. The period is characterised by entry of developing countries like India, China, South Korea, Taiwan, Singapore and Brazil who made distinctive forays in the global economy in manufactures, services and merchandise. While the period marked the high voltage drama of higher growth and investment in some of the developing countries, it also saw many countries of Asia, Africa and Latin America declining trend in Growth and investment.[19] The most encouraging development in third wave of globalisation is that some developing countries accounting for about 3 million people, have succeeded for the first time in harnessing their labour abundance to give them a competitive advantage in labour intensive manufactures and services. In 1980 only 25 per cent of the exports of developing countries were manufactures; by 1995 this had risen to 80 per cent (*Davis and Weinstein*). This is an astonishing transformation over a very short period. The developing countries exports are mostly situated in labour intensive products. Developing countries who have joined the third wave of globalisation includes countries like China, Bangladesh, and Sri Lanka, where manufacture shares in their exports are above the world average of 81 per cent, similarly countries like India, Turkey, Morocco and Indonesia have shares that are nearly as high as the world average. Another important change in the pattern of developing country exports has been their substantial increase in exports of services. In the early 1980s, commercial services made up 17 per cent of the exports of rich countries but only 9 per cent of the exports of developing countries. As in this period of globalisation the share of services in rich country exports increased slightly to 20 per cent but for developing countries the share almost doubled to 17 per cent (*World Bank Report: oxford university press*).

The factors that accounted for this shift included, trade liberalisation policies, reduction in trade barriers, FDI investments, and improved policy framework for investments. Thus Deng's 1979 announcement of opening up the Chinese economy, along the coastal region, with tax sops for multinationals provided the foundation for China's surge in economic growth of 9-10 percent annually.[20] In India the development of information and communication technologies provided the thrust for export of softwares to Europe and America, New information and communication technologies mean it is easier to manage and control geographically dispersed supply chains. The information based activities are "weightless" so their inputs and outputs can be shipped at virtually no cost. The growth in the investment climate was due to continuing technological progress in transport and communications (*Venables, 2001*). Containerisation and airfreight brought a considerable speeding up of shipping, allowing countries to participate in international production networks. By the end of the millennium the third wave of globalisation was instrumental in throwing many of the developing countries on the road of growth and investment. Scholars and economist attribute this to general reduction of tariff barriers, by easing controls on imports for strategic technologies, rise in the educational standards, better health facilities and investments by the governments in human resource development. The foreign exchange crisis faced by many countries such as India and China, with falling remittances from Gulf countries, due to war, emboldened them to open their economy by rolling down the state sector, and initiating privatisation.[21] All these provided the needed base for the economies of the countries like China, India, Singapore, Malaysia, South Korea, Taiwan to forge ahead in terms of investment and growth.

However, most countries are not just victims of their location. The newly globalising developing countries helped their firms to break into industrial markets by improving the complementary infrastructure skills and institutions that modern production needs. So, to some extent those developing countries that broke into world markets just happened to be well located, and to some extent they shaped events by their own actions. To get some understanding of this distinction it is useful to look at the characteristics of the post-1980 developing globalisers.

We rank developing countries by the extent to which they increased trade relative to income over the period, and compare the top third with the remaining two thirds. The one-third/ two thirds distinction is of course arbitrary. We label the top third "more globalised" without in any sense implying that they adopted pro-trade policies. The rise in trade may have been due to other policies, or even to pure chance. By construction the "more globalised" had a large increase in trade relative to income: 104 percent, compared to a 71 per cent for the rich countries. The remaining two thirds of developing countries have actually had a decline in trade to GDP over this period.

The more globalised were not drawn from the higher income developing countries. In fact, in 1980 they were poorer as group. The two groups had very similar educational attainment in 1980, Table 1.5.

**TABLE 1.4. Characteristics of more globalised and less globalised developing economies (population-weighted averages)**

| Socio-economic Characteristics | More Globalised (24) | Less Globalised (49) |
|---|---|---|
| Population, 1997 (billions) | 2.9 | 1.1 |
| Per capita GDP, 1980 | $1,488 | $1,947 |
| Per capita GDP, 1997 | $2,485 | $2,133 |
| Inflation, 1980 (per cent) | 16 | 17 |
| Inflation, 1997 (per cent) | 6 | 9 |
| Rule of law index, 1997 (world average = 0) | -0.04 | -0.48 |
| Average year primary schooling, 1980 | 2.4 | 2.5 |
| Average year primary schooling, 1997 | 3.8 | 3.1 |
| Average year secondary schooling, 1980 | 0.8 | 0.7 |
| Average year secondary schooling, 1997 | 1.3 | 1.3 |
| Average year tertiary schooling, 1980 | 0.08 | 0.09 |
| Average year tertiary schooling, 1997 | 0.18 | 0.22 |

*Source* : Dollar (2001).

Since 1980 the more globalised have made very significant gains in basic education: the average years of primary schooling for adults increased from 2.4 years to 3.8 years (*World Bank Report: Oxford University press*). The less globalised made less progress and now lag behind in primary attainment. The spread of basic education tends to reduce inequality and raise health standards, as well as being complementary to the process raising productivity. It can also be seen in table (1.5) that both groups reduced inflation to single digits over the past two decades. Lastly, as of 1997 the more globalised fared better than the less globalised on the index of property rights and the rule of law.

During the third wave of globalisation the cut in the import tariff, also distinguishes, as new globalisers cut import tariffs to 34 points on average, compared to 11 percent for the countries that are less globalised, fig. (1.5).

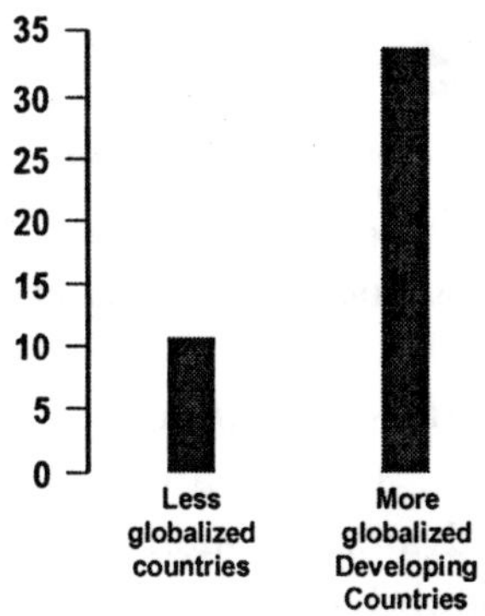


**Fig. 1.5 Decline in average import trrifiaes mid-1980s to late-1990s**

*Source:* Dollar and Kraay (2001)

The list of post-1980 globalisers includes such well known reformers as Argentina, China, Hungry, India, Malaysia, Mexico, the Phillipines and Thailand which undertook reforms involving investment liberalisation, stabilisation and property rights.

The "more globalised" developing countries started to grow more rapidly, with initiation of reform and integration, globally. They accelerated steadily from 2.9 per cent in the

1970 to 5 percent in the 1990s, Fig. [1.6]. These countries extend into a viscious circle of growth and development through educational expansion, reduced trade barriers, and strategic sectoral reforms.

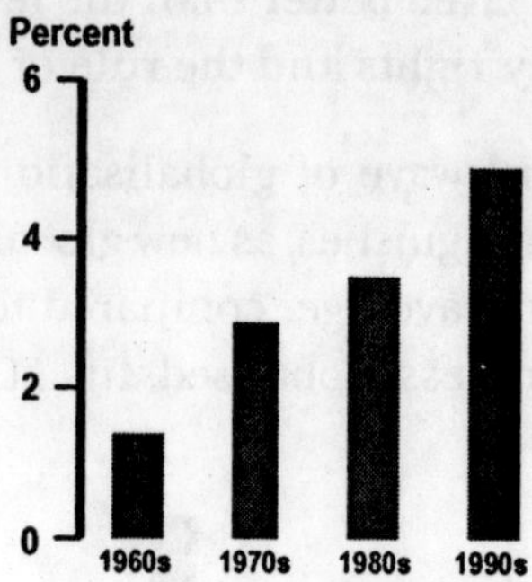


**Fig. 1.6.** **Per capita GDP growth rates: more globalised Developing countries**

***Source:*** **Dollar and Kraay (2001).**

The integration and development of "more globalisers" such as China, India, Taiwan and South Korea can be attributed to certain advantages, such as better infrastructure, growing literacy, social peace, political stability, and locational advantages. "Slow globalizers", mostly in Africa lack on these aspects. Thus Collier and Gunning (*1999, pp. 71-72*) document these infrastructure deficiencies in Africa:

> "There is less infrastructure than elsewhere, for example, the density of the rural road network is only 55 kilometers per thousand square kilometers compared to over 800 in India and there are only one-tenth the telephones per capita of Asia. The quality of infrastructure is also lower. The telephone system has triple the level of faults to Asia's and the proportion of Diesel trains in use is 40 percent lower. Prices of infrastructure use are much higher. Freight rates by rail are on average around double those in Asia. Port

> charges are higher (for example, a container costs $ 200 in Abidjan as opposed to $ 120 in Antwerp). Air transportation is four times more costly than in East Asia. Much of international transport is cartelized, reflecting the regulations of African governments intended to promote national shipping companies and airlines. As a result of these high costs, by 1991, freight and insurance payments on trade amounted to 15 percent of export earnings, whereas the average for developing countries is only 6 per cent. Further, the trend has been rising for Africa whereas it has been falling elsewhere: the comparable figures for 1970 were 11 per cent and 8 per cent."

Thus "slow or weak globalisers" have missed the third wave of globalisation, whatever may be deficiencies, they are in for hard times, as space for reversal in the age remains less and less.

Regardless of whether the disadvantages faced by the weak globalisers were intrinsic or could have been altered by better policy, their growth rates were even lower during third wave of globalisation than during the second wave. One reason is that many countries dependant on primary commodities suffered declining prices for their exports. This was probably due to slowdown in growth in developed nations. Could globalisation, also add to the marginalisation of African countries, Collier, Hoeffler and Patillo (2001) say that most marginalised countries integrated into world capital markets not through attracting capital inflows but through capital flight. By 1990, Africa, the region where capital is most scarce, had about 40 percent of its private wealth held outside the continent, a higher proportion than any other region. This integration was not a policy choice: most African governments erected capital controls, but they were ineffective. The main drivers of capital flight have been exchange rate misalignment, poor risk ratings, and high indebtedness. Another contemporary factor seems to be the very component of trade among the slow globalisers whose excessive dependence on primary commodities, has been self-defeating, especially during a civil war or strike, as rebel groups have taken advantage by occupying the centers of primary commodities production for financing their wars. It would be reasonable to assume that third wave of globalization entails some minimal conditions, which includes policy support, political stability, industrial peace, capital friendly atmosphere, and resilience and faith in the economy, for globalisation to be meaningful in the long run. Any pitfalls may be an open invitation to the crisis, as one witnessed in Mexico, South-East Asia, Thailand, Russia etc. The mobility of capital with lightening speed: to and fro, will be the order of third wave globalisation, as financial institutions, banks, exchange rates, and corporation will be the boss.

## References

1. J. Sachs and A warner, 'Economic Reform and the Process of global Integration, Brookings Paper on Economic Activity, 1995, pp. 1-118.
2. N. Woods, 'Globalisation : Definitions, Debates and Implications, in N. Wood (ed.), Globalisation, Special Issue, Oxford Development Studies 26, pp. 5-16.
3. Cited in World Bank Report, 'Globalisation, Growth and poverty', Oxford University Press, 2002, Washington DC.
4. Keith Falks, 'Political sociology : A critical Introduction, 1999, Edinburg University Press, Edinburg, pp. 57-94.
5. *Ibid.*
6. A. Harrison, 'Openness and Growth: A Time Series, Cross Country Analysis for Developing Countries, NBER working paper No. 5221, May.
7. The economics of South-East Asian countries have seen a good, growth in 1990s, they were opined as 'East Asian Tigers'. The growth among these countries was largely fuelled by FDI. Due to

monetory crisis, in 1997, the countries such as Korea, Thailand, Indonesia, Malaysia faced severe balance of payments crisis, robbing them of their growths. The globalisation with unfettered freedom of capital came to be questioned.

8. J. Gray, 'False Dawn: the Delusions of Global capitalism' 1998, London, Granta, pp. 42-67.
9. R. Robertson, ' The Globalisation paradigm, Thinking Globally,' in DG. Broomley (ed.) Religion and Social order, Greenwich, CT: JAI Press, pp. 207-24.
10. G. Ritzer, 'The Macdonaldisation of Society', 1993, London, Sage, pp. 32-80.
11. Perhaps the greatest of fears are reserved in the domain of ecological sustainability. Many scholars believe that the current process of globalisation is leading the world towards an unsustainable path of resource destruction and climate change. This puts the future generation existence to perilous limits.
12. The developing countries, in particular did not like the economic prescriptions imposed by IMF. The monetarist measures such as devaluation, liberalisation, capital account convertibility, reigning inflation at the cost of growth and investment have particularly been distasteful to developing countries.
13. IMF and World Bank have generally been proclaimed as watch dog of global integration. The lessons of 1930 depressions, strengthened the view that global economy need to be directed by international financial agencies, if economic pitfalls are to be avoided.
14. Cited in world Bank Report, ' Globalisation, Growth and poverty, Oxford University Press, 2002, Washington DC, pp. 23-35.
15. *Ibid.*
16. *Ibid.*
17. This is the period when Germany emerges as a new power after unification. Its persistent demands for a colonial share, brings new power alignments in Europe. Militarisation and Protectionism, to enhance ones gains ruled the order of the day leading to economic chaos and anarchy.
18. Cited in World Bank Report, 'Globalisation Growth and poverty', Oxford University Press, 2002, Washington DC, pp. 23-42.

19. Dani Rodrik, 'The new Global Economy and Developing countries: Making Openness Work, Washington DC : 1999, Overseas Development Council/ Policy Essay No. 24.
20. China inaugurated its liberalisation of economy in 1979, with Deng-Xiao-Peng's exhortation, that it doesn't matter whether the cat is black or white, as long as it catches mice. This was an indication that China will do everything for growth, even if it had to compromise on ideology.
21. In 1990 India faced a severe balance of payments crisis, due to falling remittances from Gulf countries, loss of Russia as an economic adjunct, and unbridled import of consumer durables. The government of India was left with 1 billion dollar of foreign exchange sufficient enough for two weeks reserve. This forced government of India, under the directions of IMF to open up its economy (Liberalisation).

# 2

# Political Economy of Globalisation

The term political economy is used in multifaceted manner in order to describe a number of different things in political science and international relations: from the application of rational individualism to the study of politics, to debates over policy with an economic dimension.[1] Here the term is used to describe the changing relationship between political systems (both national and international) and economic forces. This chapter is concerned with, public policy choices as they are ingrained in the economics for their instrumentation.

The current processes of globalisation are largely driven by the forces of the market economy supported by neo-liberal ideology. First and foremost the underlying economic structure of globalisation is the shift from the "national economy" to the "global economy". National economies are so upon by the forces of globalisation that their earlier ability of intervention and regulation has come under a scanner due to new role assumed by the international multilateral agencies such as IMF, World Bank and the GATT, rechristened WTO. Since 1945 the twin Bretton wood institutions, IMF and World Bank acquired preponderant economic power to tame countries under the pretext of stabilisation, and harmonising economies. One of the most dramatic aspects of globalisation over the past 40 or 50 years has been the extent to which private capital flows have dwarfed official flows in the global economy.[2] In the process, the central institutions of the Brettonwood's order, the IMF and World Bank, have been marginalised in the economic relations among industrialised countries. Several factors contributed to the growth in private capital flows. New informational technologies increased the speed and efficiency of transactions. Expansion of the demand for international financial services accompanied the growth in trade and multinational corporate activities in the 1960s.[3]

The range of maneuvering for managers of the national economy is being undermined by the growing power of globalised capital, also known as 'global finance' or 'transnational capital'. This money is highly mobile across state boundaries. Heightened mobility of capital has privileged and rewarded financial speculation at the expense of fixed investment. Arrighi (1994) links this shift to the onset of "financialisation" a contagious preference for liquid rather than fixed capital on the part of private and institutional investors under specific historical conditions (*usually associated with the decline of a hagemonic state*). Most recently the decline of the United States is pegged to the rise of offshore money markets in the 1970s. Recent data indicate the Chinese surpluses in Dollars have eroded the confidence in Dollar, and despite Obama's requests, the Chinese are not ready to cooperate in the recent currency turmoil. The currency markets stimulated the rise of unregulated financial institutions alongside of traditional (nationally regulated) banking systems. Arrighi, characterises this as the subordination of the "territorial" principle to the "capitalist" principle. It marks a new stage of competition among states and firms in an unstable, post hegemonic world order. When the center of accumulation (the US home market) erodes, speculation on an unknown financial future heightens.

As money capital decoupled from productive capital, financiers consolidated power and reshaped modern political and economic institutions in the 1980s, including farming (*Bienefield, 1989; Marsden and Whatmore, 1994*). Growing financial securitisation (i.e. trading in securities, including debt) heightened the authority of debt-security rating institutions, which meant in effect that all firms and states found their credit ratings subject to a global "informational standard" (*Sinclair, 1994*). Corporate downsising and relocation and state restructuring programes, in the service of credit-worthiness, have rippled across the global social landscape. The new power of financial institutions has been at the expense of the sovereignty of state monetary authorities. In 1992, the former chairman of Citicorp described the 200,000 currency traders across the world, as conditioning "a kind of global plebiscite on the monetary and fiscal policies of the governments using currency". This is far more draconian than any previous arrangement such as Gold standard or Brettonwoods. The scope for a nation to opt out of this system virtually shuts down (*quoted in Brecher and Costello, 1994:30*) This in fact means that the states are handicapped due to non-territorial character of finacialisation, wherein they have to deal according to global principles.

Under these circumstances, state organisations transmitted the effects of financial restructuring through the relatively circumscribed institutions of the "formal" economy and beyond, where communities depend on "informal" markets, subsidies, public lands and casual employment on the fringes of the "formal" economy.

The elites associated with the globalisation project are a different nut to crack. In addition to state managers (those embracing liberalisation) there are the new financial and transnational and corporate elites combined with the managers of newly empowered multilateral institutions like the IMF, the World Bank and the WTO. Fears have been expressed in various quarter that collusion between these officials has undermined the open policy making in developing country democracies.

## Globalisation and the Nation State

One of the crucial questions being asked in political science, is, whether, globalisation is eroding the sovereignty and autonomy of the state. The talk of the town is 'borderless world economy', 'global politics', and global 'civil society'; all of which militate the conventional notion of the state. There are opinions that are contrary to this, and which even suggests, that globalisation has reinforced the state, as the global forces will always require an authority to regulate, the financial order, to shape the globalisation with the onset of multilateralism, the processes of globalisation had varied differentials by way of impact on the nations. The weak states, have buckled, while the strong states like USA, China, France have shaped the globalisation processes, according to their needs. The 'strong', states in this context have a capacity to influence the rules of the international economy, and/or a capacity to control their own integration into the world economy. United States role in shaping the world globalisation is noticeable, through bodies like G-7, OECD, and multilateral institutions like IMF, where decisions are taken on the basis of voting power. At the same time, globalisation imposes limits even on strong states. A key example is the way international capital markets can exact a swift and devastating punishment on any government undertaking, inappropriate monetary or exchange-rate policy. Yet the extent to which markets, punish other kinds of policies undertaken by strong states is often overstated, for example, there is no evidence that maintaining the welfare state is an offence which the markets will punish. On the contrary the globalisation of markets has been undertaken mostly by governments who have simultaneously increased their welfare state. The logic is that a government opening up to world trade has needed to 'buffer' its citizens from the dislocations and vulnerabilities of world markets in order to avert political protests and reactions against the global economy, such as that which occurred in the period of depression in 1930s.

Strong states are also those which can control to some degree the nature and speed of their integration into the world economy. Here it is pertinent to point out that some states have managed to slow down or to control the speed and terms on which they have integrated in world capital markets. Often these states are ferocious guardians of their independence in foreign policy, human rights and security issues, as well as, their own domestic political arrangements, such relatively 'strong' states include not just industrialised countries, such as France and Britain, but also a wide variety of developing countries from the likes of Brazil to Malaysia, China, Iraq and Iran. What is striking about these 'strong states' with the exception of the United Kingdom is that each has propounded a powerful national ideology and rationale, for rejecting what some call 'Anglo-American Capitalism'. In other words, they come ready armed to the world economy with ideas of their own in what Robert Wade has called 'coercive Liberalism'. In the case of France, Brazil and Iraq the leadership has employed spate of protective economic measures in important sectors of the economy.[4] Their capacity to do this depends upon a matrix of factors which includes their size, resources, geostrategic advantages and economic strength and equally their national ideology and domestic power of the state, be it coercive or consensual.

In comparison, weak states suffer from a lack of choice in their international economic relations. They have little or no influence in the creation and enforcement of rules in the system and they have exercised little control over their own integration into the world economy. Rather, in the aftermath of the debt crises of the 1980s, many weak states opened up their economies, liberalised and deregulated, more as a result of the coercive liberalisation than of democratic policy choices. In the 1990s, as Dani Rodrik has described this continues with 'forced harmonisation', whereby for instance, in the case of trade negotiations on intellectual property, developing countries were coerced into an agreement which transfers 'billions of dollars' worth monopoly of profits from poor countries to rich countries under the guise of protecting the property rights of inventors.[5] To sum up, the impact of globalisation on the Nation states, sovereignty and autonomy, has varied according to state strength and leadership initiative, across various issue areas.

## Neo-liberalism : Ideology of Globalisation

Globalisation and liberalisation, is depicted as the road map to higher levels of development and growth. With the collapse of communism, in the 1990s, the neo-classical liberal model emerged triumphant and began to beget the replication worldwide. The proponents of neo-liberalism argued that the debt ridden countries in Africa and the newly emerging countries of Eastern Europe can pull themselves out of poverty and underdevelopment by shifting their development planning, with an active and commanding role for the state, to devolution, deregulation, liberalisation and privatisation– in short, installing market fundamentals under the iron discipline of the trinity of the IMF, World Bank and WTO. This exercise would help member nations to replicate the successful experiences of the newly industrialising countries of East Asia.

Fantu cheru (2001), rightly points out the following excerpts:

> ...... Since the early 1980s, a large and growing number of developing countries have embarked (some reluctantly, under pressure from the multinational development Banks) on the liberalisation of their trade and foreign investment regimes, as well as the adaptation of their domestic economic structures and strengthening of their export capacity. Between 1980 and 1986 alone, 36 sub-saharan African countries initiated 241 adjustment programmes. Most have had multiple programmes, with 11 implementing 10 or more. One decade later, the role of the state in Africa, has been significantly curtailed, the dominance of the market forces is now in place and economies have been opened wide to external penetration. In short, globalisation and structural adjustment are mutually reinforcing.

While neo-liberal economic theory assumes that the market is a neutral institution and that there is thus no need for a critical theory of the market in regard to the question of power, a critical view of the market begins by rejecting the social neutrality of the market. Historically markets are institutions that tend to reflect the pre-existing inequalities in the social structure, whereby those who are already advantaged, e.g., through ownership of property or control of capital and technology, tend to have more power in the market (*Dong-sook, S.Gills,* 2007, p.192). Those who are already disadvantaged, e.g., by the absence of property, capital or technology, tend to become powerless. The market ideology that accompanies neo-liberal globalisation promotes a value system which is based on extreme individualism. This doctrine preaches that individual freedom is the supreme human value above all others. In neo-liberal or 'market' ideology the primary emphasis is given to individual freedom and specifically to the freedom to compete and consume. Theoretically, in a truly free market society, everyone is equal and equally free to make their choices. Only the individuals own efforts and abilities determine the 'winners' and the loosers. Since the market alone can not meet all human needs to satisfy fundamental social rights, a political process is thus necessary to insure basic guarantees of social rights. For example, in developed countries, a state pension for old age is regarded as entitlement of citizenship. After the great depression, which was a global crisis of capitalism, a new social compromise was reached between labour, capital and the state which resulted in the expansion of welfare states and social democracy. However, neo-liberal economic globalisation by giving primacy to the market, undermines the social rights and entitlements as states have to squeeze out' social expenditures (Pension, Health subsidy on agriculture and transportation etc.) e.g. India. Thus Neo-liberalism has transformed market freedom to a type of comparative advantage in the drive, towards market liberalisation and privatisation in the third world. The definition of market freedom in these neo-liberal terms, covers a wide array of issues, including market – decontrol, labour decontrol and a catch all of imperatives aimed at removing all forms of government limitations on private sector reforms. To put it more vividly but less subtly, market freedom has come to mean that free-wheeling, free-dealing and fast-moving capital must have the freedom to control state policies (*Bryan and Farrell, 1996; Schmidt, 1995*; *Horseman and Marshall, 1994, Rinehart, 1995*). States that do not confirm to this dogma run the risk of being blacklisted as international economic and political pariahs.

## Multinational Corporations

Multinational Corporations stand at the heart of the globalisation process. The multinationals activities, their merits and demerits, have been the hallmark of various literatures on globalisation. Their critics portray them as bullies, using their clout to exploit workers and natural resources with no regard for the economic well being of any country or community. Their advocates see multinationals as triumph for global capitalism bringing advanced technology to poorer countries and low cost products to the wealthier ones.

There is no doubt that multinationals matter, as they are the most important conduits through which globalisation takes place.

The most common explanation for multinationals growth is economics of scale. In certain industries, the argument goes, firms can become more efficient by becoming bigger and producing more, another reason cited is vertical integration. In some industries, the interdependence of suppliers and users of a particular resource makes it difficult for such forms to co-operate at arms length since there is always the risk that one will undermine the other. This is the reason; many firms integrate vertically, buying up their suppliers or customers. Sometimes, these suppliers or customers will be abroad, turning the acquiring firms into a multinational. For example, Reliance Industries began its operations in textile manufacturing, later it occupied the petrochemical production, for manufacturing yarns and now it has made foray into oil exploration. This is called backward integration wherein, the company enhances maximum cost advantage beginning from primary exploration to the finished products, thereby acquiring preponderant advantage in terms of cost, and economy of scale.

Although the number of MNCs have increased from 7000 in 1970s to 38000 in the mid 1990s. Some 500 are responsible for three quarters of world trade. The table (2.1) gives the list of leading multinationals.

**Table 2.1 Top 15 MNCs by foreign assets, 1995**

| *Company* | *Industry* | *Foreign Assets as % of total* | *Foreign sales as % of total* | *Foreign employment as % of total* |
|---|---|---|---|---|
| Royal Dutch/Shell | Energy | 67.8 | 73.3 | 77.9 |
| Ford | Automotive | 29.0 | 30.6 | 29.8 |
| General Electric | Electronics | 30.4 | 24.4 | 32.4 |
| Exxon | Energy | 73.1 | 79.6 | 53.7 |
| General Motors | Automotive | 24.9 | 29.2 | 33.9 |
| Volkswagen | Automotive | 84.8 | 60.8 | 44.4 |
| IBM | Computers | 51.9 | 62.7 | 50.1 |
| Toyota | Automotive | 30.5 | 45.1 | 23.0 |
| Nestle | Food | 86.9 | 98.2 | 97.0 |
| Bayer | Chemicals | 89.8 | 63.3 | 54.6 |
| ABB | Electrical Equipment | 84.7 | 87.2 | 93.9 |
| Nissan | Automotive | 42.7 | 44.2 | 43.5 |
| Elf Aquitaine | Energy | 54.5 | 65.4 | 47.5 |
| Mobil | Energy | 61.8 | 65.9 | 52.2 |
| Daimler-Benz | Automotive | 39.2 | 63.2 | 22.2 |

**Source:** UNCTAD

In a wide range of industries or product groups the world market is controlled by 10-12 firms, often fewer, a structure of competitive or collusive oligopoly where concentration of control is often underestimated by the absence of statistics on franchising and licensing.[6] According to Ley's, one third of world output is now under the direct influence of MNCs. But John kay starts from the fact that the largest and most successful global manufacturing companies rarely hold that ranking in terms of capitalisation more than a few decades at the most. Instability at the top has intensified.[7]

Another reason for the spread of multinationals is that they tend to be successful. In any business, inefficient firms will fold, giving way to those that can earn higher profits. As the world becomes more integrated, it is to be expected that the companies most adept at crossing borders are those that prosper. This is the reason that firms from richer countries do the best. These firms have been exposed to more competition in their home markets, and therefore well equipped for international competitive battles.

Multinational's size and scale give them the potential to exert power in an exploitative way. A multinational company has enough maneuvering power to shift its operation from a country where policies are detrimental to its interest. A multinational in America can move its production, if America's worker's safety law is too restrictive, by shifting it to Mexico. It can also lower its tax bill by using internal pricing to shift profits from high tax countries to low-tax ones. This maneuvering and flexibility may make it harder for governments to raise revenue, promote worker safety and protect the environment. Critics fear an undesirable "race to the bottom" with government reducing desirable social protections to attract investment by multinationals. Another criticism in that multinationals are exporting jobs, to low-wage countries.

None the less despite the above criticism the foreign direct investment by transnational corporations in developing countries grew twelve fold between 1970 and 1992 (*world investment report 1996*). It then trebled between 1992 and 1997 rising to US $149 billion out of a worldwide FDI total of US $400 billion (*world investment report, 1996 and 1998*). Thus the rate of multinationals in terms of investment can not be discounted. Trade has consistently outpaced growth in output, to the extent that merchandise trade in 2004 was worth 44.9 percent of world gross domestic production (GDP) up from 32.4 per cent as recently as 1990– with trade in services growing even faster. The global stock of FDI, valued at 6 per cent of world GDP in 1980, grew to 9 percent in 1995 and reached 22 per cent by 2003.[8] The way multinationals are operating to achieve the scale of economies, new form of synergy is visible, as intra-firm international trade joint ventures, alliances, acquisition, mergers, subcontracting have become the order of the day. The number of cross border mergers and acquisitions tripled between 1990 and 2000, and the value of these transactions increased by even greater magnitude. As Stephen Brooks has observed, of all the trends associated with globalisation, the globalisation of production is the most historically unprecedented.[9]

The global growth is intimately connected with the internationalisation of production by the multinational corporations; some 40 percent of the volume of trade in manufacturing is accounted for by intra-firm trade among the subsidiaries of these corporations. The MNCs become important for countries as they help in bringing updated technologies in newly industrialised nations. Moreover, multinational corporations are increasingly engaged not only in international production activities, but also in finance. It is often easier for a domestic firm in a developing country to raise commercial loans internationally through joint ventures, and to obtain a better, internationally approved credit rating, if it is linked to a well-known multinational.

The awesome financial power of the multinational corporations, sometimes even eclipses the financial autonomy of the host nations. Since many of the multinationals are in good informal coordination with the Banks and Brettonwood institutions, any unfavorable economic regulation by the national governments can draw MNCs together to exert pressure for favorable policy shifts, often to the detriment of domestic industry.

Most of the largest companies, by revenue, are either American or Japanese. In 1996 (*Fortune magazine*) 162 of the 500 largest companies globally were from US, while 126 were from Japan. Only a few of the largest companies are from developing countries. An exception to this is China, which has three entries in the top 500 list. Measured by foreign assets, the distribution of the largest companies looks very much the same. Most of the top 100 companies with largest foreign assets are from US, Japan, UK, France and Germany. In 1995, the list of the top 100 multinational corporations measured by foreign assets, included two companies from developing countries for the first time. These were Daewoo and Venezuela Oil company. Total Foreign assets of the top 100 MNCs in 1995 amounted to $1.7 trillion, while total foreign sales of $2 trillion, and total employment 5,80,0000. In 1996, the total revenues of the 500 largest companies globally were $ 11.4 trillion, total profits were $ 404 billion, total assets were $33.3 trillion, and the total number of employees was 35,517,692. The top ten companies accounted for 11.7% of the total revenue of the top 500, 15% of profits and 13.6% of employment (*Fortune*). America was home to 31 of 50 most profitable firms, and seven of the top ten. The most profitable, however, was Shell (Netherlands) with profits $8.9 billion. In 1996, the top 500 companies did not get bigger, they got richer. Their profits increased by 25.1% while revenues increased only by 0.5%, assets by 3.5%, and the number of employees by 1.1%.

## Mergers, Acquisitions and Joint Ventures of MNCs

Mergers and acquisitions, continue to be a highly popular form of corporate development. MNCs follow three general procedures when seeking to access new markets. Merger with or direct acquisition of existing concerns, sequential market entry, and joint venture. Merger or Direct acquisition of existing companies in a new market is the most straight forward method of new market penetration employed by multinational corporations. Such an entry known as FDI allows multinationals, especially the larger ones to take full advantage of their size and the economies of scale, this provides multinational corporations to make use of a procedure known as sequential market entry, often also includes FDI, and involves the establishment or acquisition of concerns operating in niche markets related to the parent companies product lines, in the new country of operation. Joint ventures are undertaken with firms already operating in these markets. This kind of arrangement is especially popular among communist nations such as China, where equities are held by foreign corporations along with the host nation firms.

In 2004, 30,000 acquisitions were completed globally, equivalent to one transaction every 18 minute (*Agarwal and Jaffe,*). However, in a paradox to their popularity, acquisitions appear to provide at best a mixed performance to the broad range of stakeholders involved, while target firm shareholders generally enjoy positive short term returns, investors in bidding firms frequently experience share price under performance in the months.

## Brettonwood Institutions: IMF and World Bank

The context for the creation of Brettonwood institutions clearly lay in the aftermath of great depression of 1929, which caused untold miseries and bruises to the European economy and US. The principle objective of John Maynard Keynes and Dexter White, was to manage the international payment systems and to assist in the reconstruction of Europe. There was an underlying worldview about the pursuit of full employment which was shaped by memories of the great depression. This conception also recognized the logic of international collective action in situations where markets did not work and there was a role to government intervention. Since then the world has changed considerably, and so have the Brettonwood institutions, but their concerns have become narrower wherein, it has always been suspect in the eyes of the developing countries.

The dimension of labour established for the IMF and World Bank at Brettonwood in 1944 was such that the IMF was responsible for providing international liquidity and maintaining a stable exchange rate system, and the World Bank for financing economic development. The IMF's facilities were originally intended purely for stabilisation purposes and its programmes were designed for short term balance of payments support to cushion the domestic economy from temporary imbalances in its external accounts through the use of deflationary measure.[10] In the mid 1960s, stand by arrangements of (6-12) months duration were virtually the only means by which the IMF extended financial support to members on a conditional basis.[11] This was the old orthodoxy in the IMF's approach to adjustment. The 1970s saw changes, in IMF's policy of lending, that established a new-orthodoxy by the mid 1980s. These changes were in response to the problems created by the 1973 and 1979 oil price increases, and faltering debt position of many, Latin American nations, Asian nations and African nations. Most of the private Banks (European and American) who had landed funds to these nations found it difficult to get their money back. Their influence and lobbying was primarily responsible for, IMF extending larger amounts of fund, with longer period of adjustments. The origins of the neo-orthodoxy can be traced to the creation of the extended fund facility (EFF) in 1974.[12] with the EFF and its descendants–the structural Adjustment facilities (SAF) created in 1986, and Enhanced Structural Adjustment Facility (ESAF) created in 1987 came more expansive conditionality affecting a broad range of policies.

The neo-orthodoxy encompassed a shift in the approach to adjustment, from the old orthodoxy of demand management to structural adjustment emphasising supply-response through changes to a broad range of macro-economic policies, and removing what the IMF considers structural constraints (i.e. political and institutions) on the economy based on market-oriented principles. A change in duration of programmes also occurred from the short-term (6 months to 1 year) emphasised by standby arrangements, to the medium-term (up to three years) under EFF/SAF/ESAF. An increase in the resources available to member states also occurred.

One can also see the neo-orthodoxy in the lending policies of the World Bank, in the duration of the programme and the approach to lending. World Bank's introduction of structural adjustment loans in 1979 and sector Adjustment loans in 1980 marks the shift from the long term emphasis of project lending to medium term lending.[13] One also finds in this period a marked shift in World Bank lending and financing from capital-intensive projects, especially in the mining, energy and transportation sectors to policy based lending, emphasising changes to domestic macro-economic policies and institutions. It is in this regard that World Bank came under the fire from developing countries, that this neo-orthodoxy was meant to roll down the state sector, from its traditional, role of reserving the strategic sector for welfare goals. Some countries like Kenya accused World Bank of employing these measures to shift them from the path of socialistic development.

Two trends are noteworthy from this survey of IMF and World Bank lending. First, the expansion in the scope and content of conditions attached to loans under the neo-orthodox definition of structural adjustment is geared towards reducing the forms and extent of state intervention in the economy to freeup markets. Second, the two institutions have been reactive rather than proactive, largely guided by the undesirable effects of shocks and crises in the financial market and currency.

However, the pre-occupation with the instability and volatility of capital flows associated with financial crises is so great that there is a tendency to understate the importance of managing exchange rates and current account deficits. These policy prescriptions can only change if the governance structure of the IMF is made democratic and transparent. The representation embodied in voting rights, that are based on quotas, is far too unequal between member countries. The lenders are the principal shareholders in the IMF but the borrowers are the principal contributors to the income of the IMF. There is a clear need to restructure voting rights so as to make them more broad based and representative. Similarly the operations of the IMF lack transparency and its decisions are clouded in secrecy, which needs to be changed if it has to acquire the needed legitimacy of nations across the board.

Adrian Leftwich writes, the aim of adjustment was to shatter the dominant, post-war, state-led developmental paradigm and overcome the problems of developmental stagnation by promoting open and free competitive market economies supervised by minimal states.[14] Between 1980 and 1990, World Bank structural adjustment flow increased from 7 to 187 in 60 countries.[15] The inventory of IMF/WB prescriptions is well known. It includes currency devaluation, deregulation of prices and wages, reduction of public spending on social programmes and state bureaucracies, removal of food and other subsidies on basic necessities, trade liberalisation, privatisation of state enterprises, and the expansion of the export sector, the latter in the case of agriculture often at the expense of food production. The officially stated aims of these polices were to stabilize domestic economies, to stimulate economic growth and to ensure the country's ability to earn the foreign exchange needed to service its foreign debts.

The conditionalities attached by the IMF/World Bank to the developing countries, have drawn all round criticism from many sections in these countries. Their sentiment was even echoed by Horst Kohler, former IMF Director, on trade double standards.

> "It is unconscionable for the United States, Japan, and the European union to spend hundreds of billions of dollars on agricultural subsidies to maintain marginal activities for the benefit of a small segment of their population, while undermining agricultural sectors that are central to peace and development in poor countries. Yet this is exactly what is happing now.
>
> "For example, in the US, price support payments for cotton cost more than $2 billion a year. This is larger than the annual cotton production of all Sub-Saharan Africa. Subsidised US Production has taken over 30% of world cotton exports, while cotton sectors that are crucial for economic life in some of the world's poorest countries, like Benin, Chad, Mali and Togo are devastated.
>
> "In the EU, governments spend over $2 billion a year to buy up excess domestic sugar production, and the resulting surplus is dumped on world markets. A few developing countries get preferential access to the EU market, under a quota system, but this just means that other sugar producer's in Latin America, Asia and Southern Africa lose even more.
>
> "Japan's agricultural subsidies are the highest of any advanced country, so that rice prices, for instance, are 8 times as high as the word market price. This means

that developing countries–especially in Asia–lose major trading opportunities.

*Source:* Kohler, 2002:7

Thus the IMF promotes trade liberalisation throughout the south, yet is ineffective in getting the core capitalist states to implement similar polices and play by the same rule. The IMF managing Director Christine Lagarde, while visiting New Delhi, and China, reiterated her emphasis of interconnectedness of the economies to fight the Euro Zone crisesf.[16] She was skeptical when questions were raised regarding reform of IMF quotas and governance, which has been struggling due to lack of adequate support from developed nations.

## GATT and the WTO

GATT was established on 30 October, 1947 to deal with cross-border trade in goods. Its premise was based on the principle of non-discrimination in matters of tariff reduction. This obvious stated goal was sought to be achieved through seven rounds of trade negotiations. The large number of commodities, with differences in economic level of nations, made the settlement on tariff reduction a difficult proposition. Starting from 1950 to next twenty two years witnessed a remarkable era of economic growth. Undoubtedly the major stimulus to economic growth in this period was trade, which expanded due to infusion of inflows from America to the European Nations, as a reconstruction agenda after the war. Given the GATT philosophy and the procedure of non-discriminatory tariff reduction, the American Industries enjoyed the prospect of maintaining their leading position, while letting the European economies share the growth. For them free trade promised nothing but expanding exports (*Reich* 1983: 780). The tariff reductions undertaken under the various rounds of GATT negotiations also provided the base for increase in the value of trade. Refer to Table (2.2). Impressive tariff reductions were achieved during the Kennedy (1963-67) and Tokyo (1973-79) rounds.

**Table 2.2 GATT held a total of 8 rounds**

**GATT and WTO trade rounds**

| *Name* | *Start* | *Duration* | *Countries* | *Subjects covered* | *Achievements* |
|---|---|---|---|---|---|
| Geneva | April 1946 | 7 month | 23 | Tariffs | Signing of GATT, 45,000 taruffcince ssions affecting $10 billion of trade |
| Annecy | April 1946 | 5 month | 13 | Tariffs | Countries exchanged some 5,000 tariff concession |
| Torquay | September 1950 | 8 months | 38 | Tariffs | Countries exchanged some 8,700 tariff concessions, cutting the 1948 tariff levels by 25% |
| Geneva II | January 1956 | 5 month | 26 | Tariffs, admission of Japan | $2.5 billion in tariff reductions |
| Dillon | September 1960 | 11 month | 26 | Tariffs | Tariff concesssions worth $4.9 billion of world trade |
| Kennedy | May 1964 | 37 month | 62 | Tariffs, Antidumping | Tariff concessions worth $40 billion of world trade |
| Tokyo | September 1973 | 74 month | 102 | Tariffs, non-tariff mesures, "framework" agreements | Tariff reductions worth more than $300 billion dollars |

| | | | | | |
|---|---|---|---|---|---|
| Urguay | Septe-mber 1986 | 87 month | 123 | Tariffs, nontariff measures, reles ser-vices, int-ellectual proerty, dispute settllem-ent, text-iles, agri-culture, creation of WTO, etc. | The round led ted to the creation of of WTO, and exten-ded the range of trade negotions, leading to major re-duction in tariffs (about 40%) and ag-ricultural subsidies, an agagreement to to allow full for tex-tiles and clothing from developing countries, and an extension of intellectual properity rights. |
| Doha | Nove mber 2001 | ? | 141 | Tariffs, measures, agricultu-re labor standards, enveron-ment, competi-tion, investm-ent, tran-sparency, patents etc. | The round is not yet concluded. |

The unique problems of the developing countries, and their increase in numbers after 1950, raised new issues in the GATT. Among these, two initiatives were undertaken, first was the incorporation of Article XVIII in 1954-55, recognising the rights of developing countries to use import restrictions to protect infant industries and to safeguard balance of payments position. Secondly, an expert panel under the chairmanship of Mr. Haberler furnished a report in 1958 on developing country trade problems, such as low export growth, fluctuating commodity prices and protectionist policies of the industrial countries in terms of agriculture (*S.P. Shukla, 2002*). It was the Haberler Report which triggered a discussion and eventually led to the establishment of UNCTAD (United Nations Conference on Trade & Development) in 1964. Some of the issues agreed by GATT in 1965 under part IV, were impressive enough to meet the requirements of developing countries, but certain exceptions added by the advance countries nullified the gains of the developing countries. Particularly noticeable in this area were textiles and agriculture, which were important for developing countries, for they were crucial for the economy, here again the tendency of developed world was to extend the time period, as they felt, their industry in this zone would not be able to match the developing countries. The period of 1980-94 in the GATT's history was turbulent because of new pressures in the economic front. Competition and tension between the EEC, Japan and the US were becoming sharper, the economic space needed for the expansion of the trade could be only filled by the developing countries, who held the promise of expanding markets.

The fissures in the 1990s in trade, caused by entry of new players and as, South Korea, Brazil, Taiwan, Mexico and Singapore, threatened to reduce the market share of the American companies. To obviate such threats two trading majors could negotiate outside the GATT framework with mutual consent and agree to partake mutual advantages on reciprocal basis. Under protectionist pressures, the coverage of these measures— anti-GATT, but not strictly GATT—illegal- expanded to industries such as iron and steel, automotive, electronic products, footwear and even semi-conductors (*S.P Shukla*). The tensions between America and Japan ruled the order of the day after 1990, over the issue of US trade deficit vis-à-vis Japan.

The purported tensions and issues finally cleared the scope for the last round of GATT negotiations to be undertaken at Uruguay. This round undertook several new areas, at the instance of USA, such as high technology industries, banking, insurance services, telecommunications, TRIPs (Trade Related Intellectual Property Rights) and TRIMs (Trade Related Investment Measures). The negotiations also included agriculture in its ambit, which brought EEC, Brazil and India together. After a series of meetings at Brussels and Montreal, the final draft was prepared by Arthur Dunkel (Director General, GATT) on a take it or leave it basis with some modifications, pertaining to agriculture, the final draft was adopted by the ministers at Marrakash in Morocco in April, 1994, Henceforth GATT acquired a new name, WTO, and unlike its predecessor the current system in the WTO forbade MFN status accorded to its members. Similarly domestic policy decisions which remained immune through certain safeguards, was also taken away, and henceforth even domestic policy decisions would be within the purview of WTO. Similarly WTO is armed with the power of expulsion of member states, if they are found to have acted against the principles of WTO guidelines.

Doha round which began in 2001, was supposed to be about trade led and trade facilitated development of the world's poor countries.[17] After five years of negotiations, the talks collapsed because of unbridgeable difference among the EU, the US and developing countries led by India, Brazil and China from the developing countrie's perspective, the problem is that the rich countrie's want access to the poor countries, resources, market and labour forces at the lowest possible price.[18] Some countries were agreeable to deep cuts in agricultural subsides but resisted opening their markets, while some others reversed this. Developing countries are determined to protect the livelihood of their farmers—farmers suicide has been a terrible human cost and a political problem for state and central governments in India for some years already – and rural development. The rich countries pledges of flexibility failed to translate, as they were bent on protecting the interests of the tiny agricultural minorities. By contrast, in developing countries, farming accounts for 30-60 per cent of GDP and up to 70 per cent of the labour force. This is why labour rights protection is at least as critical for developing countries as intellectual property rights protection is for the rich, it is also to be borne in mind that Western countries for centuries relied on public regulation, social investments in order to protect the interests of the vulnerable caused by the market failure.

In 1995 the WTO Agreement on Agriculture (AOA) was introduced. A major element of AOA Discipline was substantial reduction in the level of subsidies granted by the WTO members.[19] It is alleged that developed countries provide domestic support of the order of $ 320 billion to their farmers, thus enabling them to an unequal bargaining power against farmers of developing countries. Rich countries comprise only 3-5 per cent of farm population in developed countries and receive huge domestic and export subsidies. This is in contrast to the millions of resource poor farmers (who constitute the bulk of the population) in developing countries for whom agriculture is the only means of sustaining their livelihoods. Further developing countries subsidies keep the global agricultural prices suppressed and make farm activity in the developing countries non-remunerative. Therefore it is not surprising that the developing countries are not able to compete with the developed countries even in the agriculture sector where they have natural competitive advantage just because the developed countries are artificially sustaining uncompetitive agriculture in their economies, by creating distortions in the world economy through the channel of subsidies. The new patent regime under WTO has exposed the third world countries to bio-piracy theft of the indigenous knowledge of the third world countries. MNCs are using WTO to take away bio-diversity from the people of developing countries. By treating seeds plants, cells etc. as human inventors they are being patented, to the detriment of the farmers in developing countries.

## Human Security

The traditional concept of "security" has been couched in neo-realist terms thereby meaning the safeguarding of territorial integrity and sovereignty of nations. However, at the demise of the cold war, new questions pertaining to security have been raised. At the basic level, the security of states is dependant upon whether or not their citizens feel secure and unthreatened. A conceptualisation of security that is centered primarily on individual or the community can be understood as human security. Globalisation has induced phenomenon that is affecting security not only at the state level but at the end of individuals day-to-day lived experience. While this is true across the globe, in specific ways it may be particularly significant for the people of the South, where the twin challenges from freedom of want and freedom from fear are the most pervasive. Broadly speaking, human security as freedom from want describes a condition of existence in which basic material needs are met, and in which there is a reasonable expectation that protection will be afforded during any crisis or downturn—natural or man-made so that survival is not threatened. Human security as freedom from fear describes a condition of existence in which human dignity is realised, embracing not only physical safety but going beyond that to include meaningful participation in the life of the community, control over life and so forth. This suggests a radical account of politics as freedom from domination/exploitation, not simply the freedom to choose as advocated by the liberal tradition. Thus, while material sufficiency lies at the core of the human security, in addition the concept encompasses non-material dimensions to a qualitative whole. In other words, human security embraces the whole gamut of rights, civil and political, economic and social and cultural (*Caroline Thomas : 2007*).

The condition presupposes a situation of vulnerability, in which natural disasters (cyclone, earthquake, floods, volcanic eruption) and the man-made such as disasters (rising sea levels, oil spills, nuclear and chemical explosion, war) may cause conditions of horrible proportions that can play havoc, with individuals and communities, who are especially located in region, in a symbiotic ways. The uprooting caused by these agencies, may spill psychological and economic disruption which can take a heavy toll on individuals. The insecurity can also be caused due to the very structure of the global market, which is developing a tendency of cycles of recessionary interregnum. The period of recessions, across the board at global level have necessitated downsizing of the organisation leading to unemployment and informalisation of the labour.

The table (2.3) provides a comprehensive understanding of human security as understood in contradistinction to the earlier orthodox approach (state-centric).

**Table 2.3 Key elements of orthodox security and human security**

| | *Orthdox, state-centric security* | *Human Security* |
|---|---|---|
| Refresh Operating principal | The State<br>The state and national security | Humanity<br>Global connectivity |
| Agend | Justification and status military power and national defence | Explanation and transformation (exonomic and social welfare) |

| | | |
|---|---|---|
| Means | Self-help by states | Collective, integrated, multifacted response at multiple level |
| Input | Military expenditure and arms | Redistribution structural reform |
| Output | Secure bords | Enjoyment of Economic, social civil and political and cultural human rights |
| Outcome | Interstate stability order Interstate conflict international instability Unsustainable resource use | Global social Justice Sustainable Peace. |

*Source:* Thomas, 2000.

Caroline Thomas succinctly explains the approach.

> "...... concern with individuals and communities–not simply states–has been growing on the international agenda since the second cold war. However, it was in the mid 1990s that use of the term "human security" took hold, in the context of the political space, which opened post-cold war. Significant humanitarian crises, especially the genocide in Bosnia in 1992-95 (200,000 people killed), and in Rawanda in 1994 (500,000 deaths), coupled with growing acknowledgement of the uneven distributions of the benefits of economic globalisation, drew attention to human insecurity. The downside associated with particular aspects of globalisation, such as rapid liberalisation of financial flows, hit the headlines with the East Asian crises in 1947. During the 1990s, therefore, protection of the vulnerable whether physical or material—gained attention from several important constituencies, ranging from NGOs to middle ranking powers, the G-7 states, the international financial institutions and the UN."

The two core strands of interests in human insecurity have found different champions. The Canadian government, for instance, has emphasised more attention to acts of violence, in choosing its primacy, thus leading to landmines treaty. The Japanese government, on the other hand, heavily influenced by the effects of the Asian currency crisis at the end of the 1990s, has paid more attention to the economic aspects of human insecurity and threats to survival, and the need to protect people from sudden economic downturns.

With the end of the cold war it was apparently felt that the agenda of development would acquire the center-stage of global arena, as the money spent on arms and armaments could be utilised to fuel development goals. Such hopes were dashed to the ground, as war industry remained as it is, while a chunk of finance meant for developing countries was gradually channelised towards East European economies, who had undertaken the path towards market economy.

It was in this period that the then UNDP Director Mahbub-ul-haq, and his team of visionary economists and researchers, formulated the human development approach, in order to draw the attention of the world community to the idea that development consists in enhancing peoples quality of life, and considered economic growth as a mere means to that end. It is no less than a social irony that a country registering impressive rates of economic growth leaves a sector of its population illiterate, malnourished, socially marginalised and in poverty. Can this be called genuine development in the age of globalisation?

Since 1990, with a view to shifting the focus from the traditional "income-centered" accounting to "people oriented" programmes and polices, the United Nations development programme (UNDP) has been publishing the annual human Development Report (HDR) focusing on the conceptual issues and policy strategies, to tackle poverty and deprivation. One important component of the HDR is the Human Development Index (HDI), which ranks countries on the basis of three basic capabilities, life expectancy (ability to live a long and healthy life), educational attainments (ability to acquire knowledge through literacy, basic and secondary education) and economic standard of living (to have access to the resources needed for a decent living standard).

This index illustrates that the orthodox income based GDP per capita measure is an imperfect indicator of human development, and that the addition of capability based indicator shows quiet different results. When, for example, countries and regions such as Poland, Costa Rica, Brazil and the state of Kerala in India manage to achieve higher levels of 'human development' in comparison to countries and regions with similar or higher income levels, it reveals the stark disparity between 'human' and economic development that is prevalent in many countries. This index speaks much of the quality and performance of respective governments, and policy makers–right from the origin of the UNDP's human development approach. Amartya Sen has closely collaborated with Haq to strengthen its theoretical edifice by envisioning development as an expansion of human capabilities and freedoms for many social justice groups, the market can never deliver human security, and in fact it is a cause for insecurity.

Noted sociologist Ankie Hoogvelt believes that over the course of the next generation, as wages fall by up to 50 percent, 30 percent of people in societies regarded as advanced will be marginalised within a new non-spatial social periphery that had once been the sole spatial presence of the third world. Perhaps 20 per cent of people in societies once collectively called the third world will form part of a new globalised core. Columnist Larry Elliot of Guardian also perceives the danger—unless the market delivers what people want: a living wage, job security, quality of life, decent environment, dignity in old age, a thriving welfare state—then it stands to lose not just public support but its entire legitimacy.

The statistics tell its own tale. James Galbraith's research shows—Inequalities declined in 45 out of 64 countries during the 1960s and 1970s, but increased during the next twenty years.[20] One in six children in the world's richest countries now live in poverty; in Sweden the proportion is only 3 per cent, but in Britain it is 14 per cent, and in the united states 22 per cent, poverty presents these children with learning difficulties, encourages their early withdrawal from education, and leaves them more susceptible to drugs, crime and unemployment.

The growth in inequalities is greatest outside industrial democracies, where some 20 per cent of people (1.2 billion) survive on less than $1 per day, and 50 per cent (3 million) on less than $2. Twenty three per cent of America's adult are obese, and 55 per cent over weight. Treating the obesity costs the United States US $ 96 billion each year, or 10 per cent of its health bill. Thirty two billion dollars are spent annually on diet pills. In India, however, 49 per cent of adults are underweight, losing the economy some 9 per cent of output.[21] Aid can never resolve inequalities but, like the Marshall plan, it can provide the basis for growth. Unfortunately since the end of the cold war, international aid has fallen 21 per cent, US non-military aid by 50 per cent.[22]

In Sub-Saharan Africa the situation is more dismal. Although the data point to a worldwide net-reduction of poverty stricken people, polarisation is evident in African continent. Truncated globalisation combined with local dynamics bar the bulk of Africa from gaining access to the world's productive process. For the countries of Africa, the greatest challenge is to demarginalise when national options are severely constrained by the forces of globalisation. Some 50 per cent or 265 million people on the continent are mired in poverty, and with little hope for escape in sight, they are likely to continue in the future. Two decades of economic stagnation, cuts in public spending, debt servicing, civil wars, the AIDS epidemic, and demographic pressures have seen educational outlays per people fall one third since 1980. Daniel Cohen believes that the gap between the world's wealthiest countries and its poorest has grown, continuously. In 1800 the difference may have been as little as 30 per cent, but by 1870 industrial powers were eleven times as wealthy; in 1995 fifty times as wealthy.[23]

The reasons for Africa's plight are not far to decipher. War expenditure alone absorbs 2.6 per cent of the world's gross national product, with devastating consequences for countries affected. During the 1980s Iraq spent eight times on defence, what it spent on health and education; Somalia five times. Around the world unexploded mines kill 26,000 people and the tragedy mostly effects countries such as Angola and Cambodia. Angola is estimated to have ten million unexploded mines, one for each member of its population.[24] Much of the money devoted to warfare can easily be diverted to provisioning health and education, but politics aggravates this position.

Apart from the war, corrupt ruling elites have played their part, even in countries where wars have not been an immediate issue. In Nigeria, the former military leader General Sani-Abacha and his colleagues stole US $2.2 billion from their country. This is a country which has an air force of 10,000 men, but only 20 functioning planes, and a navy incorporating 52 admirals and commodores but only 8 serviceable ships. During the 1980s, 469 members of the Nigerian National Assembly voted themselves a US $ 25,000 furniture allowance. Nigeria's average monthly wage is US $30.[25] In the Congo, Mobutu Sese Seko tucked away US $ 4 billion from his cash starved people. In the Ivory Coast, one long ruling president spent vast sums of money transforming his village with motor ways, hotels, a vast airport, and the world's largest Christian church.

Despite the apparent failure of globalisation on human security front in many regions, there are chances for optimism. At the UN General Assembly's millennium Assembly in 2000, specific targets were set for development—the millennium Development Goals (*UN/OECD/IMF/World Bank,* 2000:5). The notion of freedom from want as integral to global justice was gaining ground, as is the recognition that growth with equity only can redeem globalisation, and pure neo-liberalism with its emphasis on the market can not be relied to enable broad based human security.

Since 1995, the Human Development Report (HDR) by introducing the Gender-related Development Index (GDI) and the Gender Empowerment Measure (GEM) have tried to underscore through facts and figures, the gender based character of poverty and deprivation, and how in many parts of the world girls and women are much more disadvantaged in terms of nutrition, education, health and self-respect than boys and men.

## Democracy and Democratisation

Globalisation over the period has impacted the process of democratisation and democracy. So widespread was the move to democracy in the developing world, in the 1980s and 1990s that Huntington (1991) gave it a name the "third wave of democracy". The third wave followed two earlier waves (the first was in late nineteenth century and the second directly after world war II) and began with the shift from authoritarian to democratically elected governments in Greece, Portugal and Spain in the mid 1970s. In the 1980s and the 1990s, democracy spread to numerous Latin American, East-European, Asian and African countries. In most of the developing countries, domestic political arrangements are to some degree, affected by globalisation, but the precise impact vary from country to country. The extent of the changes in this regard can be gauged from the fact that in 1973 only a quarter of countries had democratically elected governments. Twenty years later the proportion of democracies had grown to more than half and, by 2001, it had reached about 75 percent, that is around 150 countries. Democracy here refers to the holding of relatively free and fair elections following which a victorious party or parties takes power. Because the process of democratisation has deeper roots in Western world, we often associate democracy with the first world only. Some people argue that with the cold wars end, the inevitability of democracy has finally been accepted, globally. In 1980 only 35 percent of the world's population lived within democracies, twenty years later 54 percent did.[26] In another twenty years the proportion will be still higher. Thus democracy is inevitable, it has become the universal modern condition. Dictatorship regimes have also manipulated polls, to claim their dispensation as legitimately "democratic republics".

For one, the situation of arrogation of power and authority without having regard to public opinion, underwent considerable change with the advent of technology. East European nations, with communist overtones and faltering economic growth, could not stop the entry of stories that was abound with Western nation's prosperity and great economic leap. People who visited the West European countries were mesmerised by West's advance in consumer goods, enjoying a better life style, and social security along with myriad aspects of autonomy. It was this class of core motivated by the desire to imitate West, that constituted the civil society groups comprising of authors, theatre artists, film actors, managerial class, and technocrats of various hues, who led the protest against authoritarian regimes in Poland, Bulgaria, Czechoslovakia, Hungary, Romania and Yugoslavia. The so called colour revolutions with emphasis on liberal-democracy become the leitmotif of expanding base of democracy in the communing blocks. These happenings were watched with great interest by Western nations, and they welcomed the change with open heart with liberal economic aid so that democratic take over sees a stable and peaceful transition.

Jeffrey Haynes appropriately states:

> "Since the late 1980s, the US government has provided more than $ 700 million to over 100 countries to aid democratisation (Carothers, 1991): Carother argues that such assistance was focused in a standard democracy template, involving financial support to underpin the electoral process and democratic structures. Constitutions political parties, state institutions, the rule of law, legislatures, local government structures, better civil-military relations and civil society organisations. Leftwich (1993: 612) Points out that it takes more than money to develop democracy, as it is not easy to create and embede concrete manifestations of what he calls 'good governance'. Such an outcome is not simply available on 'order', but requires a particular kind of politics...to institute and sustain it. This raises an important issue: external funding for democracy will be insufficient to achieve its aims if target regimes are content to 'acquire democratic legitimacy internationally without substantially changing their mode of operation" (Lawson 1999: 23).

The changing political, economic and strategic considerations within the developing countries have altered the monolith appropriation of power and authority. The relative insignificance of national autonomy due to a mosaic of interdependencies, at levels of economic structures makes singular defiance of world community rather difficult. Any non-cooperation, or defiance is bound to unleash a chain of reactions causing difficulties to recalcitrant nations, thereby unfurling movements from below, led by civil society groups. The chain of events in Pakistan, Bangladesh, Indonesia, Philippines, Burma and recently in Egypt, Libya, Yemen and Syria, are an increasing pointer to this new dispensation, wherein the authoritarian regimes have been at loss to provide genuine reasonable grounds to world organisations and civil society groups for not conceding space for democratisation. Here the example of Libya whose political stability in the past four decades was based on the assumption that economic growth is assured. That didn't happen because of Gaddafi's profligacy and his desire to extend political patronage to all of Africa. He squandered the country's lavish resources in toppling governments. But for his ambitions, a country flush with oil and having a population of just six million should have had a standard of living rivalling Switzerland. Instead the country grovels in poverty; its quality of health care and education has progressively declined. The unemployment rate has remained 30 per cent for years fraught with dangerous consequences in a country where the young comprises 70 percent of the population. Moreover, Libyans lacked freedom of expression and association, Gaddafi, who described the rebels as rats and germs, drug addicts and drunkards, who needed to be eradicated, was not prepared to extend to his people the basic freedoms enjoyed by people in the West and even in those African nations that have a much lower standard of living. It is they who took enmasse to twitter and facebook to give a boost to the revolutionary zeal that the authorities sought to curb by cutting off the internet. But it was late, and suffered the same fate as that of Egypt and Tunisia. The uprising in Syria and Yemen by the civil society groups and youths contains similar undertones. The warnings of sanctions by the global community for coming heavily on protestors, sans complete disdain for politics of protest, may have telling effects on the outcome of political establishments in Syria and Yemen. These instances are a grim reminder to authoritarian regimes that widening of democratic space is sine-qua-non to stabilising them in power and authority, reversals can take its toll as in Egypt and Tunisia.

An interesting study undertaken by Freedom House to measure the spatial distribution of democratic outcomes across the continents has interesting results, as depicted in the following table (2.4).

**Table 2.4 – Regional breakdown of 'free' and 'partly free' countries in the developing world, 2000**

| *Region* | *Total "free" new demo-cracoes* | *% 'free'* | *Total 'Party new democ-racaies* | *% partly free* | *Over total: 'free' and 'partly free' newdemo-cracies* |
|---|---|---|---|---|---|
| Asia | 4 | 57 | 3 | 43 | 7 |
| Latin America | 5 | 44 | 9 | 56 | 16 |
| Afroca | 5 | 28 | 13 | 72 | 18 |
| Middle East | 0 | 0 | 4 | 100 | 4 |
| Total | 16 | | 29 | | 45 |

*Source:* Based on Freedom House survey data available at www.freedomhouse.org

In Sub-Saharan Africa, the democratic transition consists of peculiar set of factors, encompassing structural economy (dependency), social fragmentation (tribal loyalties), military establishment and foreign aid. The relative admixture of aforesaid variables have largely been responsible for political transition towards democratisation. see (table 2.5).

**Table 2.5 Decocracy in Sub-Saharan Africa, 2000**

| *Country* | *Political rights* | *Civil liberties* | *'Freedom status'* |
|---|---|---|---|
| Cape verde | 1 | 2 | free |
| Sao Tome Principle | 1 | 2 | free |
| South Africa | 1 | 2 | free |
| Benin | 2 | 3 | Partly free |
| Namibia | 2 | 3 | Partly free |
| Mali | 3 | 3 | Partly free |
| Malawi | 2 | 3 | Partly free |
| Seychelles | 3 | 3 | Partly free |
| Ghana | 3 | 3 | Partly free |
| Mozambique | 3 | 3 | Partly free |
| Central African | 3 | 4 | Partly free |
| Burkina Faso | 4 | 4 | Partly free |
| Guinea-Bissau | 3 | 5 | Partly free |
| Lesotho | 4 | 4 | Partly free |
| Tanzania | 4 | 4 | Partly free |
| Madagascar | 5 | 3 | Partly free |
| Gabon | 5 | 4 | Partly free |
| Zambia | 5 | 4 | Partly free |

1 = most free, 7 = least free; 'free' = combined political rights and civil liberties total of 2-5; 'partly free' = 6-9; 'not free' = 10-17.

*Source: Based on Freedom House survey data available at www.freedomhouse.org*

South Asian countries greatly differ in terms of size, geography, economic structures, political traditions, forms of rule, relations with external power and culture. With a long period of political apprenticeship during the colonial period, the liberal democratic gains till 2005, have been exemplary, in countries such as Pakistan, Nepal, Bhutan and Bangladesh Table (2.6).

**Table 2.6 New Democracy in South Asia, 2000**

| *Country* | *Political rights* | *Civil liberties* | *'Freedom status'* |
|---|---|---|---|
| Bangladesh | 3 | 4 | Partly free |
| Nepal | 3 | 4 | Partly free |

1 = most free, 7 = least free; 'free' = combined political rights and civil liberties total of 2-5; 'partly free' = 6-9; 'not free' = 10-17.

*Source:* Based on Freedom House survey data available at www.freedomhouse.org

Unlike Sub-Saharan Africa, the region's countries had many factors unpropitious for democracy, including poverty, under-development and widespread ethnic and religions strife.

In East and South-East Asia the 1980s and 1990s witness, the widening of democratic spaces in countries such as Taiwan, Thailand, Indonesia, Philippines and Singapore. President Suharto had paved for the transition to democracy, due to protests by students, on issues of corruption and misgovernment. In Phillipines the US support aided the transition to elected government. Thailand and Taiwan witnessed the roll back of authoritarian regime and consequent transition to democratic dispensations (see Table 2.7.)

**Table 2.7 New Democracy in East and South-East Asia, 2000**

| Country | Political rights | Civil liberties | 'Freedom status' |
|---|---|---|---|
| South Korea | 2 | 2 | free |
| Taiwan | 2 | 2 | free |
| The Philippines | 2 | 2 | free |
| Thailand | 2 | 3 | free |
| Indonesia | 4 | 4 | Partly |

1 = most free, 7 = least free; 'free' = combined political rights and civil liberties total of 2-5; 'partly free' = 6-9; 'not free' = 10-17.

***Source:*** Based on Freedom House survey data available at www.freedomhouse.org

The Latin America presents the picture of economic regression and political repression, generally at the hands of military dictators. The US support and the activism of the civil society groups, students and intelligentsia, was instrumental for paving the way towards democracies. An interesting feature has been the trend towards social democracies, a feature that combines democratisation with pro-poor and pro-people policies—generally a reaction to neo-liberal policies. Many of the ultra-leftist, who were engaged in guerilla warfare against the governments, were catapulted to power, see table (2.8).

**Table 2.8 New Democracy in Latin America, 2000**

| Country | Political rights | Civil liberties | 'Freedom status' |
|---|---|---|---|
| Urugay | 1 | 2 | free |
| Panama | 1 | 2 | free |
| Bolivia | 1 | 3 | free |

| | | | |
|---|---|---|---|
| Chile | 2 | 2 | free |
| Argentina | 2 | 3 | free |
| Dominican Republic | 2 | 3 | free |
| Ecuador | 2 | 3 | Partly free |
| El Salvador | 3 | 3 | Partly free |
| Honduras | 3 | 3 | Partly free |
| Nicaragua | 3 | 3 | Partly free |
| Brazil | 3 | 4 | Partly free |
| Guatemala | 3 | 4 | Partly free |
| Mexico | 3 | 4 | Partly free |
| Paraguay | 4 | 3 | Partly free |
| Colombia | 3 | 4 | Partly free |
| Peru | 5 | 4 | Partly free |

1 = most free, 7 = least free; 'free' = combined political rights and civil liberties total of 2-5; 'partly free' = 6-9; 'not free' = 10-17.

***Source:*** Based on Freedom House survey data available at www.freedomhouse.org

With the revolution in Eastern Europe, the release of Nelson Mandela, assertiveness of the human rights movements, the drive towards democratisation has won legitimacy. More importantly, pro-democracy forces have gained confidence. However, the consensus on adapting the versions of democracy, have differed from a liberal perspective, democracy centers on the principle that the right to rule should be based on the consent of the governed. Liberal democracy calls for public influence on government through such institutions as political parties, regular elections, and an alternation in power.

The rise of social movements from below have altered the traditional notion of democracy, based on liberal economic conceptualisation of globalisation, as it allows for tolerance of social inequality. The disruptive effects of globalisation on environment, women, tribals and marginalized sections seem to challenge the classical Greek theory-notion of democracy of rule by the people.

## Civil Society

Civil society is more generally understood to denote that sphere of human interaction or association which stands apart from the formal activities and structures of the state. The idea of civil society gained currency in the 1980s, in Poland, where the solidarity protest movement under Lech Walesa was regarded as a manifestation of an emerging civil society pressure group, specifically opposed to the communist state and seeking a measure of autonomy from it. While there are many interpretations of civil society, as explained by Hegel, Gramsci etc., in simple terms civil society is the contested political space established and extended by collective action, and composed of voluntary associations distinct from economy and, while not completely separate from, nonetheless outside the direct control of the state.

The idea of civil society has been imported into the politics of globalisation, partly because of multiple signs of the disintegrations of social orders. Civil society has acted as the watch dog, whistle blower, and voice for citizens, by taking recourse to agitation, peaceful protests, media sensitisation, and at times by undertaking mass movements in the zone of protest. The common target of all civil society groups, in one way or another, is global capitalism, and the increasing and unaccountable power of the multinational corporations in the current world order. The inequality explicit in the globalisation project between countries and among populations has been seriously castigated by the civil society groups.

The WTO held a ministerial meeting in Seattle in November and December, 1999 to launch a new round of trade liberalisation talks. Over 135 countries were represented. The event seemed to galvanise a wide body of opinion, almost 1,200 non-governmental organisation in 87 countries signed a petition calling for a fundamental reform of the WTO. Groups as varied as the Self Development of Indigenous People in Mexico and the Friends of the Earth joined common cause to condemn the present system of world trade and the closed and regressive nature of WTO rules and regulations. The planning of such groups as the Direct Action Network organised effective public protest. On Tuesday, 30 November the official opening of the conference was delayed as almost 20,000 people blocked the delegates entering the meeting at the Washington state convention and Trade center and effectively closed down the center of the city. Over the next few days protest actions were seen around the world, and the WTO, which had been an organisation unknown to the wider public, was pushed into the hard glare of media attention. The next day estimates of the crowd had increased to 50,000.[27] The demonstration in Seattle had succeded in shifting public opinion towards a closer scrutiny of the WTO and the supposed benefits of free trade.

The debate at Seattle widened to a critique of consumerist society, declining environmental quality and the power of multinationals. The talks were cancelled due to protest, and delegates could not sign an agreement.

The success of the Seattle protests emboldened civil society groups to plan protests of the joint IMF/World Bank meeting in Washington DC on 16-17 April, 2000. Estimates of the number of demonstrators varied from 35,000 to 10,000. Learning from the past experience of Seattle the police was able to manage avoid disruption of the meeting, but not before the message of the protestors received welcome audience by the officials. On 16 April, the IMF issued a communiqué that acknowledged the growing discontent with globalisation and that prosperity was not reaching everyone. The IMF announced new initiatives to place a renewed emphasis on debt relief for poorer nations and tighter auditing of IMF loans to avoid abuse. The IMF next day issued a more comprehensive plan that included more money to fight AIDS and speeding up debt relief for developing nations.

Prague, Seattle, Washington DC, all represented among many things, the emergence of the international civil society.

In the third world, civil society groups have made the transformation of the state their top priority. There is a sense among these groups that political transformation that empowers local communities may be the firststep towards poverty-alleviation. Civil society groups have been very effective in forming global alliances to counteract the excess of the state, and contest for widening the political space. This has had a positive fall out effect in the form of transparent and open elections, better accountability of public finance, independence of the judiciary, and inclusive economic policy, which is pro-poor. The recent 'Anna Hazare' movement in India under the banner of 'India against corruption' had shaken the very foundation of the government in Delhi, for the implementation of Lokpal (agenda of demands to lower corruption in government). The large scale mobilisation of people across India, from a variety of sections, represented the mood and tenor of the people. The government was forced to table a bill which will combat corruption in the government system. Earlier the same group has succeeded in getting the RTI (Right to information) Act passed, which enabled people to access information pertaining to the government functioning.

There are other laudable achievements that mark the vigour of civil society, from Central and South America through Africa, the Middle East and South and South-East Asia, the civil society groups have started to turn their attention on the excesses of market. From local to global issues pertaining to environment, displacement, marginalisation, social security, have begun to catch the limelight in media, TV and Conferences, thereby democratising and widening the narrow space which marked the political and economic dispensation of yester years. Thus Latin America has seen the burgeoning of indigenous, environmental, peasant, community association of the urban poor, as well as other key social movements that will play a central role in forcing any prospective egalitarian outcome. It is also worth noting that less coordinated mass protest is also the order of the day throughout the region. Hunger strikes, sit-ins, land invasions, marches, blocked street and mass meetings in both the cities and the countryside are regular occurrences (*Craig N. Murphy, 2002*). The following interventions undertaken by civil society organisations, are a pointer to their notable success in global platforms.

1. The Jubilee 2000 petition was launched during the 1998 G-8 summit in Birmingham, England. The demonstration reportedly involved 70,000 people linked together in a chain of arms to persuade the world leaders to provide debt relief for third world countries.
2. The Africa summits held in various American cities between 1998-2000 around the theme, 'Africa matters', focused on the investment potentials of African countries—civil Disobedience of WTO meetings in 1999 and 2001 and World Bank/IMF meetings in 1999-2000 also drew worldwide attention to the debt burden of third world countries and the need for debt relief for the poorest countries.
3. During the 2000 International AIDS conference in Cape Town a global coalition linked the debt burden and its

subsequent impacts on health care to the rapid rise of AIDS amongst the poor. The call for debt relief was again reissued here and at the 2000 G-8 summit in Japan (*B. Ikubola Jeh Logan, 2002*).

4. Despite notable achievements of the civil society groups in marshalling community mobilisation and international political activism, there are legitimate doubts on the ability of civil society to represent the interests of the poor effectively. For one thing, civil society covers a wide array of groups and agendas. Like the state and the market, elements of civil society tend to be self-serving and engage in a lot of turf protection to secure donor funding. Thus Glenzer notes that civil society is often beset by a number of short comings. Local organisations tend to be led by individuals with strong ties to the state and with agendas that are sometimes antithetical to the needs of the poor, many groups lack the managerial and organisational skills required to tackle, headlong, the grand project of poverty-alleviation; many groups lack the capacity to replace the state as provider of the basic social needs of the poor, and their reliance on the market (or agents of the market) for funding, encourages an agenda that is likely to impoverish the poor even further.

## Regional Organisations

The past two decades have seen a strengthening and deepening of regional trade arrangements as almost every country in the world has joined some kind of preferential trading arrangement.[28] The European Union (EU) has moved towards a single market. The North American Free Trade Agreement (NAFTA) has cemented a free trade area among Canada, the United States and Mexico, and is now further extending its membership. A large but less formal arrangement, which has come to the fore is Asia Pacific Economic Cooperation Group (APEC). In South, American countries have joined MERCOSUR. In other parts of the world, list includes the Economic Community of West African States (ECOWAS), the Southern African Development Coordination Conference (SADCC), the Preferential Trade Area for Eastern and Southern African States (PTA), the Association of South-East Asian Nations (ASEAN), the South Asian Association for Regional Cooperation (SAARC), the Gulf Cooperation Council (GCC), the Latin American Integration Association (LAIA), and the Carribean Community (CARICOM).

The encouragement to undertake regional grouping, was the formation of European Economic Community. Its successes, in reducing the trade barriers and enabling nations to reap a rich harvest in sectors of their advantage, helped the cause of proliferation. Moreover, many of the developing countries who were sidelined by the GATT, found in these groupings a future for their market, by granting reciprocal treatments to each other. Some scholars are of the opinion, that emergence of regional organisations will favourably offer basis for multilateral harmonisation of trade. The task of combining various regional organisations into single multilateral trading system would apparently be easier, than dealing with individual participating nations. In fact, the presence of regional organisations, with prior understanding and experiences, would be like a pre-emptive homework thus leading to less brainstorming among the financial interlocutors. They would act as 'building blocks' (*Ngaire Woods:* 2004) towards global free trade. The optimists highlight that regionalism has increased the depth of liberalisation since regional free trade agreements frequently involve the integration or harmonisation of a number of loosely assorted trade related policies. This has led to negotiations at the international level on policies regarding intellectual property, as well as investment rules, labour rights, tax and competition policies, and the treatment of the environment. In other words, regionalism is assisting the passage from shallow to deep integration.[29]

The contrarion view holds an opposite view. They cite, that regional economic blocks impede the emergence of single multilateral integration, and thereby derail the process towards integration of the global economy. The states who are hostile to the prescriptions of WTO due to the distinct advantage of US, UK, Japan and Germany might well be tempted to use the regional grouping to torpedo the WTO regulated financial system. The universal set of rules for trade under the trinity of the IMF, World Bank and WTO, may be challenged by powerful regional organisations, which can roll back the process of global integration. Furthermore, if powerful states focus attention towards their region then they are likely to neglect international fora and organisations. Although there is little evidence of this, indeed Mexico and Canada are using the WTO against the United States, and Brazil is taking two cases against Argentina to the WTO.

While academic reasons are easier said than done, not withstanding the above negativities in the case of economic regional block the statistics shows that no country has a clear cut choice in order to either opt for regional trading block or multilateral scheme.[30] All regions are heavily dependant on each other due to varying incidence of mineral resource availability, agricultural practices, manufacturing agglomeration and comparative cost advantages. The only guiding factor that plays a role in deciding the economic course of action is the advantage of the market. The EU relies heavily on North American markets as does Japan, NAFTA offers too small an area of trade for the USA. The interest of the USA in promoting the Uruguay round was to open up newer markets, to extend coverage to agriculture and services and to fix up areas like intellectual property rights, and foreign investment.[31] In the 1990s, the US companies were facing a stiff competition from Japan, Germany and South-East Asian nations such as Taiwan, Korea and Singapore. The loss in manufacturing was intended to balance with the new sectors of economies, such as TRIPs, TRIMs and services. At the same time, the evidence suggests that powerful states gain important bargaining leverage from participation in regional blocks. (*Diana Tussie and Ngaire Woods, 2000*). The United States, for example, used the threat of NAFTA and APEC to force other countries to take the Uruguay round seriously (*Jeffrey Schott; 1989*).

Furthermore, the new regionalism (*Diana Tussie and Ngaire Woods,* 2000) helps in bridging the traditional division, between the industrialised and developing countries, and paves the way for a more cosmopolitan economic grouping encompassing rich and poor countries alike. Richer trade blocks have long been presented as one solution that might enable poor nations to access richer markets, while maintaining some degree of protection for domestic producers. It is quite possible that by the end of the 21st centuries first decade, we shall witness the consolidation of an embraced European Union (28 countries and 600 million people), an American Free Trade Association (34 countries and 880 million people), and East Asian Free Trade Association (13 countries and 2 billion people). WTO Director General Mike Moore believes that regional blocs help officials to prepare for global liberalisation and enable them to develop the necessary negotiating skills.

Regionalism may have a role in augmenting the power of powerful nations such as USA and Japan, but smaller countries may also reap advantages by way of regional grouping, and consequent enlargement of the market. Since the forthcoming period, essentially, would rest on the strategic width of market, the smaller nations can increase their bargaining in multilateral forums with joint efforts.

The implications of regionalism for multilateralism and consequent process of globalisation would ultimately depend upon the degree to which regionalism effects global economic integration and governance. The regional associations may prove to be a strong vehicle for multilateral cooperation, as the experiences and maturity in their regional setting could remove the ostensible fears and distrust. This would open the door for much confident interrelationship, exchange and intersection.

## References

1. The term 'political economy' gained currency with Karl Marx's interpretation of the nature of state, wherein he opined that political actions are ingrained in the respective economic matrix, which in turn is reflection of class formation.
2. As cited in Business week, 26 January, 1998, p. 28.
3. For details see the opinion piece by Mahatir Mohammed, Prime Minister of Malaysia, in the wall street Journal, 23 sep., 1997.
4. Robert Wade, 'National Power, Coercive Liberalism and Global Finance' in Robert Art and Robert Jervis (ed.), International politics; Enduring concepts and contemporary issues (New york: Addison/Wesley Longman).
5. Dani Rodrik, 'The New Global Economics and Developing Countries Making Openness Work (Washington DC: Overseas Development Council), 1999, p.148.
6. Leys, (ed.) Barbara Harris White, 'Globalisation and Insecurity, Palgrave, 2002.
7. Lograin, 2000.
8. World Bank, World Development Indicators, 2006, table 6.1, UNCTAD Statistical Handbook.
9. Brooks, "The Globalisation of Production", 654; Deibert, Parchment, p.26.
10. Eichengreen and Kennen, 'Managing the World Economy',

pp. 33-6, Mahbub-ul-Haq, "The Brettonwood Institutions and Global Governance in Kennen, Managing the World Economy, p. 410.

11. IMF, Selected Decisions of the Executive Board, (Washington DC: IMF, 1991), pp. 105-34; Joseph Gold Standby Arrangements (Washington DC: IMF, 1970).
12. Miles Kohler, 'Orthodoxy and its Alternatives : Explaining Approaches to Stablisation and Adjustment' in Joan Nelson (ed.) Economic Crisis and Policy Choices : The Politics of Adjustment in the Third World (Princeton University Press, 1990), pp. 42-3.
13. Elliot Berg and Alan Batchelor, Structural Adjustment Lending: A critical view; World Bank-CPD Discussion Paper No. 1985-21 (Washington DC: World Bank, 1985) pp. 9-11.
14. A Leftwich, 'Governance, Democracy and Development in the Third World' Third World Quarterly, 14 (3), 1993, p. 607.
15. TR Papola, 'Social Dimension of Globalisation, IASSI, Quarterly, 2007, Vol. 25, No.23.
16. Hindu, 19 March, 2012.
17. Rajendra Kumar, "Failure of the Doha Round -Looking Back to Look Ahead, South Asian Politics, 2007, January, No. 9.
18. *Ibid.*
19. V. Mathew Kurien, "AOA, TRIPs and the Third World Agriculture", Mainstream, Dec. 22-28.
20. Galbraith, Inequality Employment and Growth.
21. Guardian, Weekly, 9-15 March, 2000, p. 7.
22. *Ibid 2-8* Dec, 1999, p. 3.
23. David Cohen 'The Wealth of the World and the Poverty of Nations, Cambridge, MIT Press, 1998.
24. Ramon-Luis Acuna, A culture of peace, Le monde Diplomatique, Nov, 1999, p.16.
25. Karl Maier, This House has Fallen: Nigeria In Crisis, London, Penguin, 1999, Guardian weekly, 25-30 June, 2001, p.16.
26. Jeoff Haynes, Politics in the Developing World, Blackwell Publishing, 2002, United Kingdom, pp. 81-93.
27. Business Standard, Dec. 1, 1999.
28. World Trade Organisation (1995); see Frankel, Regional Trading Blocs.

29. R. Lawrence, Futures for the World Trading System : Implications for Developing Countries, in M. Agosin and D. Tussie (eds.), Trade and Growth : New Dilemmas in Trade Policy (London: Macmillan, 1993), pp. 43-68.
30. On NAFTA see Jeffrey Schott, Free Trade areas and the US Trade Policy (Washington DC: Institute for International Economic, 1989) and Jorrod Weiner, Making Rules in the Uruguay Round of GATT (Aldershot, UK: Dartmouth, 1995). On APEC see I. Dastler, American Trade Politics, 3rd ed. Frankel, Regional Trading Blocs in the World Economic System (Washington DC: Institute for International Economic, 1998).
31. Guardian Weekly, 6-12 January, 2000, p. 2; 3-9 January, 2002, p-14.

# 3

# Economics of Globalisation

The years of war and depression in the early twentieth century produced consensus among policy makers that unemployment should be kept as low as possible. Economists were of the opinion that by putting money in the economy, growth could be achieved. Underlying this presumption the governments spent money to create jobs. The impact of this was unprecedented rise in living standards across the industrialised parts of the world and very low levels of unemployment. The relationship of capital, investment, growth and employment convinced policy makers, and rulers that peoples destiny could be altered by introducing suitable pills of economic medicines.

The more people are unemployed, the greater pressure on workers in employment to moderate wage demands, and since wages formed a large component of costs across most economies, any tendency for wage rates to decline would similarly impact on inflation (*Robbie Robertson, 2004*). The relationship between inflation and unemployment demonstrated the existence of a natural equilibrium, which could be manipulated by policy instruments such as tax rates, public spending and varying interest rates to ensure continuous growth.

In spite of this new understanding of economies the man-made interventions went astray in the 1970s. Unemployment and inflation instead of balancing each other rose at the same time, it was called as stagflation and economists were at pains to explain it. The monetarists who had fallen apart due to 1930 depression debacle joined the debate with vengeance, arguing that Keynesian economists had misled governments into believing that they could spend their way out of recession. Milton Friedman (noted Chicago economist) exhorted that spending fuelled inflation.To stop inflation government had to slow monetary growth by raising interest rates and by reducing public expenditures. Many governments including Britain fell under the spell of monetarism, in order to curb and curtail inflation, which was eating at the roots of profit. The time honoured practice of reducing unemployment gave way to, hurried attempts, curbing and reigning inflation.

The period of 1970s marks an important turn around for the global economy. USA's war in Vietnam and Indo-china, had decidedly thrust economic pressures, so much so that USA'S dollar lost its confidence in international market due to balance of payment deficits. The 1973 oil crisis triggered a shock to the global manufacturing. Unemployment soared to a new height, so did inflation, although at different levels in different countries. Paul Ormerad contends that there is no relation between economic growth and unemployment over a period of time. Between 1970 and 1992 the US economy grew 76 percent and employment 45 per cent. European economic communities economies grew by 75 per cent, but employment only 7 per cent. The ghost of stagflation caused panic, and the confidence of the governments was at its low ebb. The unfolding of Japan and West European countries, with their newfound wealth, and emergence of developing countries among which, few made rapid strides in the economic realm, unfolded the drama of contentious economic engagements. The coming of Ronald Reagan and Margaret Thatcher in US and Britain respectively marks the advent of heydays of monetarists, who dominated the multilateral bodies such as IMF and World Bank. The Keynesian sops of guiding the market with the state intervention again goes to the background and the virtues of the market were held is esteem. The cheap fund made available through World Bank to the third world countries to modernise by building infrastructure suddenly began to dry up, due to increase in the interest rates. This marked the advent of period when World Bank was well positioned to insist from its clients, to undertake structural adjustments (winding up state sector, opening up markets to private capital and balancing budgets) in lieu of loans.

Despite the claims of the monetarists, of having the clue to economic travails, the general economic climate takes a beating. The United States intensified its wind back of social programmes and injected vast resources into the renewed cold war (*Starwars programme*) through debt and borrowings. US went deeper and deeper into debt. Debt sustained the US economy, but as the costs of servicing debt rose, social services declined (*Robbie Robertson*). Debt also sustained domestic consumer spending, jumping from US $155 billion in 1993 to US $795 billion in 1989. Monetarism also failed to roll back the state in Britain. Public expenditures remained at 42 percent of GDP during the 1970s and 1980s.

In the end, public support for the permission of state services weakened the monetarist push.[1] One fact that cannot be lost sight of is that both in Britain and West Europe, the maintenance of welfarism served their societies well by preventing exactly the kind of devastating social shocks that had destabilised European societies during the 1930s.

The failure of the monetarists, in halting the wreck, through their economic prescriptions, paves the way to a mix of economic doses, enabled by multilateral order to make their economies globally competitive to hold on to their respective share of the world market, nations increasingly resorted to policies, that reduced wage costs, shifting the tax burden from corporate businesses, disposing of state assets, rolling back uncompetitive employment sectors which had acted to cushion societies during recessions. The assets of the state were to be privatised and labour markets were made more flexible to the privilege of capital. Henceforth workers employment conditions deteriorated, unemployment rose, state expenditures on health and education fell, and in many cases the more expensive services provided by the now privatised utilities declined in quality. The twin strategies of state planning at home, and trade liberalism internationally, which had been the central feature of the post-war years, disappeared. Now only one strategy officially existed – regulation for both the nation and international relations (*Robertson,* 2004).

The deregulation introduced after 1980s at the level of the policies (industrial, finance, capital, services, investment), has heralded a new era of financial globalisation. Unregulated capital has reacted to the volatility of its own markets by increasingly emphasising short-term profit at the expense of investment, the resulting decline in growth feeds volatility further and the consequent result has been crises and financial shocks, causing economic downturns globally with few exceptions like China and India, who were able to absorb the shock, by their own style of statism and governmental management of fiscal and monetary policy. The structure of the trade has undergone a fundamental change in the 1980s. In the four decades running from 1945 to 1985 global economic expansion was taking place mainly within and among OECD countries. However, in the wake of the 1980s debt crisis, a large number of developing countries began to liberalise their economies, dismantling trade barriers, as well as domestic production subsidies, subsequently, these countries enjoyed an increase in exports as well as imports including more trade with OECD countries and perhaps yet more markedly, an increase in trade with other developing countries (*Dianna Tussie and Nagaire Woods*).

The world economy has witnessed transformation, in terms of increase in capital flows along with merchandise. The growth of capital flows has been explosive, with an almost fourfold increase while capital now have seen a great speed, their consequent flight in unfavourable economic environment or better opportunities elsewhere, shad been a cause for recurrent cycles of shocks, and downturn in the capital markets all over the world.[2] The crisis in Mexico, South- East Asia, Europe, Russia are a grim reminder of the financial integration of capital and consequent impact on people, state and business environment.

The growth, investment and trading patterns have enhanced the stakes, the countries have in global integration, at global and regional levels. Overall, globalisation has set in new processes, new participants, new kinds of transnational exchanges, and new sets of relations into the international trade area. While many states face new opportunities (India, China), they are also constrained by new kind of vulnerabilities, extending to include the poor, marginalised, labourers, environment etc. to estimate the length and breadth of the globalisation on economic parameters, pertaining to inequality, poverty, growth, food security and migration, one has to extend the analysis beyond statistical data and carefully explore the intertwining of possible linkages embedded in the history and economic specificities of countries concerned.

## Foreign Direct Investment (FDI)

The increased influence of private interests, especially the multinational corporations, is arguably the most interesting aspect of the current process of global financial integration. During the 1980s according to (*Cobus-de-Swardt-Kraus, 2000, p. 62*) government not only changed their policies on Foreign Direct investment (FDI), but also turned FDI into a competitive terrain as a source of capital and technology. Some of the general changes in regard to FDI regulations include the following:

(*i*) The number of activities and industries closed to FDI, or with major restrictions on FDI, has been considerably reduced. Earlier many governments felt threatened due to the monopolising powers of FDI. The drying up of concessional loans from multilateral institutions, provided the ideal setting for FDI;

(*ii*) Compulsory joint ventures with governments and / or local private enterprises are now limited to a small number of strategic activities;

(*iii*) The establishment of global legal standards which offers protection to foreign investors, particularly in the area of expropriation and state contracts. Countries like China with their communistic ideological orientations were feared but with formalisations of international rules, China became a preferred destination for FDI;

(*iv*) Entry of authorisation requirements are being eliminated and replaced by registration aimed at facilitating the repatriation of capital and remittances of profit. The earlier restrictions imposed on the remittances of multinationals, to their station of origin, acted as the chief stumbling block, for FDI investments.

The above mentioned changes in the management of FDI have led to dramatic increase in FDI. The FDI multinationals quadrupled between 1985 and 1995 and increased by 40 percent in 1995 alone (*John H, Dunning 2000*). Thus Cobus-De-Swardt-Kraus (2000) offers following interesting details:

> "During the 1980s, around 97 percent of all outward direct investment consistently originated from companies 'based' in one of only ten countries (OECD). While there were no major changes in the geographical origin of outward direct investment, the geographic destination of FDI, has however changed considerably. For example, until 1960, the 'Third World' received about half of the total FDI flows. By 1966 this percentage had declined to one third, and to one quarter in 1974. By the late 1980s it had dropped to 16.9 per cent, with more than half of this figure going to the regions of East, South and South-East Asia. Africa's share declined to less than 2 per cent during the 1990s due to a substantial loss on investment. By mid 1990s, 91.5 per cent of FDI flows went to the more advanced industrialised countries composed of 28 percent of the world's population."

In general, investment and trade liberalisation, as facilitated by the multilateral institutions, such as GATT and Later on WTO, diminished the influence of local policy tools, such as tariffs and quotas. The capacity of governments to protect domestic producers and domestic workers consequently declined. Moreover, most of the governments were in crucial need of foreign exchange and technology to initiate competitive manufacturing of goods and services, hence they began to offer a range of incentives, tax holidays, investment zones with cheap land and one window clearance of projects. For example, the French government subsidised a quarter of the cost of recently developed Mercedez-Benz plant in Lorraine.

The FDI by multinational corporations in developing countries grew twelve fold between 1970 and 1992 (*World InvestmentReport, 1996*). It then trebled between 1992 and 1997, rising to U.S $149 billion out of a worldwide FDI total of US $ 400 billion (*World Investment-Report, 1996 and 1998*). The table 3.1 shows US FDI flows.

**Table 3.1 US International Direct Investment Flows**

| Period | FDI Inflow | FDI Outflow | Net Inflow |
|---|---|---|---|
| 1960-69 | $ 42.18 bn | $ 5.13 bn | +$ 37.04 bn |
| 1970-79 | $ 122.72 bn | $ 4079 bn | +$ 81.93 bn |
| 1980-89 | $ 206.27 bn | $ 329.23 bn | - $ 122.96 bn |
| 1990-99 | $ 950.47 bn | $ 907.34 bn | +$ 43.13 bn |
| 2000-07 | $ 1,629.05 bn | $ 1,421.31bn | +$ 207.74 bn |
| Total | $ 2,950.72 bn | $ 2,703.81bn | +$ 246.88 bn |

***Source:*** *BEA (Bureau of economic Analysis, US Dept. of Commerce).*

A recent paper published by the commonwealth secretariat discusses the situation of the least developed and land locked countries in the global economic system. It quotes WTO data to show that even after removal of systematic biases against trade and the dismantling of barriers since mid 80's, India's share in world merchandise increased by only 0.5 per cent in 1983 to 1 per cent in 2006. In 1948, soon after the conclusion of GATT, India's share was much higher at 2 per cent. More generally the paper, by Stanford University visiting professor TN Srinivasan, said the total share of world merchandise trade for Mexico, South and Central America, Middle East, Africa and Asia (excluding Japan) that together broadly cover the developing world, was 31.4 per cent in 1948, 26.8 per cent in 1983 and 35.4 per cent in 2006. If South, East Asia, which has been more open since 1960s and China, which opened in 1978, are excluded, the share of the remainder of this group was 27.1% in 1948, 19.8 per cent in 1983 and 19.6 per cent in 2006 (*T.N. Srinivasan*).

The paper also refers to World Bank data that suggests a similar recent trend, "It is clear that although the period after 1980 is one of growing integration of the developing world with the world trade – certainly it resulted in halting the decline and has in fact, raised the export share of the developing world – the gain in export share has largely been in China, and South-East Asia, Africa and South and Central America have experienced a steady decline in their share of world trade ever since 1948."

John Dunning cites three important factors that alters the course of multinational FDI. He says that the direction of the FDI or its destinations would rest essentially on three factors, i.e., change in their own competitiveness, alterations in what they seek from countries in which they invest, and a transformation in the way they link production to local markets.

**Table 3.2 The Largest Recipients of Inward FDI 1975-1980 and 1990-1996 (annual average)**

| *Country* | *1975/80 $m* | *Developed Countries %[b]* | *Country* | *1990/96 $m* | *%* |
|---|---|---|---|---|---|
| USA | 7894.0 | 32.0 | USA | 44757.1 | 29.2 |
| UK | 5795.4 | 21.1 | UK | 19613.4 | 12.8 |
| France | 2127.3 | 8.6 | France | 19080.1 | 12.4 |
| Nether-ands | 1276.6 | 5.2 | Belgium[b] | 10012.1 | 6.5 |
| Australia | 1271.4 | 5.2 | Spain | 8579.3 | 35.6 |
| Belgium[b] | 1203.1 | 4.9 | Netherlands | 7770.9 | 5.1 |
| Germany | 1052.6 | 4.3 | Canada | 6185.3 | 4.0 |
| Spain | 970.5 | 3.9 | Australia | 6118.9 | 4.0 |
| Top[8] | 209916 | 85.2 | Top[8] | 122117.1 | 79.6 |
| All | 4642.0 | 100.0 | All | 153380.9 | 100.0 |
| Brazil | 1835.8 | 24.4 | China | 22424.7 | 30.0 |
| Mexico | 2023.5 | 13.5 | Singapore | 7081.7 | 9.5 |
| Malaysia | 524.3 | 7.0 | Mexico | 5622.1 | 7.5 |
| Singap-ore | 502.0 | 36.7 | Malaysia | 34289.0 | 35.7 |
| Egypt | 376.8 | 5.0 | Argentina | 3690.3 | 34.9 |

| *Country* | *1975/80 $m* | *Developed Countries* | | *1990/96 $m* | *%* |
|---|---|---|---|---|---|
| | | *%[b]* | *Country* | | |
| Iran | 315.5 | 4.2 | Brazil | 3222.7 | 4.3 |
| Indone-sia | 289.9 | 3.8 | Indonesia | 2842.6 | 3.8 |
| Hong-Komg | 241.1 | 3.2 | Thailand | 2197.9 | 2.9 |
| Top 8 | 5108.2 | 67.8 | Top 8 | 51353.0 | 68.7 |
| All | 7539.1 | 100.0 | All | 74777.6 | 100.0 |

**Notes:**

(a) Bermuda was, in fact, ranked higher - Sixth - but we have excluded the tax haven from our ranking

(b) Of all developed country investment

(c) Of all developing country investment.

(d) And Luxemburg

***Source:*** UNCTC, Transitional Corporations and World Development (New York, UN, 1988); UNCTAD, World Investment Report, 1995: Transitional Corporations and competitiveness (New York and Geneva, UN, 1995); UNCTAD, World Investment Report, 1998 (Geneva and New York: United Nations, 1998).

In the years 1975-1980, the ten largest recipients of FDI identified in the above table account for 74.1% of all FDI inflows, and in 1990-1994 they accounted for 68.8%. In the former period, Japan accounted for only 0.6% of all inflows into developing countries; and in the latter for 1.0%.

Table 3.2 gives details of the leading recipients of inward direct investments in the two periods in developed and developing countries. Overall in 1975-80, the ten largest recipient countries accounted for 74.1 per cent of all FDI flows; with just over one half being directed to the United

States, the United Kingdom, France and the Netherlands. By the first-half of the 1990s, the geographical concentration had decreased to 66.5 per cent, although from leading countries, viz., the United States, the United Kingdom, France and China, still accounted for 46.4 per cent of the total FDI flows. Table (3.1) also shows that, among the most significant changes in the distribution of inbound FDI between developed countries over the past two decades have been, first the rise of China to the position of second largest recipient and second, the declining drawing power of Brazil and Egypt. Among the developed countries, France, Spain and Canada have both increased their share of FDI over the past two decades, while of the developing countries, Singapore, Argentina and Thailand have considerably strengthened their position. An important fact which needs to be taken into account, is the phenomenal increase in the Chinese share of FDI investment. The advantage with the Chinese lay in the repatriation of investments by NRI Chinese based in Makau and Hongkong. The policy of the Chinese government to create free trade zones across the coastal China with tax cuts, for FDI related production and comparable industrial peace are primarily the reason for its turn around.

Over the years, the nature and character of the competitive advantage of multinational corporations has changed. In general their country of ownership has become a less important determinant and their degree of multinationality which is firm specific variable a more important one. Moreover, although part of the core competencies of firms continues to be the exclusive or privileged possession of specific assets, it is the way in which these assets are governed and coordinated with the assets of other firms, and with the specific endowments of countries or regions, in which they operate, which is increasingly driving the global strategy of MNCs and the location of their various value added activities (*John H. Dunning*).

Kuemmerle, (in the drivers of Foreign Direct Investment) has detailed, that over the last two decades, not only has the percentage of innovatory activity undertaken by multinationals outside their home countries risen sharply, but the reason for conducting such activity at least in industrialised countries have broadened to include both the creation of new core products/processes and the acquisition of Research and Development facilities necessary to advance the productivity and remain in the market. The share of FDI, in Research and Development related activities in developing countries has fallen compared to rich nations.

## Poverty and Inequality

The relationship of poverty and inequality with globalisation is one of the heated areas, constituting the hot spring of debate on the various dimensions of poverty. The notion of a self-regulating market is most fundamentally misapplied to labour, when labour is assumed to be a commodity in abundance and variable supply that responds primarily to market signals. Poverty is then explained as a preponderance of underutilised labour, the solution to which is increased employment through macro-economic growth. The World Bank defines poverty as the inability to attain a minimum standard of living with poverty gauged in terms of the expenditure necessary to procure nutrition and basic necessities, and at a more country specific level the cost of participating in every day life.

How the poor derive and spend their income is the stated topic of the World Bank, and World Development Report.

The follow up report on poverty reduction (World Bank, 1996, 2) also centers on income and consumption. In both the documents, expenditure has been taken as the benchmark for measuring poverty.

There is another school of thought that problematises poverty, as it is embedded in the social and market structure (Neo-liberal). This conceptualisation of poverty departs from the World Bank defined perspective in that it focuses on production in order to portray poverty as arising within work relations (*Ashwini Tambe and James H. Mittleman*), however, constrained and not simply occurring simultaneously with unemployment and underemployment. Secondly, it links poverty to the process of marginalisation, rather than limiting it to a category of people. It takes the preliminary step of dissociating poverty from static geographical and cultural categories to conceive in relational terms. The powerlessness of the poor may then be partly explained by the disembedding of market forces from society. They are excluded from the very realm of production processes. The very rigidity of structures (production, hierarchy) help in keeping them marginalised. Due to the very nature of social structure the rewards from labour are less than the amount of work expended. Thus the process of globalisation in this context, pushes the people to edges of the economy (informalisation, retrenchment, underemployment) beyond which returns from work are lower than the effort expended. When people live in poverty, their work consistently incurs a higher cost than its return. Implied here is all work, whether wage earning or not, and all costs, especially those of health and the ability to survive. In this case it is pertinent to note the case of India, Where there was a national furore over government's decision to announce the benchmark of poverty as 28 rupees for cities per day and 22 rupees in rural areas, for the purpose of policy making. The government of India had to announce the necessary roll back of this figure, due to media and civil society intervention. Thus many people are of the view that the statistical indicators, adopted by World Bank and countries, in fact do not portray the real picture of poverty, rather these are figures for legitimising the neo-liberal agenda at global level.

If we countextualise poverty and inequality then it encompasses different terrain, such as inequality among the citizens of the world, distribution within countries, distribution among wage earners.

David Dollar, (2007) presents evidence in support of five trends in inequality and poverty since 1980:

- Growth rates in poor countries have accelerated and are higher than growth rates in rich countries for the first time in modern history;
- The number of extremely poor people (those living on less than $1 a day) in the world has declined significantly;
- By 375 million people for the first time in history though the number living on less than $2 a day has increase;
- Global inequality has declined modestly, reversing a 200 year trend towards higher inequality;
- Within country inequality is generally not growing;
- Wage inequality is rising worldwide. This may seem to contradict the fourth trend, but it does not because there is no simple link between wage inequality and household income inequality.

The globalisation trend after 1978, which coincides with the oil shocks, rising inflation, external debts of Latin

America, South Asia and African nations, marks a critical rethinking of economic policy from protectionism to increased openness and liberalisation. The openness adopted in this period leads to increase in trade and economic turn around, as depicted in the figure (3.3). China's ratio of trade to national income has more than doubled, and countries such as Mexico, Bangladesh, Thailand and India have seen large increases as well.

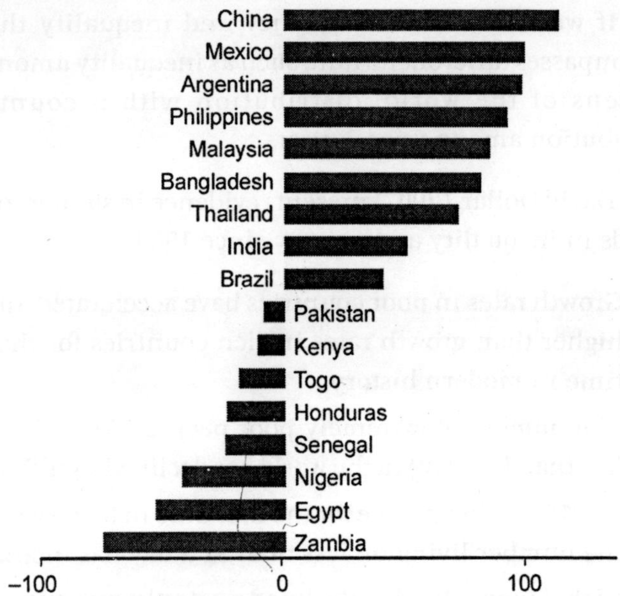


**Fig. 3.3. Change in trade as a share of GDP, selected countries, 1977–1997 (%).**

***Source :*** World Bank (2002).

The perceptible change according to David Dollar has been not only in the amount, but also in the nature of what is traded. Twenty years ago, nearly 80 per cent of developing country merchandise exports were primary products. The stereotype of poor countries exporting tin or bananas, has paved the way towards big increase in merchandise exports in the past two decades, in terms of manufactured products, So that 80 percent of today's merchandise exports from developing countries are manufactures. figure (3.4) Garments, from Bangladesh, CD players from China, refrigerators form Mexico, and computer peripherals from Thailand. In services sector India has made an important dent in software exports.

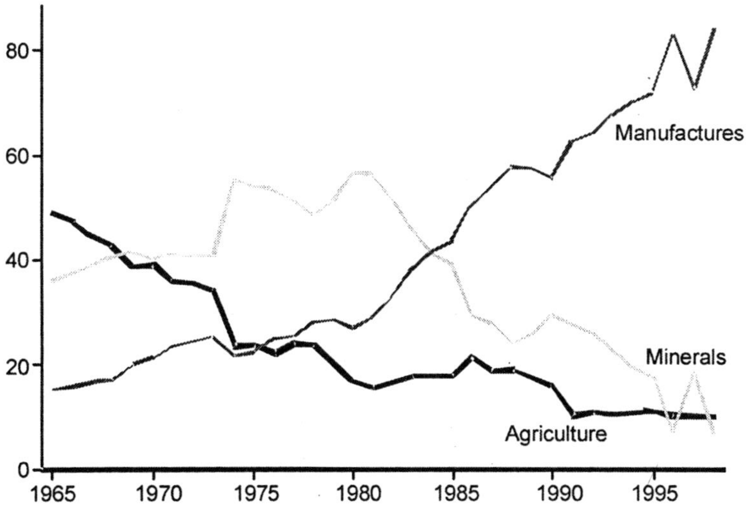


**Fig. 3.4. Developing country exports by sector, 1965–1999 (% of Total).**

***Source:*** **World Bank (2002).**

The change in the composition of trade towards value addition in developing economies, was greatly facilitated by reduction in tariff barriers, across the board, simplification of licensing procedures and favorable tax sops to business. The multinational enterprises took the location specific advantage with cheap supply of labour to bring the turn around in the exports of goods and merchandise. The figure (3.5) indicates the trade and tariff barrier relation in the last two decades (1980-2000).

The impact of globalisations on the poor people is complex enough to elude sweeping statements,(*David Dollar*).

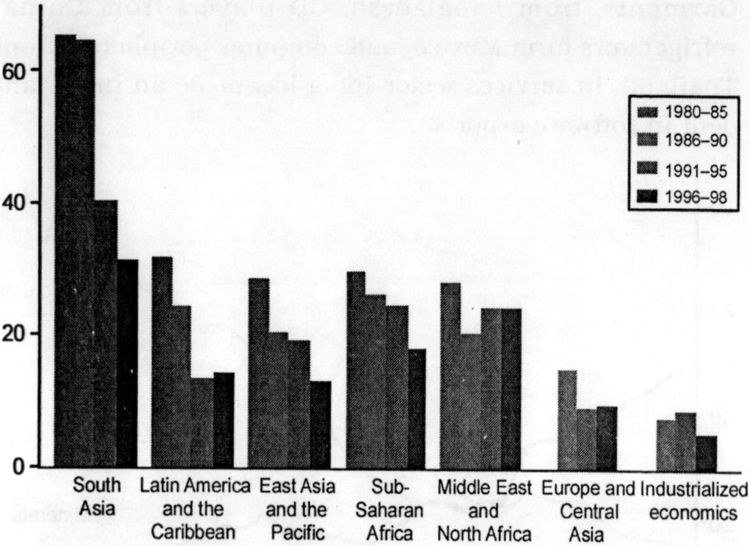


**Fig. 3.5. Average unweighted tariff rates, by region, 1980–1998 (%)**

***Source:*** **World Bank (2002).**

The trends of the last 20 years highlight following features:

- Growth rates of developing economies have accelerated and are higher than those of industrialised countries.
- The number of extremely poor people (those living on less than $1 a day) has declined for the first time in history, though the number of people living on less than $2 a day has increased;
- Measures of global inequality (such as the global civil coefficient) have declined modestly, reversing a long historical trend towards grater inequality;
- Within-country inequality in general is not growing

though it has risen in several populous centers (China, India the United States);

- Wage inequality in general has been rising (meaning lesser) wage increases for skilled workers than for unskilled worker. The data shows the relative faster rate of growth of developing countries as compared to industrialised countries. In the 1990s, developing countries growth at 35 per cent was twice the rate of rich countries. The poverty reduction is closely related to the GDP growth rates. Poverty incidence has been gradually declining throughout modern history, but in general population growth has outstripped the decline in incidence so that the total number of poor people has actually risen. Even in 1960-80, a reasonably prosperous period for developing economics, the number of extremely poor people continued to rise.

The 1981-2001 decline in the number of extremely poor people is unprecedented in human history. At the same time many of those who rose above the very low $1 a day threshold are still living on less than $ 2 a day. The number of people living on less than $2 a day increased between 1981 and 2001 by nearly 300 million. About half the world population still lives on less than $2 a day. Overall picture is so dismal that public spirited citizens must hang their heads in shame. Despite a glut of food and spectacular increase in the globe's capacity to grow more, hunger remains one of the world's major problems.

Scholars and policy makers are now discussing the disparities issue with a level of concern and keenness not seen since the 1970s. Notable here is the publication last December of the world Distribution of Household Wealth report by the World Institute for Development Economics Research, Helsinki which makes the shocking disclosure that the richest 2 percent of the world's adults own more than half of global household wealth.

The richest one per cent alone owned 40 percent of global assets in 2000, and the richest 10 per cent accounted for 85 per cent of the world total. In contrast, the bottom half of the world adult population owned barely 1 per cent of global wealth.

Among the most revealing and disturbing recent analysis of India's disparity scenario is "patterns of wealth disparities in India during the liberalisation Era" (*Economic and Political Weekly, Sep.* 22)—this shows on the basis of national sample survey data, that there was a perceptible (and probably underestimated) increase in inter personal wealth inequality in India between 1991 and 2002. The top 10 per cent of the population increased its share of total national wealth to 52 per cent, while the share of the bottom 10 fell to just 0.21 per cent. Some of our high gini coefficients (for instance, 0.92 and 0.99 in respect of ownership of machinery, transport or bank deposits) are probably the highest anywhere (1.0 represents total inequality). The Distressing figure are also contained in the Asia-Pacific wealth report just released by (*Merrill Lynch-Capgemini*) which indicates that the number of India's High Net-worth Individuals (HNIs) has increased by 2.05 per cent over the year 2007 to reach 100,000 (HNIs have net financial assets of at least $ 1 million excluding primary residence and consumables). Even more important than the rapid increase is the disclosure that this miniscule minority holds $ 350 billion in assets—or about half of India's entire gross domestic product.

Although overall decline in extreme poverty is a positive news, performance has varied by region. South Asia, East Asia and Pacific grew well and reduced poverty, but Sub-

Saharan Africa had negative growth between 1981 and 2001 and a rise in poverty. The number of extremely poor people there increased from 164 million (41.6 percent of the population) to 316 million (46.9 percent of the population). Two thirds of extremely poor people still live in Asia, but if strong growth there continues global poverty will be increasingly concentrated in Africa. Inequality has risen in several populous countries such as China, India and US. This means that a majority of citizens of the world live in countries in which inequality is rising. Similarly the picture of inequality is not favorable to rich countries in the last decade, due to fall in the wage income of workers as a result of competitions from developing countries wage payments to skilled workers. The pressures on the rich countries, in terms of inequality is bound to escalate, with the roll down of social security measures by the governments in developed nations.[3]

Globally the income inequality takes an interesting profile, if we look at its evolution within specific countries in a comparative perspective. In a global approach, there has been over the past three decades, increasing inequality and polarisation in the distribution of wealth. According to UNDPs 1996/99 Human Development Reports, in 1993 only US $5 trillion of the US $23 trillion global GDP were from the developing countries even if they accounted for nearly 80 per cent of total population. The poorest 20 per cent of the world's people have seen their share of global income decline from 2.3 per cent to 1.4 percent in the past 30 years. Meanwhile the share of the richest 20 per cent has risen from 70 per cent to 85 per cent. The ratio of the income of the 20 per cent richest profile in the world over the poorest 20 percent–increased from 30:1 in 1960 to 74:1 in 1997. In 1994 the assets of the world's 358 billionaires (in US dollar) exceeded the combined annual incomes of countries with 45 per cent of the world's population. The concentration of wealth at the very top accelerated in the second half of the 1990s. The net worth of the world's 200 richest people increased from US $ 440 billion to more than US $ 1 trillion between 1994 and 1998. Thus, in 1998, the assets of the three richest people in the world were more than the combined GNP of the 48 least developed countries, comprising 600 million people.[4] The gap in per capita income between the industrial and the developing world tripled from US $ 5,700 in 1960 to US $ 15,000 in 1993.[5] Between 1960 and 1992, all but the richest quintile (of the world's people) saw their income share fall, so that by 1991 more than 85 per cent of world's population received only 15 per cent of its income yet another indicator of an even more polarised world (Manuel Castells, 2000).

One can also find considerable disparity in the evolution of intra-country inequality in different areas of the world. In the last two decades (1980-2000), income inequality has increased, in the United States, United Kingdom, Brazil, Argentina, Bolivia, Venezuela, Peru, Thailand and Russia and in the 1980s[6] in Japan, Canada, Sweden, Australia, Germany and in Mexico (*Manuel Castells*). The table (3.6) shows income inequality after 1979 in OECD countries. The income inequality decreased in the 1960-90 period in India, Malaysia, Hongkong, Singapore, Taiwan, and South Korea (*UNDP,* 1996). The data shown by Deininger and Squire, in terms of Gini coefficient, by major regions of the world between the 1990s and the 1970s, one discerns that in 1990s it was much higher in Latin America, but lower in all other regions, when analysed at highly aggregate level.

**Table 3.6 Change in income inequality after 1979 in OECD countries**

| *Country* | *Period* | *Annual change in Gini coefficient*[1] | |
|---|---|---|---|
| | | *Relative (%)* | *Absolute (point change)* |
| United Kingdom | 1979-95 | 1.80 | 0.22 |
| Sweden | 1979-94 | 1.68 | 0.38 |
| Denmark | 1991-90 | 1.20 | - |
| Australia | 1981-89 | 1.60 | 0.34 |
| Netherlands | 1979-94 | 1.07 | 0.25 |
| Japan | 1979-93 | 0.84 | 0.25 |
| United States | 1979-95 | 0.79 | 0.35 |
| Germany[2] | 1979-95 | 0.50 | 0.30 |
| France | 1979-89 | 0.40 | 0.12 |
| Norway | 1979-92 | 0.22 | 0.05 |
| Canada | 1979-95 | -0.02 | 0.00 |
| Finland | 1979-94 | -0.10 | -0.02 |
| Italy | 1980-91 | -0.64 | -0.58 |

1. Measured as the relative change in the Gini Coefficient, where growth reflects more inequality.
2. Western Germany.

*Source:* Gottschalk and Smeeding (1997) elaborated by Mishel et.al. (1999: 374).

An interesting variation occurs, with regard to inequality when it is measured in terms of Gini coefficient, for most OECD countries during the period of 1970 and 1990s. In United Kingdom the inequality increased the fastest. Similarly two of the Scandinavian countries Sweden and Denmark also witnessed inequality despite the fact that the internal policies are regarded considerably egalitarian. Similarly the transition economies in East European countries and CIS, experienced in general faster rise of inequality in this period. By the end of the twentieth century, in Russia, the income share of the richer 20 percent was 11 times that of the poorer 20 per cent (*UNDP* 1999: 36).

The above data clearly brings out the fact that the pattern of inequality has widened within the countries with a notable exception of China. The uneven development and replacement with technology has considerably added to the pressures on the population and has led to the Informalisation and Casualisation of labour. The capital has prospered at the cost of equity and social justice.

Thus according to UNDP (1996:1-2) :

> "since 1980 there has been a dramatic surge in economic growth in some 15 countries bringing rapidly rising incomes to many of their 1.5 billion people, more than a quarter of the world's population. Over much of this period economic decline or stagnation has affected 100 countries, reducing the incomes of 1.6 billion people, again more than a quarter of the world's population. In 70 of these countries average incomes are less than they were in 1970. During 1970-85 global GNP increased by 40 pe rcent, yet the number of poor increased by 17 per cent while 200 million people saw their percapita incomes fall during 1965-80, more than one billion on people did in 1980-93.
>
> During the 1995 if we take the extreme poverty line indicator of US $1 as consumption level, then 1.3 billon people accounting for 33 percent of the developing world's population, were in extreme misery. Among these poor people, 550 million lived is South Asia, 215 million in Sub-Saharan Africa, and 150 million in Latin America (*UNDP*; 1996: 27). In a similar estimate, using the one dollar a day as benchmark for extreme poverty, ILO estimated that the percentage of the population below this line increased from 53.5 percent in 1985 to 54.4 per cent in 1990 in Sub Saharan Africa;

and decreased from 61.1 per cent to 59 per cent in South Asia, and from 15.7 per cent to 14.7 per cent in East/South-East Asia (without China). According to UNDP, between 1987 and 1993 the number of people with incomes of less than one dollar a day increased by 100 million to reach 1.3 billion. If we consider the level of income of less than two dollars a day another billion people should be added. Thus at the turn of the millennium, well over one third of humankind was living at a subsistence or below subsistence level.

(Mannel Castells; 2000, 81) extensively quotes the data from the ILO, pertaining to poverty.

"In addition to income poverty other dimensions of poverty are even more striking : in the mid 1990s about 840 million people were illiterate, more than 1.2 billion lacked access to safe water, 800 million lacked access to safe health services, and more than 800 million suffered hunger. Nearly a third of the people in the least developed economies mainly in Sub-Saharan Africa were not expected to survive to the age of 40, women and children suffer most from poverty: 160 million children under five were malnourished and the maternal mortality rate was about 500 women per 100,000 live births (*ILO:* 1995). The largest concentration of poverty was, by far, in the rural areas in 1990, the proportion of poor among the rural population was 66 per cent in Brazil, 72 per cent in Peru, 43 per cent in Mexico, 49 per cent in India and 54 per cent in the Philippines (*ILO*; 1994). As for Russia, the CIS countries and Eastern Europe, a report issued by the World Bank in April, 1999 calculated that there were 147 million people living below the poverty line of four dollars a day, the equivalent figure for 1989 was 14 million.

The juggernaut of globalisation as the above mentioned data reveals, is more complex than it appears. When we think of it in terms of gains, we can not overlook the sustained process of exclusion and marginalisation that it entails in countries like Latin America, Sub-Saharan Africa, South Asia and CIS states. The figures of poverty and inequality make the process of globalisation bereft of legitimacy. Can the world afford to leave the business of Economics (Production Exchange) in the hands of multinationals, with governments presiding departments of charity, it is only the gods who can steer the ship of growth with equity. The increase in the global inequality can be accounted for due to following factors, technological change and financial liberalisation result in a disproportionately fast increase in the number of households at the extreme rich end without shrinking the distribution at the poor end. Population growth meanwhile, adds proportionately to the numbers at the poor end. These deep causes yield an important intermediate cause that makes things worse. The prices of industrial goods and services exported from high income countries are increasing faster than the prices of goods and services produced in low income countries that do little international trade.

Growing inequality is analogous to global warming, its effects are diffused and long-term, academic analysts have a responsibility to counter the current neglect by analysing the relationship between trends in world income distribution and poverty as a way of getting distribution issues on the world agenda.

## Labour

Debates about global employment patterns are dominated by two agendas. On the one hand there is 'relocation' debate which focuses on the extent to which jobs in industry in the core regions of the world economy are being relocated to the periphery. While there are debates around the restructuring of the labuor market in the core countries, where core activities in manufacturing are increasingly either shed or 'externalised' into produced 'service' activities.

At the beginning of 1994 there were at least 120 million people registered unemployed world wide (*Ankie Hoogvelt; 1997*). To this figure must be added an estimated 700 million workers who were underemployed that is engaged in an economic activity that does not permit them to reach a minimum standard of living. What is new about these statistics is that they include some 35 million people who are registered unemployed in the advance countries.

Technological advances continue to contribute substantially to the restructuring of work relations. The automated enhancement and fragmentation of production processes, and the superior speed of Technological Production Process Innovations (TPPI) relative to retooling practices are two of the most important development in this regard. The automated enhancement and fragmentation of production processes are characterised by contemporary automation technologies which engender new forms of production process flexibility. Examples in this regard include programmable machines that control their own operations, and the ability of management to centrally control and electronically monitor labour functions and task performance (*Cobus-De-Swardt-Kraus, 2000*). The new science of management entails that companies are continually experimenting with new methods to generate new possibilities of achieving economies of scale, by introducing interface between employees and their work tools such as computers. Consequently, visual displays are employed, to understand the task between worker and machines.

The 1970's and 1980's marked the global restricting of industry and a redistribution of jobs in the international production system , to maximise production and attain scale of economies, in order to take an edge in the increased global competition. Kotthoff argues that the new pattern reflected a form of "self directed Taylorism". The superior speed of technological production process innovation (TPPI) relative to retooling practices is a new phenomenon of work reorganisation that emerged during the 1980's and 1990's. In the current scenario, the decrease in the tariff barriers, homogenisation of labour laws, and integration of production process at many sites, gives preponderant leverage to multinationals to dictate terms to government and labour unions. The contemporary technological innovations occur at such a rapid rate that incremental retooling practices are often an expensive option compared to the development of a completely new production site. The tempo of change in technological inputs renders single purpose production equipment more and more obsolete and provides corporations with unprecedented process flexibility. New production sites most often allow corporations to simultaneously reduce their labour component and the collective organisations of workers by closing a site with collectively organised labour and by opening a new site where workers are employed on individual contracts. The threat of plant closures increases the competition among governments who baulk and provide wide ranging concessions to the corporations that includes tax reductions, subsidies, low cost infrastructure and more importantly anti-labour laws.

According to some studies, integrated international production has hurt the core and benefitted the periphery, particularly Asia Pacific. A French government report in 1993 estimated that in the last 20 years no less than 6.6 million jobs left the European Community and the US for the Far

East. US manufacturing employment in the developing countries as a whole grew almost five times the rate of such employment in the developed economies. Today the developing world as a whole contributes 19 percent of manufacturing exports as against only 7 per cent 20 years ago (*Ankie Hoogvelt*). Two thirds of this comes from just one region in Pacific Asia, namely South Korea, Taiwan, Singapore, Hongkong and the regions in mainland China near Hongkong.

*Robert Reich,* in his best selling book, The work of Nations, comes up with interesting statistics. Between 1975 and 1990 America's 500 largest industrial corporations failed to create a single net new job, and their share of the civilian labour force fell from 17 per cent to under 10 per cent. At the same time the number of people describing themselves as 'self employed' began to rise, and by the late 1980's America was adding about 1.3 million new enterprises to the economy each year (compared with a mere 93,000 in the 1950's) most of them small businesses (*Ankie Hoogvelt*). The same transformation is in evidence in other advanced countries.

Current mechanisation and automation strategies need to be evaluated in the light of the global unemployment trends. The inclusion of high proportion of world's population into the orbits of global capitalism provides it with billions of potential workers as well as billions of potential unemployed workers. This could jeoparadise growth with social stability. In the early 1990s the global labour force stood at 2.8 billion people which is about, half the total population of the world. Of the 2.8 billion people, about 800 million (30 percent) were not productively employed, and more than 700 million were unemployed (*Cobus-De-Swardt-Kraus;* 2000). According to (*Simai's 1995*) analysis of the population projections of the United Nations, the number of people in the working age group will increase by 1360 million people in the years up to 2010. Of the total increase, only about 60 million (i.e,. less than 5 per cent) will be in the so called developed world, with 1300 million people (i.e.; more than 95 per cent) in the so called developing world. On calculation it goes that the existing pattern if maintained over next twenty years, the relative number of people in the category of underemployed and unemployed is going to increase by about 30 to 40 million people per year. In real numbers, this would mean a 50 per cent increase over the next 20 years. The projected figures of current and future figures, in both developed and developing parts of the world, suggest that maintenance of current levels of employment generation would be a difficult task to manage. Similarly, agriculture which has been the most fertile source of employment throughout the history is also going to face daunting challenges in the forseeable future. Farm mechanisation and automation in relatively advanced industrial economies, has led to the reduction of the farming population from approximately 60 per cent in the 1850s to less than 3 percent in the 1990s. (*Cobus-De. Swardt–Kraus, 2000, p.86*). The details show that half the population still earns its living by farming the land today (*UNDP, 1999*). The livelihood of a large section of these potentially engaged people is going to be threatened by current and potential mechanisation and automation.

In addition to the impact of technical advances in rural and agricultural sector, some important changes in the general pattern of unemployment can be observed. During the last three centuries the labour that was displaced by new technologies were mostly absorbed by new emerging sectors. But the current trend does not reflect the same pattern. The newly emerging sectors, so called 'knowledge sectors', consist mainly of a small group of industries and professional disciplines related to new high-tech, high-skill and selectively automated activities. (*Rifkin 1996*) explores extensively the developments in this sector, over the last two decades. He argues that while the numbers of these so called symbolic analysts or knowledge workers (from the field of science, engineering, management, consultancy, teaching, marketing, media and entertainment) will continue to grow, their absolute numbers will remain small compared to number of workers displaced by the new generation of thinking machines (Rifkin, 1996:35).

The data and figures given by Cobus-De-Swardt-Kraus (*2000*) aptly sums the dangers to employment:

"In contracts to the period from the 1960s to the 1980s, the service sector is no longer absorbing the large numbers of workers who become redundant in the industrial sector. On the contrary even with-in the service sector, computer based and telecommunication processes, accompanied by electronically integrated work, exchanges and consumption practices drastically reduce the human labour component. For example, in advanced industrialised spaces electronic banking and other changes in commercial banking endanger the immediate employment of 30 to 40 per cent of workers in this service sector. As the real cost of automation technologies and their costs relative to labour costs, continue to decrease, automation technologies seem likely to substantially increase unemployment and underemployment in the forseeable future. Similarly, automation technologies continues to decrease enterprises relative dependency on labour in general and on mass labour in particular. Furthermore, it is often these people who are socially the most variable, such as unskilled and underskilled workers, women, migrants, blacks and peasants, where job categories are most affected by automation technologies, thus facilitating marginalisation".

An International labour organisation (ILO) report, "Labour and social trends in Asia and the Pacific 2006: Progress towards decent work" brings out interesting pattern on labour. Referring to labour productivity, it says that of the 1.71 billion workers in the region, over one billion still do not earn enough to lift themselves and their families above the $ 2 a day poverty line. In fact in 2005, as many as 336 million families among the working poor or every fifth worker in the region lived on less than $ 1 a day. Similarly, despite strong economic growth, unemployment rose by 1.4 million in 2005 in the region; in percentage terms, it was 1.7 percent higher than the previous year. In fact, the rate of unemployment rose in East Asia, went down marginally in the Pacific and South-East Asian region, and remained stagnant in South Asia. The most interesting finding of the ILO report is that there has been a rise in wages, especially in the manufacturing sector, but the increase has not been commensurate with labour productivity. The increased workers productivity has not translated itself into shorter working hours, better conditions and better bargaining power. Collective bargaining in fact has shown a marked decline. It is an irony, that despite the economic crisis and slow down the level of unionisation has registered a marked decline, the report says that workers in "developing Asia" still put in considerably longer working hours than their counterparts in the rest of the world.

Thus the current scenario, increasingly points that capital has gained an overarching influence to that of labour in the current process of globalisation. As the cost of industrial relocation drops, productive capital has migrated from the triad heartlands; first textiles, then the assembly stages of secondary industry, followed by capital intensive industries, electronics and now information technology and software.[7] The impact of re-structuring has impacted the conditions of labour, and gradually led to the marginalisation and disempowerment. The capital has hastened the process of casualisation of the labour force and marked informalisation. Unorganised, irregular employments, the hallmark of women's wage work has proliferated. Unions have also been suppressed, the labour laws in the countries have been circumvented to serve the interest of capital, taking recourse to legislative measures, on grounds of stability peace and growth.

## Agriculture and Food Security

By far an important sector, which has been able to keep globalisation, at a distance, in the economic realm is agricultural sector. The very nature of its spatial locations, climatic uniqueness, farming practices and a secure means of livelihood, for minimal security has made national governments to adopt a cautious approach in integrating agriculture. A sizable section of the farming community in developing countries, also decides the configuration of politics and power. In many cases general agricultural policy goals seem to be incomparable and incommensurable with general economic policy goals. On the one hand, farmers try to follow the principle of sustaining capital in the long run (i.e.; the main focus lies in the aim to run a farm over as many generations as possible— thus implying a need for economic and social sustainability). On the other hand, in other sectors of the economy (assuming the business is not privately owned) the principle of profit maximisation dominates i.e; economic benefits are consumed and used by a person immediately without considering whether the business or profession that originally produced these benefits will continue to do so in the long run. The questions of food security and secure farming incomes are therefore always a subject of discussion regarding agricultural policies, especially during the process of designing and providing reasonable explanations for the required market regime and intervention measures.

On account of the low price elasticity between supplies and demand, and on account of the strong shifts in supplies, the prices for agricultural products are highly unstable, with price fluctuations appearing, at the same time, that are disproportionately pronounced. Since there is a little chance of steering production in the short term and because markets are weak, agriculture is radically different from other branches of the economy. Essentially the special feature is that farmers cannot adopt on a short term basis to changing conditions in view of the close links with natural development and growth process, while at the same time they are extremely vulnerable to short term vagaries in weather conditions.

Experts agree that the current global food production could be sufficient to feed the world's population if it were distributed equally (*Oltersdorf and Weingartner 1996:45*). In order to provide the necessary amount of energy (c.2500 cal perday) and proteins (c. 55 g per day) for the approximately 6 billion people, living today even the total cereal production of slightly over 2 billion tonnes (1996) would be sufficient if it were to be devoted to human nutrition only (*Theodor Quendler, 2002*). Since the beginning of the 1980s global food production has increased steadily, at an annual rate of about 2% which is slightly higher than the rate of population growth 1.7% (*Oltersdorf and Weingartner, 1996:29*). This has resulted in a slowly increasing per capita food production.

The developed countries of the North produce 45% of world cereals yet their share of world population is only 23%. The difference is even more marked in the meat and milk sectors, in which developed countries hold share of 56% and 68% respectively (*Oltersdorf and Weingartner, 1996: 26,108*).

The major increase in world food production has however taken place in the developing countries, especially in Asia. Growth in food production has virtually remained constant in developed world. Per capita food production consequently increased by 25 per cent in Asia and 38 per cent in China between 1980 and 1993. This trend is ongoing, China increased per capita food production by a further 40 per cent between 1990 and 1996 (*FAO*, 1997). Notwithstanding these healthy growths, more than 800 million people in the world suffer from inadequate access to food (Beck, 1997: 27), mainly in Sub-Saharan and South Asia.

Given the above figures and data, clearly the situation of undernourishment, malnutrition and hunger can be ascribed to the imbalance between production and supply. Many analysts point that the failure of the market and institutions, in supplying the requisite quantum of food, is the reason for hunger. The people lacking in food necessarily do not have the purchasing power to buy the food commodities. In addition of the economic factors, there may also be social, cultural and political-organisational patterns that make access to food difficult, especially for women and children; not only is there a need for an increase in local production in countries with inadequate agricultural output, but there is also a need for the creation of jobs outside agriculture in order to raise the buying power, as well as to improve transport and storage facilities.

According to the World Bank and Development Aid Organisations, despite the regional differences several recurring reasons for insufficient food production and supply (which often occur at the same time) can be identified.

- A low production output for natural reasons, made worse in recent decades by a widespread reduction in soil fertility, as a conseqquence of inappropriate or excessive farming, erosion or deforestation.

- Low agricultural productivity attributable in past to a lack of modern technologies and suitable farming methods and in past to economic and social reasons. In addition, performance inhibiting agricultural regulations exist that result in unfair leasing conditions and a dearth of land for small farmers, a situation that in turn is a consequence of ownership structures.
- Performance inhibiting agricultural regulations, insufficient promotion and sometimes even deliberate neglect of agriculture in rural areas on the part of governments, who give preference to the urban-industrial population (a typical manifestation of such features are the often inappropriately low prices for food, which are fixed by the governments of many African states and India in order to be able to supply urban populations with cheap food products, in consequence farmers have no financial incentive to produce more and thus limit themselves to satisfying their own needs).
- A lack in many developing countries of basic infrastructure for transporting and storing food (lack of marketing structures, insufficient means of transport in the consumption centers, high harvest and post-harvest losses because of pests, spoilage, weather conditions, lack of storage and conservation facilities).
- The absolute poverty, in many countries, which acts as a detterence to purchase food commodities due to lack of buying capacity.

Given the importance of agriculture in terms of employment, livelihood and food security, the contention for policy making in WTO, suffered from incongruence of interests between USA, EEC, Latin American countries and, developing countries like India, China and Sub-Saharan Africa. The question of subsidies and exemptions granted to the agricultural inputs, remained the bone of contention between North and South. The agricultural subsidy in USA and EEC is quiet higher, as compared to the developing countries; therefore even in the area of agricultural commodities despite the comparative advantage in terms of labour, they could not access the developed market for agricultural exports. The countries of North, it is alleged, provide $320 billion to their farmers, thus enabling them an unequal bargaining power against farmers of developing countries. In 1995 the WTO agreement on agriculture (AOA) was introduced. A major element of AOA discipline was substantial reduction in the level of subsidies granted by the WTO members.[8] Rich countries farmers comprise only 3-5 percent of population and receive huge domestic and export subsidies. This is in contrast to the millions of resource poor farmers (who constitute the bulk of the population) in developing countries for whom agriculture is the only means of sustaining their livelihoods. Further developed countries subsidies keep the global agricultural prices suppressed and make farm activities in the developing countries non-remunerative. The developed countries are artificially sustaining uncompetitive agriculture in their economies by creating distortions in the world economy through the channel of subsidies.[9]

The globalisation of food and agriculture systems, in effect means, the corporate take over of the food chain, the erosion of food rights, the destruction of the cultural diversity of food and the biological diversity of crops, and displacement of millions from land based rural livelihoods.[10]

The corporatisation of the agriculture with the onerous motive of profit, by companies like Monsanto can wreak havoc, on the natural ecosystems, livelihoods and symbiotic productive relationships existing with nature.

Biotechnology companies that produce genetically modified (GM) foods have increasingly come under scanner. GM technology now enables the genes of one species to be inserted into completely different species. For example, lichen genes can be inserted into potatoes to increase their resistance to diseases. Beta carotene from carrots can be added to rice to increase production of vitamin A. These features, its proponents allege, make genetic engineering on 'evergreen revolution' capable of feeding the world's burgeoning population with less hand, fewer harmful pesticides, herbicides and fertilizers and under conditions of greater stress from drought, global warming, salination and soil infertility. It is a scientific response to global environmental dilemmas.[11]

But the technology cannot be separated from the corporate strategies that promote it. Like information technology companies, biotechnology buisnesses tried to monopolise the production of seeds by introducing a terminator gene that prevented farmers using the seed produced from their plants. The private ownership of genes and seeds have also raised fears about risks to food diversity. The dependence on a small number of genetically modified crops carries risk. For instance, in 1845 and 1846 Ireland was struck by a famine due to overdependence on one crop, potato, which was struck by a disease called blight.

GM crops had been introduced around 1994, and within five years their usage had expanded 25 fold to cover 49 million hectares, mostly in North America and China. But by then honeymoon was over, and public skepticism rose. Britain imposed a ban on the commercial cultivation of GM crops for three years. A large supermarket chain refused to stock GM products. In addition, European countries imposed a five year cultivation ban and refused entry to US gram imports.

American farmers took note and began to abandon GM crops. The shares of Monsanto fell 35 per cent in value and the company moved quickly to regain credibility by abandoning the terminator genes.[12]

The reasons for skepticism in European countries and Britain were dangers encompassing health risks. For example, Soyabean genes transplanted with nut genes, were reported to have caused allergy reactions in Brazil. Beans in France were reported to be dying because of GM seeds treated with insecticide. Hives fell dramatically in number from 1.4 million in 1996 to 1 million in 2000. Some new human allergies have been blamed on transgenic maize.[13]

GM crops may also cause environmental problems. Thus pollen might blow into fields of ordinary crops and fertilise them. Also, crops genetically modified to repel pests might spur the evolution of super pests or poison other species. Laboratory tests have shown that butterfly larvae are harmed when fed the pollen of plants genetically modified to express a toxin called Bacillus Thuringiensis (BT), which protects corn from corn borers and cotton from boll worms.

Notwithstanding such fears, among developing countries, China has been the most enthusiastic country to welcome GM crops. In 1997-99, China gave 26 commercial approvals for GM crops, including transgenic peppers, tomatoes, rice and cotton. The most commercially successful of these has been BT cotton, Cotton-chomping ball worms have grown resistant to pesticides. In 1992, these worms destroyed the entire cotton crop in some parts of China, ruining large number of farmers and banckrupting textile factories. So when Monsanto, a big American biotech firm, started selling ball-worm-resistant BT cotton seeds, the Chinese openly embraced them. BT cotton now covers, half a million hectares of Chinese soil. Production costs have fallen by 14 per cent, despite the hefty price that Mosanto charges for its seeds. It was easier in China to introduce GM crops, as the space for public protest is negligible due to communist party dictatorship. It has not been in the case of India, where NGOs and civil society group's vociferous campaign through media and mass protests have made the things difficult for corporatisation of Indian agriculture. A notable critic of the corporate take over and openness of India's agriculture has been Vandana Shiva, who has given warning signals of Indian agriculture opening to multinationals. For some time the agrarian distress in the South Indian states has already claimed thousands of lives of farmers, who have committed suicide. The Southern states such as Maharashtra, Andhra Pradesh, Kerala, have followed the commercial pattern of farming, encompassing crops like cotton, tobacco, rubber, and spices. The fall in the prices of the commodities, with high interest rate loans from money lenders and increasing input prices (pesticides, fertiliser, seeds) have taken its toll on the farmers in India.

Trade liberalisation in India has led to budget cutbacks, on extension and withdrawal of low-interest credit from cooperatives and public sector Banks, peasants have had to take high-interest rate loans from the same companies that sell them hybrid seeds and pesticides. Thus the corporations have become money lenders, extension agents, seed suppliers and pesticide salesmen rolled into one. As a result, peasants have become buried under the weight of unpayable debt. This has forced peasants to undertake epidemic suicides (*Vandana Shiva*).

Many scholars in India fear that opening of trade in agri-business to multinationals may destroy the livelihood of many millions of people, such as oil mill operators and small farmers. The small traders who have been dependent on the local production chain for years would get dismantled with the coming of multinationals. The decentralised, small scale household dependent economy of food production and processing is huge in aggregate. It generates millions of livelihood and provides fresh and wholesome food at affordable prices. The entry of the multinational corporations can break the back of millions dependent on this particular type of community economy which provides space for all and sundry.

> Thus Vandana Shiva underlines, "Agri-business has already begun to get Indian consumers to doubt their own quality control systems and to trust the brand names. They see a potential corporate controlled market that would generate 300 crore or 30 billion rupees of profits through the sale of packaged brand name wheat. The corporate agenda of India is to introduce monopolies in wheat such as those of Cargill and ADM, and in seed such as those of Monsanto, Novarties, Dupont and Zeneca. These seed corporations demand monopolistic intellectual property rights to seed, forcing farmer to pay royalties while also controlling other inputs. This trend is moving the country towards an agricultural economy in which only a small number of people are involved, and only as tractor drivers and pesticide sprayers. All other functions of farmers - as maintenance of biodiversity, stewards of sail and water and seed breeders are destroyed."

Another area, which looks threatening, to developing countrie's scholars, is the TRIPs agreement under WTO, causing anxieties to the question of bio-diversity. Under the TRIPs agreement, all countries are required to provide legal protection for potential inventions of both product and process, in all fields of technology. Patents to genetic innovations ensure the economic control of "life industries" over modified organisms and their offspring. Only through the establishment of proprietary rights over cells, micro-organism and organisms, does the genetic material of the living world become available to be marketed? Patent empowers firms to take ownerships of parts of the natural realm, to turn it into a economic resource, and as far as possible to monopolise it so that no one can use it unless they pay for an approved purpose. Life patents thus play for "life industries", the same role that land deeds played for emergent agrarian capitalism. The rules of ownerships would be decided by multinationals, and they would even decide to whom should the benefits accrue. Activities such as planting, animal raising or curative treatment, which used to be a part of public domain, thus come increasingly under the control of corporations. This would bring a global system of legal patents for generic inventions, which incorporated and irrevocably modified parts of the human biological heritage for commercial ends, would threaten to result in nothing less than a simplification of the biosphere. There would be a threat to the South's bio-diversity in the form of disappearance of floral varieties, which has sustained millions for years in history.

## Localised VS Global Food System

Within the process of globalisation shortening the distance between producers and consumers would bring immense benefits, supporters of the global, industrial model will certainly decry such a shift, claiming that it would entail too much social and economic disruption. But the current direction, on the name of "progress", is driving family farmers and rural communities the world over to extinction. Millions of people are being pulled off the land into sprawling ever-expanding cities. More and more people all over the world are coming to the understanding that corporate take over of the food system, is fraught with immense dangers. The commodification of food like industrial goods inevitably does not auger well for such societies, who are actually dependent on the ecosystem for their survival. They are beginning to see for themselves the immense costs of severing food from its cultural and environmental moorings, and then treating it as a commodity subject to lawless speculative investment.

As a result, farmers, consumers, and environmentalists, around the world are linking hands to demand shifts in policy—away from the globalised model with its bias towards large-scale, monoculture production and corporate agro-business, towards more localised food systems, that promote smaller scale, diversified forms and healthier communities.

With enough pressures being generated from bodies like WTO, NAFTA and EEC to open the doors of the developing countries, by reducing the tariff to promote agro-business, and GM food crops export, people have started galvanising themselves, to oppose the agenda of corporate take over. The precedent at Montreal, to oppose the global model—Montreal Biosafety Protocol in February 2000, by the 135 countries (like-minded group of Nations)— was significant step in this direction (*Helena, Hodge, Merrifield, Govelick, 2000*).

The "like-minded group" comprising of 135 countries succeeded in sending the message that communities and food production should be looked in an integrated way. The subsidies and tariffs should be carefully employed so as not to disturb the food-cultural synthesis, which has sustained populations.

We have already noticed that globalisation of food is being propelled by a vast array of hidden government subsidies, investments, tax breaks and other incentives that overwhelmingly favour corporations and global trade. These would need to be reformed to ensure that prices reflect the environmental and social costs of their production and distribution.

Both hidden and direct agricultural subsidies now favour large scale farms, industrial agro-businesses and corporate middlemen, allowing them to lower their prices artificially and thereby they invade local food economies, to the detriment of both farmers and consumers. The shift in the stand of the government by funding smaller scale, diversified, agriculture practices would strengthen bio-diversity, healthier soils and fresher foods.[14] If the subsidies for the large and global agribusiness is directed towards the smaller-scale and more localised producers, the shift towards more ecological and equitable food economies would be given a major boost.[15]

Even in the North, an unhealthy urbanisation continues. Rural communities are being steadily dismantled, their populations are being pushed into the spreading sub-urbanised megapolis, where the vast majority of available jobs are located. In the United States, where only 2 per cent of the population still lives on the land, farms are still disappearing rapidly. One cannot offer the same model to the world, where the majority of people earn their living as farmers.

Thus, localising the production of food along with its marketing is an urgent priority. When applied to farming, the global economic model is giving us food that is neither very fresh, flavourable, nor nutritious, that too at a price that includes depleted soil, poisoned air and water, and a destabilised global model. It is destroying rural livelihoods and hollowing out communities in both North and South. The possibility of food getting concentrated in the hands of multinationals, who subordinate every other concern before profit is a dangerous proposition. Worst of all, people everywhere are being encouraged to rely on "a single model of food production", which is dangerously lacking in diversity, can severely jeopardise the local security worldwide. Of all these the shift to the local is the only answer, which will restore the symbiotic dependence of people on bio-diversity and ecosystem thereby providing the needed base for safeguarding the renewal of Earth. The potential knowledge of restoring plural survival needs to be restored before it is late.

## Global Financial Environment

By the end of the nineteenth century an international economy was fully developed. The shift from an international one to a global one was underway by end of the twentieth century. It was neither a complete nor a uniform process. Not all companies are as footloose as shoe manufacturers and there are barriers to technology transfers between countries. Not all countries are fully globalized. Indeed, we can say that globalisation of production is a series of technology districts 'technopoles',[16] around the world in selected countries rather than in all countries. Consumption is far more dispersed. Capitalist commodities have found their way into more homes in more countries than at any time in human history. But inspite of notable success in commodity dispersal and trade, the one area where global integration has been pronounced is financial markets. Global financial integration, which we can define as the increasing freedom of movement, transfer and tradeability of money and finance across the globe, has become the leading edge of globalisation. Money today knows no boundaries. The finance system has moved from a national to a globally integrated system, with the consequent loss of national financial autonomy. The transcendent power of money to break national boundaries is one of the most pronounced features of globalisation (*Manuel Castells, 2000*).

For understanding the global architecture of financial flows, we need to understand the visions and philosophy as enshrined in Brettonwood Institutions, along with the status of the global economy in 1945. In general, the Brettonwoods system was ultimately premised on the notion that international trade would become the stimulant of enduring growth. This assumption was based on the philosophy that international trade needed to be underpinned by a unitary and stable framework for trade and financial relations among countries. This was essential in order to prevent a return to the fragmented and competing monetary blocs which exacerbated the Great Depression of the early 1930s and contributed to the social instability which formed part of the backdrop to the First World War (*R.J. Barnet, 1983*). This system was brought into practice, by bringing in a monetary system of stable fixed exchange rates and currency convertibility which facilitated trade between countries, it also prevented the kind of unilateral and competitive currency devaluations, which was the hallmark of 1930 Great Depression. The international institutions created (IMF, World Bank, GATT) between the 1945 and 1970 had the important responsibility of managing the orderly international flow of money, goods and technology.

The long term cross border flow of money and capital were to take place under the watchful eyes of the IMF. The structure and governing process of IMF facilitated the hegemony of USA, Japan, Britain and other nations of the North. The financial stability, which was key to international trade, was sought to have been maintained partially by fixed exchange rates pegged to the American dollar. The other important aspect of stabilising factor was linking the value of the dollar to a specific gold price (US $35 an ounce); at that juncture it was feasible to convert the dollar into gold since America then held 67 per cent of the world gold stock

(*Cobus- De-Swardt-Kraus, 2000*). Each countrie's Central Bank was entrusted with the important responsibility of maintaining its currency's par value to the dollar within a margin of 1 percent above or below parity. To facilitate stable exchange rates and periodic balance of payment deficits, IMF provided temporary loans to the states (*Eichengreen,B., Globalising Capital, 1998*). This actually meant that the IMF returned American balance of payments surplus to countries in deficit. This kind of fixed currency exchange rates provided a stable monetary framework which resulted in fixed domestic interest rates. This also provided enough room for national governments to implement medium to long term policies for growth and development.[17]

Another important post-war institution organising the international flow of goods and trade was GATT. Under the GATT, the regulation and promotion of trade were guided by the principles of multilateral reciprocity between the member nations. The main objective of the GATT regime was to liberalise international trade based on four basic principles, namely reciprocity, transparency, non-discrimination and the organisation of periodic negotiations between participating parties in order to further liberalise trade.[18] For instance, the GATT regime induced American tariff reductions on industrial goods from an average of 60 percent in the early 1930s to 4-3 per cent in late 1980s (*Cobus-De-Swardt-Kraus, 2000*). Between 1974 and 1980, GATT agreements reduced tariff rates on trade in manufactured goods by more than 75 per cent.

Apart form the above mentioned GATT principles, the regime also underscored two assumptions, namely that a so called open trading systems is more efficient and beneficial than a protectionist one, and that 'national economies' would prosper, and reap the harvest of growth, if they concentrate in the areas where they have comparative advantage.[19] This idea creates problems for developing countries in the context of product/labour specialisation, as this would mean that developing countries would concentrate in labour intensive product manufacturing due to cheap labour advantage, while the developed nations would confine themselves in high value added products. Thus the developing countries, caught in the vortex of low value added production will continue to stagger in terms of growth. This also means that they will have to continuously maintain the cheap-labour, framework to survive globally—which in turn means that they will have to remain in poverty in order to afford cheap labour supply. Once the conditions in these countries go for the better, thereby increasing the wage costs, they would loose the comparative cost advantage and capital from these countries and would move to new destinations, where cheap labour is available. This creates a paradox. The asymmetrical core-periphery production relation, constituted the hallmark of GATT trade regime (*Sala-i-Martin, x.2002*).

Despite the obvious anomalies which characterised the trade regime between 1945-1970s, the Keynesian model of growth along with the Brettonwood institutions, brought unprecedented prosperity and social stability to advanced industrialised countries. By the 1970s the Brettonwoods system came under increasing pressure,[20] owing to various factors, occurring at global level. Among these was the formation of a seller's cartel by the Organisation of the Petroleum Exporting Countries (OPEC), the rise of regional trading blocs, emergence of European countries as major players in the global productions and trade relations, the decline of the American comparative advantage in manufacturing compared to Japan and the emergence of multinational corporations who gain prominence globally (*Winters, L.A, 2004*; *Edward Gold Smith and Jerry Mander, 2001*).

During the 1970s American role in the international financial system changed from creditor to debtor. The costly Vietnam War meant that US was racking up huge trade deficits and suffering rapid inflation, international confidence was ebbing. The Vietnam War undermined the fiscal strength of the country and eroded international confidence. In 1971 president Nixon announced that the dollar was no longer freely convertible to gold. The devaluation of the dollar meant end of fixed exchange rates. When fixed exchange rates disappeared and every domestic currency was convertible into every other, the value of currencies was set by worldwide demand and supply. The global markets now set exchange rates. A fundamental element of national economic sovereignty, the ability to set the exchange rate of a currency, had been taken out of the hands of politicians and put into those of currency speculators.

The demise of fixed exchange rates undermined national financial regulations and thus allowed easier capital flows across national boundaries. Some other factors which lubricated capital flows, were Eurocurrencies. These were at first created in the 1950s and 1960s when the USSR and some East European countries deposited their US dollars in European Banks to avoid them being taken by the US government. Similarly the multinationals began to deposit their foreign currency earnings in the form of Eurocurrencies in order to avoid tax and regulations in their home countries. A pool of denationalised money was created, corporations and even national government, used the Euro market to borrow and to raise foreign currency. Thus a 'denationalised' money had been created. Secondly, the oil price hike imposed by OPEC in 1973, from \$2.48 a barrel to \$11.65 a barrel, meant a huge transfer of funds from oil-importing countries to oil-exporting countries. The current account balance of OPEC countries increased from \$1.5 billion in 1972 to \$ 7 billion in 1977 (*John Renne Short, 2008, p: 106*). The insatiable demand for oil meant that the revenue kept on pouring the coffers of the OPEC nations. A great pool of liquid money was created, some of it was leant to cash-poor, newly industrialising countries and the poorer oil importing countries, who were facing a cash shortfall.

The growth of Euro dollars relative to American gold reserves eventually became a liability to the American government. In addition to this the American Federal Reserve's stock of gold had fallen rapidly as it attempted to support the falling dollars. The shift from fixed to floating currency exchanges, and increased capital mobility resulted in highly volatile money markets during the 1980s. In contrast to the Brettonwood systems of fixed exchange rates, the stability of the financial assets, profits and borrowings of corporations were now relative to potentially volatile money markets and changes in currency values.

In addition to increased speculative behaviour, the deregulation of financial markets also facilitated, growth of global debt, and the debt crisis of 1980s. The current account balance of poor, non-oil exporting countries fell from minus $ 5 billion in 1972 to minus $ 36 billion. By 1979 International Banks had lost $ 150 billion to poor, oil importing countries. The fall of fixed exchange rates and the growth of Euro currencies and petrodollars together created a more liquid financial system. An institutional infrastructure of international banks and global markets was created.

## The 1980 Debt Crisis

The debt crisis of 1980 was fuelled by a combination of factors, comprising the surplus of petrodollars, with the commercial European Banks rising inflation due to increase in the prices of oil and petroleum products, served to arrest the growth in the developed nations. The low interest rates in OECD countries coupled with rising inflation, necessitated the commercial European Banks, to lend money to the developing country economies between 1970 and 1975. This marked a great shift in the money market, as the Banks who were flush with funds due to petrodollars, found the developed economies, unpalatable for investments. Since most of the developed nations, banked on the primary commodities of developing economies, for their manufacturing, hence to offset the reduced economic space, in their own countries, they connived with Brettonwood institutions to force the economies of the developing countries. The IMF prescriptions, to developing countries, to expand their manufacturing base, by liberalisation, reduction in trade barriers, devaluation of currency and roll down of state sector did not bode well, for developing economies. Many countries in the developing economy adopted the trappings of the industrial development without having the base (e.g. in terms of skills, infrastructure, markets) needed to sustain rapid industrial and commercial developments. Nevertheless, once 'third world' governments embarked on this restructuring path, they became dependant on financial support from the public and private financial institutions, of the advanced industrial world. Consequently the 'thrid world' became prime markets for commercial banks. This created a dependency wherein the private capital came to control the African and South-African economies. During this period official lending (bilateral and multilateral) were effectively displaced by the unregulated, often undersecured private bank lending. Thus in the early, 1970s bank loans accounted for 13 per cent, multilateral loans for 33 per cent and export credits for 25 per cent of third world debt.Within a decade this pattern was reversed with banks holding 60 per cent of "third world" debt by the end of the 1970s. In the case of Africa, official/ public loans fell from 40 percent in 1970 to 12 per cent in 1978. All in all foreign banks and bond financing rose form 7 per cent in the early 1960s to 65 per cent of all foreign financing in the late 1970s (*Cobus-De-Swardt-Kraus, 2000*). In real terms, private bank lending to the 'third world' increased from $ US 2 billion in 1972, to $90 billion in 1981.

The 1980 debt crisis suffered by many developing countries was largely the outcome of no holds barred lending resorted by the commercial banks. Upon this was the policies of US government (monetarist) of reducing social spending, reducing money supply, restricting credit, raising interest rates. This was adopted to counter the fall of dollar against other major currencies. For 'third world' countries this meant higher repayment due to increased interest rates as well as decreased local currency values in relations to the American dollar in the absence of fixed exchange rates. Similarly the third world loans taken for the public sector expansion, went into a limbo, as most of public sector enterprises found it hard to deliver profits. The increase in the prices of the oil accounted for more than 25 percent of the 'third world' debt (IMF survey, 1999).

The official debt crises erupted in 1982, when Mexico faltered in paying its scheduled debt. Similarly many countries in South America such as Argentina, Brazil and Peru followed suit. During the late 1980s 19 African countries had debt service rates of more than 300 per cent in which 3 had debt service ratios of more than 1000 per cent. This in turn meant these countries had to increase their exports tenfold solely to meet their debt obligations (*IMF survey, 1997*).

According to OECD estimates (1990,1991), the total resource flows to developing countries amounted to $ 927 billion in the period between 1982 and 1990. This includes official bilateral and multinational aid, grants by private charities, trade credits, direct private investments and bank loans. A substantial proportion of this inflow was not in the form of grants, but consisted of new debt and interest in old debt. (George 1997) beautifully sums up to highlight the extent of these money flows from the developing countries to their creditors. He says that by comparison, the US Marshall Plan transferred $ 14 million to war ravaged Europe in 1948; while the poor have financed six Marshal Plans for the rich through debt service alone. It is estimated that in 1998 the 'Third world' repaid US $250 billion to advanced industrialised countries whilst receiving about US $ 30 billion in public development aid (Cobus-de-Swardt-Kraus). This horrifying picture prompted 1999 G-7 decision to cancel some 'third world' debt.[21] On a macro level, debt and exponential debt profits currently constitute a large percentage of the profits of capital in general and finance capital in particular. The repayment of debt to private institutions puts severe restrictions on 'third world governments'. American governments national debt interest payments amounted to 20 per cent of governmental spending.

## New Financial Integration and Speculation

The growth of new money markets, and considerable dilution of local control over financial flows of capital across the boundaries constitute the hallmark of 1990s.[22] The technological barriers to foreign direct investment and transnational transactions in general have largely been broken down during the 1990s, thereby making it difficult for national governments to control the transnational flow of money, goods and information. New technologies currently facilitates the dissemination of detailed information to every financial center around the globe in no time. This leads to the integration of almost all major financial and banking centers into a single financial network. The contemporary money flows are not only more global but also autonomous. The movement and control of the value currencies are increasingly controlled by a new breed of global financial specialists, consisting of the financial analysts of major banks, transnational pension and mutual funds.[23] There are also capital market flows that involve international transactions in securities, bonds, notes, derivatives and currencies. By the mid 1990s these totaled almost $ 600 billion.[24] Savers have diversified their portfolios to include foreign assets in the form of bonds, equities and loans, and lenders have turned to foreign as well as domestic sources for funds. It is possible to speak of international bonds, international equities and international money markets.

Foreign exchange markets are concentrated in London, Tokyo and Newyork, with a second tier in Hongkong, Zurich and Paris. The total foreign exchange turnover increased from $ 17.5 trillion in 1979 to $297.5 trillion in 1995.[25] Currencies are traded, bought and sold, but also speculated, as investors take positions betting on the future exchange rate of one or more currencies, for unlike domestic stock markets, the foreign exchange market is a 24 hours one. Between them, London, New York and Tokyo provide a 24 hours coverage. The market is turbulent, speculative and sensitive. A small run against a currency in Tokyo can pick up steam in London, generate future speed in New York and takes a full flight when the market opens again in Tokyo. Runs against a currency can lead to a marked devaluation and consequent economic crisis; devaluations affected the Mexican Peso in 1994 and Russian Rouble in 1998. In both cases the currencies had to be bailed out by loans from other governments and the IMF. One of the most dramatic cases was Asian crisis of 1997. It began with a run against Thai currency but extended to many

East Asian countries. The South Korean, Won, for example, fell from around 800 Won to the dollar on 10 January 1997 to almost 2000 Won to the dollar two days later. In order to shore up its foreign currency reserves, and pay back short term loans, the Korean government entered into agreement with the IMF in November 1997. The IMF extended $56 billion loan package, in lieu of which, it had to undertake cuts in public spending, increase excise and other indirect taxes, relax import limitations, hold inflation below 58 percent, allow international investors to owe 50 percent or more of Korean companies and allow foreign Banks access to the domestic market. Due to the opening of Korea for foreign investment, unemployment rose, layoffs occurred and those in employment saw their purchasing ability fall by 50 percent.[26]

One of the latest and fastest process of financial restructuring is the form of derivatives since 1980. In 1986 the total outstanding value of derivatives markets was about US $ 1 trillion, decade later this amount had risen to about US $ 20 trillion.[27] Derivatives include various financial instruments which acquire their value from underlying securities such as bonds, bills, foreign currencies, bank deposits, futures, forward contracts options and swap contracts (i.e., the exchange of one type of loan, such as a fixed interest rate loan, with a floating interest loan).

Complex derivative trading and transactions have led to some spectacular financial disasters during the 1990s. In 1995, Orange county California lost US $2.16 billion on interest rate derivative contracts entered into by its treasurer (Robert Citron). Similarly in 1995, a 233 year old merchant Bank (British) Berings, collapsed because of the activities of single trader in Singapore (Nick Lesson), who lost US $1.78 billion with options on the Japanese Nikkei index.[28] Berings was a merchant Bank with long history. John Bering emigrated from Bremen in Germany to England, and in 1714, started a wool business. His son founded the family Banking firm in London in 1793. It prospered, and the Berings became Earls, Knights, Viceroys and Barons as they transformed raw capital into cultural capital, new money into old respectability. The company helped finance the British war effort, organized loans in South America and was principal agent in the financing of US foreign trade and the sale of US bonds. Berings was one of the first financial institutions to get a place at the Tokyo stock exchange. Berings wanted to take part in the Asian economic miracle. In 1984 it bought a Asian stock broking house that was the basis for Bering securities, which made money on the then bullish Tokyo stock market. The bubble economy burst in the 1990s and Bering securities lost $20 million in 1992. In the same year Nick Lesson was sent out as head of settlements, becoming head of trading with a specialty in futures trading. Lesson incurred huge losses due to trading on the Singapore, Osaka and Tokyo exchanges. Lesson had taken futures on the assumption, that Nikkei was not going to fall. Nikkei went downward and Lesson doubled the bet, Bankers asked for more money to cover the position. Berings had only $316 million in reserves and the losses were $1.4 billion. The other Banks refused to bail them out, because the losses were very large. Berings was declared bankrupt on February 1995. This sent shock waves all round the world and stock indices at Nikkei, Phillipines, Taiwan fell. British Banks and financial companies associated with Bering fell around 6 per cent (*John Rennie Short, 2001*). In 1996, the Japanese trading company Sumitomo lost $3.3 billion[29] through the electronic gambling activities of one trader (Yasuo Hamanaka).

The electrification of the contemporary techniques not only affects global corporations and direct investors, but also a large section of the so called working and middle classes, whose shares, savings, investments and pension funds, increasingly flow in the electronic arteries of the global financial system. For instance in the mid 1970s, 75 per cent of private savings in the United States were held in saving accounts or fixed interest securities. By 1985, bank deposits had declined to 50 per cent and presently about 75 per cent of savings are invested on the stock exchange.

The general movement of savings, investments and pension funds into the spheres of global speculation, alter the structure of 'financial globalisation'—money profits and social destituteness are all increasingly virtual and faceless entities. For example, on the day BHP announced the planned restructuring and downsizing of its Australian steel works with a loss of at least 8,000 jobs in 1997, the markets responded and the value of BHP immediately increased by Australian $ 1 billion.[30] This apparently makes clear who the winners (shareholders) and loosers (workers) are, neither party is forced, or has the opportunity to confront the other. The denationalisation of money contribute to the privatisation of the self interest of those who participate in the global financial markets. For them, national and geographical monetary solidarity is becoming obsolete and dysfunctional.

## Migration

Migration as a phenomenon is as old as humanity. Anthropologists will have us believe that ever since the evolution of man in Africa, continuous movement of population, from one place to another for reasons of livelihood security and faith, has been a part of human destiny. Even after mankind had populated most of the planet, migration continued to play a decisive role in history down the centuries, as people contested for territory and the resources.

In some of the biggest movements of people, the migrants were not volunteers. In the 17th and 18th century, 15 million people were taken as slaves from Africa and shipped to Brazil the Caribbean and North America. In the 19th and 20th century between 10 million and 40 million indentured workers ("coolies") were sent in vast numbers around the world mainly from China and India. The industrial revolution extended capital overseas, altering the supply of and demand for resources, including labour. The primary movement of population between 1815 and 1914 included 60 million Europeans leaving for the Americas, Oceania, East and South Asia; and 1.5 million Indians finding homes in South-East Asia, East Africa and South Africa. After 1945, however, the number of international migrants rapidly increased from 50 million immigrants in 1989, the world total doubled in 1992, representing 2 per cent of the world population.[31]

For the past century or so, the pattern of migration has shifted a good deal, with changes in government policy playing a key role in determining the movement. Until 1914 governments imposed almost no controls. This allowed for the enormous 19th century movement of migrants from Europe to North America. The United States allowed entry to everyone with the exception of prostitutes, a convict, a lunatic—or after 1882, Chinese (*Claudia, Goldin, 1994*). Between 1914 and 1945, partly reflecting security concerns migration was curtailed. The two World Wars opened up apparent security concerns, extending from social and religious make-up to informational scrutiny. After 1945 came great change, many European countries faced labour shortages. Their immigration laws by and large were not repealed, but were enforced much more liberally.

Government showed alacrity in recruiting immigrants for jobs in their expanding industries. Migration surged again, now not mainly from Europe to North America but form the developing countries to the rich ones.

Finally a big change came in the 1970s. The rich countries were no longer growing quickly and struggling with labour shortages.[32] The recessionary trend of the 1970s forced governments in America and Europe to tighten the immigration rules, which continues till today.

Between 1870 and 1914, international labour migration was enormous. During this period, more than 50 million people left Europe, out of which two-thirds went to the United States while the remaining one-third went to Canada, Australia, New Zealand, South Africa, Argentina and Brazil *(Lewis, 1978)*. Most of these, were labour displaced who did not find industrial employment. The migration was, in effect, driven by the push of land scarce Europe and land abundant Americas as also other new lands with temperate climates that attracted white settlers. This mass emigration from Europe amounted to one eighth its total population migration in 1900 (*Deepak Nayyar, 2002, p.145*). For some of the countries such as Britain, Italy, Spain and Portugal such migration went to the tune of 20-40 percent of their population (*Massey, 1998; Stalker, 1994*).

The massive labour migration was halted in the period from 1914 to 1945. Between 1919 to 1939, the introduction of passport system and immigration laws were introduced. In United States restricted immigration laws, came into force due to several economic and political reasons. The Great Depression brought the economy to a reversal, this dampened the movement of people, who were interested in getting employment opportunities. The period of the second World

War led to a massive movement (15 million) of people within Europe of population in terms of refugees. This was consequent to the policies of racial hatredness, vengeance and redrawing of boundaries by the European states.[33]

In the second half of the twentieth century, it is possible to discern two phases of labour migration, i.e., from the late 1940s to the early 1970s to the late 1990s. During the first phase from 1940s to 1970s two streams of migration can be discerned. First, people's migration from Europe to the United States, Canada, Australia and New Zealand. This migration was bolstered by search for economic opportunities, and the nature of immigration laws, wherein Europeans were preferred, with the only exception in United States. In the period from 1950 to 1970, the total immigration was almost 6 million to the United States and 3 million into Canada.[34] Secondly, people from the developing world, such as India, China, Pakistan, Bangladesh etc. moved to Western Europe where economic growth in league with better employment opportunities created labour shortages, thereby leading to labour imports (*Deepak Nayyar, 2002*). The demand for labour shortages in West European countries was even compensated for by the Southern European states such as Italy and Spain. Italy happened to be most important source of labour, in order to fulfill the larger scarcity needs of labour, the European countries imported labour from other countries, which was patterned in the very colonial nature of state relationships. Britain imported workers from the Indian sub-continent and the Carribean Islands. France imported workers from Libya and Moracco. Germany imported workers from Yugoslavia and Turkey. Available evidence suggests that total immigration into Western Europe from 1950 to 1970 was about 10 million.[35]

During the second phase from the early 1970s to late 1990s, the trend of migration virtually halts. The era of rapid economic growth combined with full employment opportunities, was marred by economic strains, caused due to oil hike and rising inflation in Western Europe. The immigration laws became tighter due to resentment in many European countries.[36] In Britain due to unemployment among native population, the social attack upon Asian communities purportedly increased in London. Similarly in Germany with the unification, large scale attacks by native Germans (East-Germany) on Turkish migrants saw an increase. In France, too, public resentment ran high against the migrants from North African communities. The public resentments in France against the migrants, took the form of anguish over wearing of scarf and the veil by women (Muslims) of North African countries. The emigration to the United States undergoes a shift, in emphasising the entry to people with technical and professional qualifications, rather than the country of origin. This paves the way for better access to people from developing countries.[37] Between 1970 to 1995, total immigration into the United States was 17 million, while to Canada it was 4 million.[38] Despite the immigration laws, the consular practices, the average inflows of foreign population into the industrialised world were 3 million people per annum during the first half of the 1990s (*Deepak Nayyar, 2002, p. 56*). It is clear that international migration lagged far behind international trade and international investment in the process of globalisation. In fact, the number of new immigrants per 1000 inhabitants in the world as a whole in 1990 was lower than in 1970. Even though globalisation has gathered momentum, the process of cross border movement of populations of labour has not been able to keep pace with it.

A study by Peter Stalker, published by the International labour organisation in 1994, says that roughly 80 million people live in countries they were not born in. Another 20 million live in foreign lands as refugees from natural disasters or political oppression. Each year sees another 1.5 million or so emmigrate permanently, and perhaps another 1 million seek temporary asylum abroad. By historical standards, these numbers are large in absolute terms, but small in relation to the now much larger population of the receiving countries, See figure (3.7).

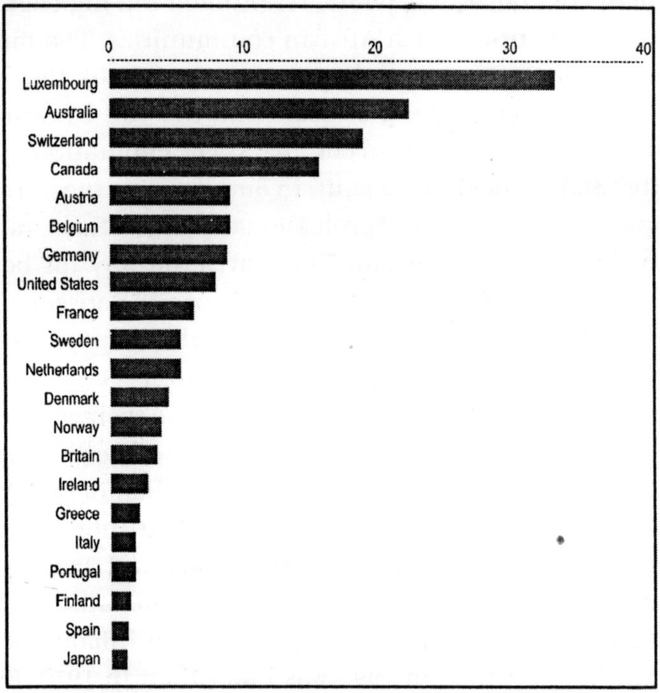


**Fig. 3.7.** Foreign population as % of total population, 1995.
***Source:*** OECD.

## Melting Pot

Mexico is the main source of migrants to the United States, with about 90,000 permanent (legal) settlers in 1995. But the former Soviet Union and the Philippines, taken together, supplied even more during that year– 55,000 and 51,000 respectively. See table (3.8).

**Table 3.8 Country of origin of immigrants 1995 in thousands**

| Australia | Britain | Canada |
|---|---|---|
| Newzealand 12.3 | Pakistan 6.3 | Hong Kong 31.7 |
| Britain 11.3 | India 4.9 | India 16.2 |
| China 11.2 | United States 4.0 | Philippines 15.1 |
| Ex-Yugoslavia 7.7 | Bangladesh 3.3 | China 13.3 |
| Hong Kong 4.4 | Nigeria 3.3 | Sri Lanka 8.9 |
| India 3.7 | Australia 2.0 | Taiwan 7.7 |
| **France** | **Japan** | **United States** |
| Algeria 8.4 | China 38.8 | Mexico 89.9 |
| Morocco 6.6 | Philippines 30.3 | Ex-Soviet Union 54.5 |
| Turkey 3.6 | United States 27.0 | Philippines 51.0 |
| United States 2.4 | South Korea 18.8 | Vietnam 41.8 |
| Tunisia 1.9 | Brazil 11.6 | Dominican Rep. 38.5 |
| Ex-Yugoslavia 1.6 | Thailand 6.5 | China 35.5 |

*Source:* OECD.

Citizens of European Union countries are free to work anywhere within the EU. The proportion of EU citizens in each member countries, foreign born population, varies widely from 25 per cent in the Netherlands to 89 per cent in Luxembourg.

In the United States about one fifth of the population in 2000 are either immigrants or the children of immigrants. With the removal of the post first world war restrictions in 1968, immigrant levels rose fourfold by 1998, and their compositions changed dramatically. Europeans now make up only 15 per cent of new arrivals, Latins and Carribeans 45 per cent, and Asians 30 percent.

The desire for security and well being drives the restless movement of humans. Saskia Sassen(sociologist) claims that people do not really want to leave the familiarity of their home territory, or their support networks if they can help it. Citizens of the European Union who are free to work and live, wherever they like in Europe, have begun to cease themselves, as less than 1.5 percent are choosing to move. Even the post-war movements north of Italians and Spaniards have creased as the economic circumstances that once drove them have been addressed.[39] Today Turks, Arabs and Africans have taken their places.

The impact of the migrants or new minorities has been profound for many nations. By the 1970s foreign migrants made up 12 per cent of Paris population, 16 per cent of Brussels and 34 per cent of Geneva.[40] By 2000, ethnic minorities composed 7 per cent of Britain's population and 34 percent of inner London's and were growing at a rate fifteen times that of the non-migrant population. Half are Asian and one third black. Some estimates suggest that by the end of the century people with some migrant background will comprise the majority of the population.[41] France does not identify people by race or religion, but it has five million migrants, or 8 per cent of its population, sixty per cent are North African. In Spain the population of migrants is only 2 per cent, in Germany it is 12 per cent.

Similarly, the scenario in United States is also varied. Some states are still dominated by their original settler communities: Mormons in Utah, Germans in Wisconsin, and Japanese in Hawai. In states such as Texas and Florida, the return of Afro-Americans and the huge inflow of Hispanics will soon turn the WASP population into a minority. Miami is already 65 percent Hispanic, 22 per cent black, 9 per cent WASP and 1 per cent Asian. California, which was 90 per cent WASP in 1950 and 80 per cent WASP in 1970, recorded only

47 per cent of whites in 2000. Hispanics made up 32 percent. WASPs still comprise 72 per cent of the US population, but they may be a minority by 2060.

## Immigrant Fears

Since migrants do not form a very large population of the overall population currently, and as they do not constitute a homogeneous bloc, they should not be construed as threatening to the advanced countries. This should neither be understood as invasion, as echoed by right wing newspapers. Yet people in varied populations in advanced nations have become sensitive to migration. This has resulted in distrust and suspicion, as to the intentions of migrants. Such fears by native population in Europe during the second world war fostered hatred and vengeance with hoary consequences for minorities. At the end of the war, twelve million Germans were, ethnically cleansed from Poland, Romania and Czechoslovakia. Two million Germans died in the exodus. Seven million of other minorities were also forced to move. After it was over, Eastern Europe's proportion of minorities had fallen from on average of 32 percent to 3 per cent in Poland, 12 per cent in Romania and 15 percent in Czechoslovakia. Anti-Jewish pogrammes continued. This ultimately resulted in the creation of Israel. Its creation did not solve the problem, rather led to another problem—exodus of Palestinians from their homelands, leading to a refugee crisis. These problems were largely due to the reassertion of ethnic homogeneity, in contra-distinction to the multiculturalism that accommodated diversity.

Similar was the case of Nigeria when oil production dropped to 400, 000 barrels in 1982, down from 3.3 million barrels in 1979, Nigerians felt the pinch of unemployment. Lagos came to regard noncitizens as competitiors for jobs as well as a strain in the economy and decided to retaliate for the 1969 expulsion of Nigerians from Ghana. In 1983, Nigeria ordered an estimated two million West Africans to leave the country within fourteen days. The repatriation of foreign workers to Ghana, Togo, Burkina Faso and Chad entailed a massive displacement of labour, enforced by inspections of households in search of defaulting aliens and emergency reception centers to help ease the human suffering (*Arthur, 1991, 72-77*).

Muslims represent one third of all immigrants in Western Europe, and allowing for inter-regional flows, two thirds of Non-EU nationals. In fact, the prospect of Islamic resurgence in the Southern countries causes serious concern. A perplexing problem is structured political participation among Muslims in these countries, because Islamic tradition differs from a secular democratic society, with its representative bodies. Attacks on immigrants in EU countries are increasingly frequent and accompanied by a swell of xenophobia.

## Production, jobs and Wages

Migration may not be new but it has become more controversial for many years. Clearly immigration brings a variety of benefits, to the receiving country. An important one for many rich countries is demographic. The average age of the advanced economies population is rising. Immigration tends to lower it, because most migrants are young. This improves the ratio of active workers to retired people, so taxes can be lower than otherwise. It is expected that between 2000 to 2025 the population of industrialised countries will remain almost unchanged at about 125 billion while the population of developing countries will increase from 4 to 7.5 billion. But this is not all. The zero population growth in the industrialised world, combined with increased life expectancy, is expected to lead to a rapid ageing of the population in these countries. Deepak Nayyer exhorts that dependency ratios (the proportion of the population aged 65 years or more) are projected to rise sharply from about one fifth to about onethird.[42] This consequently means that, shrinking working population, made up of producers and earners, would have to support an expanding elderly population made up of consumers and pensioners. The ageing of industrial societies, however, will also generate a demand for labour imports to provide services, such as health care and home care, in order to maintain the quality of life among the aged or elder in the population. Such service providers, whether permanent immigrants, guest workers or illegal immigrants, would have to come from the developing countries, the disposable force comprises workers who are employed on a transitory basis in one country, who can be repatriated when they are no longer required, thereby maintaining a high level of employment for national labour. Switzerland and the Persian Gulf region states have practised a disposable labour policy. In the Gulf region, the ratio of foreign to total population has been the highest in the world, ranging from 23 per cent in Saudi Arabia to 76 per cent in the United Arab Emirates in 1980. As a percentage of the total labour force rather than of population, the proportion of foreign (i.e. temporary) workers has been even greater, reaching around 90 per cent in Qatar and the UAE in the same year (*Tabbarah 1988, 1256*). Countries in various regions are increasingly opting for "turnkey" projects. A contractor, sometimes the state (as in the case of People's Republic of China), recruits workers, sends them to enclaves, in locales such as Botswana, and repatriates them on termination. Such kind of usage is quiet profound in the strategy of multinationals, who shift employees from country to country, they use citizens of one country to alleviate skill shortages in another.

The World Bank and some liberal economists contend that labour mobility is a means of reducing income inequality world-wide. The Bank argues that emigration helps to relieve population pressure, alleviates unemployment, funnels remittances in the country of origin and may contribute to the diffusion of new ideas and technologies, either when skilled workers return home or through an exchange of information (*World Bank, 1990, 93-94*). However, the benefits of migration have been distributed unequally to the advantage of the already more fortunate receivers. This happens when receiving countries shift their policies from favouring particular ethnic groups to emphasising highly skilled immigrants, as did the United States and Canada. This resulted in not only a marked increase in the brain drain, but also considerable upsurge of illegal migration. The polices of US and Canada, by preferring (professionals, engineers and doctors), while erecting barriers to the free flow of unskilled labour have served to cause asymmetry. The negative flow of human capital from sending countries saves receiving countries the cost of reproducing a sector of their labour force (*Griffin and Khan 1992, 57, 65-67*).

## References

1. Mark Mazower, Dark Continent: Europe's Twentieth Century, London, 1998, Allen lane, p. 337.
2. WTO, Trade and Foreign Direct Investment: Report of 16 October, 1996 (Geneva: WTO, 1996).
3. D. Dollar and A. Krany, "Trade, Growth and poverty", 2004, Economic Journal, 114 (493): f-22-f-49.
4. UNDP (1999: 37).
5. UNDP (1996: 2-3).
6. Baner and Mason (1992).
7. Leys, ed. Barbara Harris White, "Globalisation and Insecurity", Palgrave, 2002.

8. V. Mathew, Kurien, AOA, Trips and the Third World Agriculture, "Mainstream, Dec. 22-28.
9. Rajendra Kumar, "Failure of the Doha Round-Looking Back to Look Ahead, "South Asian Politics, January, No. 9.
10. Vandana Shiva, "Impacts of Globalisation", 2001, Earth scan pub, p. 204.
11. Luke Anderson, "Genetic Engineering Foods and our Environment", Australian, 22 February, 2000, p. 15.
12. Guardian weekly, 14-20 October, 1999, p.12.
13. Guardian weekly, 1-7 June, 2000, p. 8.
14. Jules Pretty, "The Living Land: Agriculture, Food and Community Reservation in Rural Europe", London, 1998, Earth Scan.
15. *Ibid.*
16. John Rennie Short, "Global Dimensions Space, Place and the Contemporary World" 2001, Reaktion Books, p.104.
17. A.I. Blownfield, "Monetary Policy under the International Gold Standar, (New York, 1959, p. 62.
18. K.W. Dam, "The Rules of Game, Reform and Evaluation in the International Monetary System", Chicago, 1982, p. 6.
19. David L.Wilfred, "The IMF Policy Paradigm", New York, 1985, Princeton.
20. Milton Gilbert, "Quest for World Monetary Order", The Gold Dollar System and its Aftermath, New York, John Wiley, 1980, p. 62-66.
21. Business Standard, 5 December, 1989.
22. David Held and Ayse Kaya, "Global Inequality patterns and Explanations", polity, 2007, p. 79.
23. Barbara Harris-White, "Globalisation and Insecurity", Palagrave, pp.13-14.
24. World Bank Report, 1996.
25. Cobus-de-Swardt Kraus, "Globalisation for Sale", Kagan Paul International, 2000, p. 55.
26. John Rennie Short, "Global Dimensions Space, Place and the Contemporary world", Reaktion Books, p.109.
27. *Ibid* p.108.
28. Business Standard, 18 Feb., 1995.

29. Financial Express, 19 Nov. 1996.
30. Cobus de Swardt-Kraus, "Globalisation for Sale: An Analysis of the Interdynamics of Globalisation, Valorisation and Marginalisation, Kagan International, 2000, p.72.
31. OECD (1998).
32. Peter Stalker, "The Work for Strangers : A survey of International Labour Migration", ILO, 1994, Geneva.
33. M. Mazower, "Dark Continent: Europe's Twentieth Century," London, 1998, Allen home.
34. The figure cited here are obtained from immigration statistics published by the United States Immigration and naturalization service and the Canadian employment and Immigration center.
35. The evidence is not definitive and is possibly based on Estimates Stalker (1994) reports that, between 1950 and 1973, net immigration into Western Europe was nearly 10 million.
36. These changes in immigrations policies are described in UN (1998). Evidence available for the period 1986-96 also shows that the proportion of foreign born population in the total population in most countries of Western Europe was remarkably stable. See OECD (1998, p. 224). Even in countries such as Germany, where it rose modestly, it was probably attributable to the slower growth in the Native population rather than to more immigration.
37. Deepak Nayyar cites that the Immigration Act of 1965 abolished national origins quotas, fixed a ceiling on western hemisphere immigration and devised a preference system that favoured relatives of US citizens and residents those with needed occupational skills,.abilities or training, and refugees. Immigrant visas were allocated on a first come first served basis, subject to seven categories of immigrants in order of preference and without any numerical limit on espouses, parents, or children of US citizens. This led to a rapid shift in the countries of origin of immigrants consequently, in the stock of foreign born population in the United states, the proposition of European immigration fell from 32.2 per cent in 1970 to 19.7 per cent in 1980 and 11.7 percent in 1990, while the proportion of Asian immigration rose from 5.2 per cent in 1970 to 10.8 per cent in 1980 and 15.2 percent in 1990.

38. The Primary sources of the data are immigration statistics published by the United States and Canada. See Deepak Nayyar (1994) and OECD (1998).
39. Sassen Saskia, "Home Truths", Guardian weekly, 27 April, 3 May, 2002, p.13.
40. M. Mazower, "Dark continent", p. 327.
41. Ojita Mirta, "Best of Friends, World Apart", How Race is lived in America, New York Times. (N.Y.T. com) 5 June, 2000, The Economist, 7 April, 2001, p. 56.
42. Simulations of population scenarios that much greater inflows of immigrants would be required, in the OECD countries– old-age-dependency (ODR), would register a significant increase everywhere between 2010 and 2000, as projected in United Nations, World Population Prospects, 1996. According to the calculation, the number of people of working age required for the ODR in 2020 to remain unchanged at the levels (2010), US would require an additional 66 million people of working age. This number is 11.5 times the actual net migration of 5.8 million people into the United States during the ten year period from 1985 to 1995. Similarly for the same period, the calculation works out to be 17.4 for France, 10.6 for U.K 7.9 for Italy, and so on. For Japan it is estimated that an additional 22 million of working age would be required in 2020. These projections are based on OECD, Report (1998:29).

# 4

# Social and Cultural Ramifications of Globalisation

## Homogenisation and Culture

Cultural diversity is of course much greater at the global than at the country level. It was possible earlier to imagine cultures as being separated from one another—with room to breathe and to develop independently—but technological change in transport and communications has for centuries been dissolving time and space, breaking down the barriers that surround even the most isolated culture. This process has accelerated due to globalisation. One consequence of globalisation is that cultures are coming into increasing contact with each other. For instance, the Chinese culture rubs against the Indian culture, the European culture rubs against the African culture and so on.

The rubbing of cultures is not a question of physical proximity, and strictly speaking cultures do not have boundaries. They interpenetrate, hence they are not homogeneous, they are rather hybrids (*Nederveen Pieterse, 1994*). It is thus particular cultural attributes that rub against one another, and not one particular reified culture (much less a singular national or state culture) that rubs against another. This kind of rubbing has been a part and parcel of our history. It would be improper to claim that technological change, and the cultural interchange that follows it, are universally beneficial. Development has always been uneven, consequently the process of cultural interchange has also been asymmetrical. Samarkand, Bukhara, and Khiva, once were centers of culture, art and architecture. This was largely silk route connecting China with Europe in the fifteenth century, with the development of organic trade these cities lost their economic status and went into a period of isolation and hibernation. The transport cost in land became unprofitable in relation to maritime trade.

While closer contact, between communities, yielded fruitful intercourse at the level of life style, thought, food habits, religion and economic interchanges, at times it has not been devoid of consequential banes. Culture contact, has often been a by-product of military encounters and has been associated with violence, pillage, war, enslavement, conquest, colonialism, imperialism (*Elsenhans; 1991*). The culture contact resulted in some cases (Maya, Inca) to the decimations of indigenous population. It has also lead to the introduction of alien diseases, racism,[1] and genocide, more often it has led to the destructions of pre-existing social structures and the system of beliefs that sustained them.[2] On the positive side culture contact has enabled cultures to enrich themselves of 'convenient diversities' which were unknown to them encompassing food, technologies, ideas, knowledge etc. Thus Latin America gave maize, potatoes, the tomato and natural rubber. Ethiopia and Yemen gave coffee, China gave tea and noodles (which the Italians transformed into Pasta) and so on. The world's pharmacopoeia draws on Botanical products from many different regions. The same holds true for domesticated animals. Chinese have provided paper, porcelain, compass, gunpowder and many other things (*Needham*, 1954). The Arabs gave system of numerals and the Indians gave zero and Buddhism. Thus all our cultures have numerously been influenced by each other.

Similar processes can be observed today. Today no culture, no society is completely closed. The question revolves around the degree of openness and the relative terms on which one culture interacts with another culture. The relationship among the culture can be one of subordination, domination and exploitation or one of equality, mutual respect and beneficial exchange. The process of globalisation with its attendant ramifications consisting of capital and technological flows has made cultural interchange more frequent than in the past. Many scholars speculate that the world is increasingly witness to the 'global culturel', with local cultures being submerged under an irresistible tide of western influence. Culture worldwide is becoming more homogeneous. Products such as coca-cola, blue jeans and North American popular music rule the roost. Local cuisines are being abandoned by Western style fast foods, traditional ways of life and livelihood habits are being abandoned in favour of pale images of the American way of life.

Globalisation has induced a rapid flow of ideas, information and knowledge, than one could perceive in the past. This has resulted in diversity—greater heterogeneity and not greater homogeneity. This overdose of diversity in manifold forms, culture, lifestyles, fashion, food etc., has led to permutations and in the process created new ways of life, new cultures.

Culture over the years in history is valued in itself, and also as a means to obtain other things that are desired or sought. Thus culture can be ascribed to possess both intrinsic and instrumental value. The intrinsic value of culture, reflects in preserving cultural heritage, respect to traditions, and cultural possessions of preceding generations who passed them on to us. It also encompasses, recorded spoken languages and to restore and maintain historic monuments, art objects and ancient artifacts. Culture as our way of life is something most of us treasure, and wish to preserve in a recognisable form; it contributes to our sense of self or who we are and to our sense of satisfaction or well being.[3]

Culture as a means is also felicitated. The instrumental value of culture is being used by leaders and spiritual inheritors in various areas of life to achieve economic, social and political purpose. This includes the appeal to tradition to forge new alliances based on ethnicity or nationality, sometimes with the objective of creating new, culturally homogeneous states, as with Serbs in Bosnia. It also includes the revival of religious and other traditions in an attempt to re-establish an old order, to recreate a golden age, and to impose ancient, fundamental values on a society regarded as immoral or godless. The rise of Christian, Islamic, Jewish and Hindu 'fundamentalist' movements can be interpreted in this way.[4]

Globalisation has intensified the cultural interchange among various communities at global level in different format such as communication (fax and internet), new ways of doing business (MNCs), new forms of political organisation (EEC) and new ways of finding a spouse (by advertising in media). These activities are implanted into the subterranean terrain of local culture, thereby acquiring a new form 'global culture'. Though culture apparently binds people in identifiable and recognisable shades, for numerous social, economic and political functions, it may not be the case always. People in search of fertile terrain of violence, find culture a useful tool for aggrandisement (political, social, economic). Call for cultural purity or cultural ascendancy can result in genocide, ethnic cleansing, civil war, repression of minorities and domestic violence. Globalisations ability of space and time compression, may prove to be a handy tool, for bigots and frenzy mongers, to take the peoples peace for a ride.

Despite the bad omens of culture, 'sitting in the hind sight', the perceptible benefits of culture far outweigh the demonic representations. Culture gives people a sense of identity and helps to define one's place in the world. It provides a degree of psychological security by enclosing each person within symbolically visible cultural boundaries. It fosters trust and cooperation within groups and facilitates collective agreements, and market exchange. The frequent closeness of cultures may produce rubbing and it may result in conflict. The formidable process of global capitalism, has brought, competing interests of various communities to the forefront. The very speed and reach of global capital provides too short a time for contemplation to communities. The very idea to cash an opportunity under globalisation is— "now or never", tends to add a high degree of Nitrate, that results in explosion of violence and retribution. The leaders of various cultures harp upon the contamination (cultural), of Western nations, which can uproot and dislodge the local indigenous life style left by their forefathers. The most widely held description of this has been labeled as – "The Mcdonaldisation of culture", or the homogenisation thesis. This indicates the "Convergence towards a common set of cultural traits and practices." The notion of "Mcdonaldisation" refers to the "worldwide homogenisation of societies through the impact of multinational corporations". This essentially indicates, cultural westernisation and in particular the Americanisation of the entire globe.

As Robert Holton notes that "consumer capitalism" of this type has been built upon a standardised brand image, mass advertising and the high status being given by many third world population to Western products and services. The birth of the global consumer has not simply been founded upon "the utilitarian convenience of global products but on the sale of dreams of affluence, personal success, and erotic gratification of Hollywood. But this thesis of homogenisation, has not been accepted by many scholars, for instance, Holton notes, "the strong association of cultural globalisation with Americanisation is overstated." He offers the example of "colonial dependency" relation. The cultural synchronisation of Western cultures is not a single monolith, rather multiple centers, such as British, French, Dutch etc. In India apparently it is the British cultural remnants which are more visible, similarly in French Congo it is the French cultural remnants. An overarching American culture domination is simplification of an otherwise complex set of cultural process at work.

Similarly Shannon Peters Talbott offers her own analysis of Mcdonaldisation, she says that it is not so much cultural homogenisation, but global localisation. The Mosco Mcdonald's varies from its American Western counterparts by catering to the consumers in Moscow.[5] Nederveen Pieterse writes that firms may be multinationals, but they adopt the business of food according to local tastes and choices. Multinational corporations, such as McDonalds have abandoned product standardisation and have developed marketing design and product strategies that are as numerous as the variations of consumer demands in differing markets. This is "glocalisation", a notion that " has been used to suggest that the global and the local may be mutually reinforcing rather than necessarily in conflict.

There is the third paradigm that views culture, as a interconnection between globalisation and culture, as a hybridisation of cultures in the world. Hybridisation according to Nederveen Pieterse, is an open-ended process of interconnection of cultural influences (Eastern as well as

Western). There is both cultural difference and a "Striving for recognition" on the global scale, which implies a claim to equality, equal rights, same treatment, or, in other words a common universe of difference.

## Identity

The existence of local, autonomous, distinct and well-defined, cultural systems specific to its unique geographical setting constitutes the hallmark of various communities prior to the processes of globalisation. The unique settings with cultural interactions gave one's community its unique "cultural identity". This identity was something people simply 'had' as an undisturbed existential possession an inheritance a benefit of traditional long dwelling, of continuity with the past.

John Tomlinson (1999) states:

> ..."Identity like language, was not just a description of cultural belonging. It was a sort of collective treasure of local communities. But it was also discovered to be something fragile that needed protecting and preserving, that could be lost. Into this world of manifold, discrete, but to various degrees vulnerable, cultural identities there suddenly burst (apparently around the middle of the 1980s) due to the corrosive power of globalisation. The power of globalisation has swept like a flood tide, through the world's diverse cultures, destroying stable localities, displacing peoples, bringing a market driven "branded" homogenisation of cultural experience, thus obliterating the differences between locally-defined cultures which had constituted our identities. Though globalisation has been judged as involving a general process of loss of cultural diversity, some of course did better, some worse out of this process. whilst those cultures in the mainstream of the flow of capitalism-

> i.e., West and specifically, the United States saw a sort of standardised version, of their cultures exported worldwide. It was the 'weaker' cultures of the developing world that have been most threatened.Thus the economic vulnerability of these non-western cultures is assumed to be matched by a cultural vulnerability".....

The fact contended by John Tomlinson in the above paragraph underlines the advantage of cultural power that lays with the Western world. The Western world's cultural system and capitalist version of economic development have finally triumphed over any other system prevailing in the world. This clearly gives the Western system a cultural edge in promoting its own version of culture (consumerism) over the non-western culture. While the West has enjoyed a relatively longer period of engagement with market economy, hence they needed time for cultural adaptation. The non-western societies did not have the secure time lag, hence their cultural and social systems are finding hard to negotiate the forces of globalisation. This has facilitated the process of cultural rejuvenation and cultural reversals in the form of progressive and fundamentalist versions of culture. The spiritual and political leaders in several cultures have fed upon their people the notions of subjugation, thereby causing revival of ethno-religious conflicts.

The collapse of communism is often interpreted in political - economic terms as a reaction to step change in the global advance of capitalism. The increasing power and the integration of the global capitalist market made it impossible for the control of economies of eastern bloc to survive outside the dominant economic system (world system). Arguably as many analysts have us believe that most East European countrie's ills lay, as a result of static economic environment with fixed wages, and absence of incentives to the entrepreneurship. The public sector failed to deliver goods in terms of quality, pricing and marketing strategies. On the other hand due to globalising media, and the attraction of Western consumer culture, the populations in these countries, were a dissatisfied lot just waiting for the moment to vent their anguish.

The rapid disintegration of the Yugoslav federation revealed deep divisions in cultural and religious identities—Serbs, Croats, Bosnians, ethnic Albanians, Christians and Muslims—which became rapidly inflamed into what *Kaldor (1999)* has aptly called the 'new wars' of the era of globalisation. The key point of Mary Kaldors assertion is that 'globalisation wars' are fought around a vicious particularistic form of 'identity politics' in which 'movements—mobilise around ethnic, racial or religious identity for the purpose of claiming state power (1999:76).

Such examples of identity formation can be seen in most of the countries in diverse forms. In Sri Lanka, the Tamils have been waging a war against Sinhalese majority, Pakistan has witnessed Baluchi and Sindhi, in India, Sikh and Assamese, Indonesia has witnessed the Timori revolt, among few to cite. Such examples of the violent assertion of, and the struggle over, cultural identity seem, on the one hand, to fit the argument about the generation of modern institutionalised forms of identity rather well. Far from being simply atavistic reversions, the deliberate aim of such ethnic conflicts is as, Kaldor says, to claim state power—that is to institutionalise a particular cultural identity in a modern political form.

Tomlinson (2000), enunciates a similar typology of identity formation along ethnic religious lines, but, has a point, in stating that, there are examples of projects of cultural 'reterritorialisation' the claiming and reclaiming of localities—

which don't involve claims to state power. For example, the land rights movement of aboriginal groups in Australia, the USA, Canada and elsewhere that have come to prominence in recent years. Though in such examples the claims of identity are inextricably mixed with issues of political and economic justice. If they are dealt in cosmopolitan fashion then they can co-exist within single national identity.

## Islamic Fundamentalism

Islamic fundamentalism has been viewed by many scholars and sociologists as reaction to globalisation (westernism and consumerism). In order to understand the recent political and cultural history of Islamic societies, two related arguments must be considered. The first attempts to recognize the profound problems of having, within a world cultural system, competing world religions which claim exclusive and largely absolutist truths or values. The second argument is concerned with the problem of relationship between the cultural, aesthetic, and stylistic pluralism of globalisation and fundamentalist commitment to the coherent and unified world organised around values, styles, beliefs which are held to be incontrovertibly true.

The globalisation with its culture of consumerism (*Bryan S. Turner, 1994*) is making alternative life styles, beliefs and attitudes appear as a set of commodities for sale on a world cultural market. The Islam has not been able to resolve its dilemma, of engaging itself with the culture of globalisation, as it threatens the religions uniqueness, and diversity associated with it. People in Islamic societies have not been able to come to terms with the juggernaut of globalisation, which attacks local culture, traditionalism and downgrades versions of truth. Hence rise of fundamentalism in Islam according to many scholars is a cultural defense against forces of globalisation which can shake the foundation of Islam.

The other explanations for the rise of fundamentalism are conditions of poverty, deprivation, and alienation that exist in the Muslim world. Islamist rebellions and violence, it is commonly claimed, are the result of socio-economic impoverishment and psychological alienation and stem from the failed modernisation and excessive westernisation (*Ansari, 1948; Davis, 1984; Arjomand, 1988; Ayubi, 1991; Casandra, 1995*). Rapid dislocations that have taken place in the Muslim world during the globalisation era, have contributed to this sense of relative deprivation and alienation. These social transformations entailed the expansion of secondary and university education, development of public sector employment, implementation of land reforms and Western style legal systems, nationalisation of religious institutions, modification of personal status codes and promotion of state led industrialisation (*Mohammed, Hafez,* 2005).

A nationalist and technocratic elite with an affinity towards Western models of development usually carried out these reforms. During the globalisation period, the technocratic elite often equated successful development with secularisation and westernisation of society and saw institutions rooted in rural economies and religious traditions as impediments to modernisation. Such examples can be found in Iraq-Saddam Hussain, Syria-Hafez-Al-Asad, Iran-Shah Reza Pahelvi, Tunisia-Habib Bourguiba etc.

These post-colonial transformations, under globalisation despite improving the lot of many people, manifested serious contradictions. Industrialisation initially a source of national pride, quickly turned into a heavy burden on society that could only be sustained through national debt.

The expansion of education increased literacy, thereby producing doctors, engineers and lawyers, but they could not find gainful employment and their skills were underutilised.

Similarly's land reforms did not improve the lot of peasants, instead many were forced to migrate to already overcrowded cities where they ended up in shanty towns. Moreover, the rhetoric of progress, that accompanied efforts at modernisation produced high expectations among people. Only a well-positioned few were able to take advantage of state led development and many were left with unfulfilled expectations and broken promises. The failure to meet the rising expectation of ordinary people and the crude emulation of Western lifestyles, it is commonly argued, resulted in feelings of deprivation and 'normative disorientation' (*Arjomand, 1988*), which made many Muslims susceptible to Islamist radicalism and militancy. As *Kepel (1984:128)* explains in relation to Egypt, "in the ramshackle dwellings of the suburbs ringing the large Egyptian cities, people by passed by progress and development turned towards other, more radical tendencies of the Islamicist movement. Others point to psychological alienation as an equally important factor. Ansari (*1984:140-141*) asserts that Islamist militancy is by product of the breakdown of traditional solidarity caused by "rapid urbanisation and rural migration" By and large, even a casual glance at events in central Asia comprising of countries such as Egypt, Algeria, Tunisia and Jordan etc. portray tendencies of rebellion among the Muslim youths to apparent, unemployment, poverty, marginalisation coupled with political corruption. In the 1980s and 1990s most of the central Asian economies witnessed negative rate of growth thereby compounding the problems of educated youth. The repression let loose by the government in these countries with the Western support, further added to the alienation. The treatment of Muslims in many of the European countries such as Germany, France and Great Britain on some popular issues such as scarf and veil, further accentuated the belief that West was demonising Islam. Western countries treatment of politically sensitive issues concerning Muslim world such as Palestine, Bosnia-Herzegovina, Iraq, Afghanistan etc. was viewed with skepticism by Muslim youth. The revulsion of all that is Western, (Globalisation, Modernisation, Westernisation) became an obsession. 9/11 attack on the US marks the culmination point, George Bush's rhetoric after 9/11 further aggravated the situation, as action and pronunciation reminded us of the battle drawn during the crusades between Christianity and Islam. Islamic fundamentalism while different in its national and local manifestation, shows a common rejection of the modernist secular period on a variety of grounds. These include the perception that modernisation has failed because its secular character could not alter coherent values. In addition modernisation failed, because too rapid urbanisation and inadequate agricultural policies produced gross inequalities of wealth and power, leaving the peasantry often in a precarious economic situation. In addition, there is the notion that liberalism has failed because the policies of the nationalist Arabic state systems did not allow genuine political expression and democracy, for example, it is suggested that Egypt, despite radical changes, remained dominated by traditional elites who manipulated the electoral system to maintain political power under the slogan of political participation.

An interesting development during the globalisation has been the re-introduction of Islam into the mass media and the regulation of broadcasting and advertising by Islamic institution and norms. In this area Islamisation is distinctively anti-consumerist and against globalisation (Western led). The growth of a global system of communication has made possible for the majority of Muslims the ritual necessity of Pilgrimage to Mecca, thereby reinforcing the concept of Islam as a global system. At the same time, these institutions of global communication spread the message of pan-Islamic unity.

> "Ironically, the technological tools of modernisation have often served to reinforce traditional belief and practice as religious leaders who initially opposed modernisation now use radio, TV and print to preach and disseminate, to educate and proselytise. The message of Islam is not simply available from a preacher at a local mosque. Sermons and religious education from leading preachers and writers can be transmitted to every city and village" (Esposito 1984: 212).

## Gender

Gender is fundamentally a relationship of power. It is a social stratification system that places most women in subordinate positions. Gender ideology consists of ingrained beliefs that order power relation between men and women. As with other kind of ideologies, structures of domination are preserved in an often-unconscious manner through commonsense assumptions. In the case of gender ideology, some common assumptions are that household work is the natural domain of woman and that women are non-productive social actors.[6]

Reinforced by global communications internal and international migrations, rising levels of formal education for women and increased personal autonomy and mobility, feminism has become a powerful social movement in its own right. World conference on the international year of the women in 1975, and the UN decade for the women (1975-85), served to bring the issue of women representation in economy, governance participation (political) on the plank of equity. By the 1990s hundreds of feminist organisations were operating locally, nationally and transnationally.

Women have made tremendous gains in formal equality, as measured among other indicators, by the UN gender development index. This composite index ranks nations according to the share of total income that women earn, women's life expectancy and literacy compared to men's as well as women's enrolment in primary, secondary and tertiary schools (UNDP, 1995).

A general outcome of discourses that address the issue of gender is that gender ideology not only structures power within social relations, but also articulates and connects in distinctive ways to the ideology of globalisation. The ideology of globalisation lends legitimacy to shifting functions in the realm of social services from the state to women, as well as to prying open markets, liberalising trade and reducing state intervention in the economy. In economies that structurally restrict women's economic participation to subsistence activities, the rolling over of the state, which is sometimes theorised as the institutionalisation of patriarchal power, in fact, works against augmenting this participation. Even in economies where women's economic participation, has increased, under pressures arising out of the liberalisation of trade and industry. The terms of this participation are highly exploitative. The gendered division of labour is actually one of the factors that make globalisation possible, (*Mittleman*).

There are various interpretations that are offered for women being paid less, in the current era of globalisation one of these is, that most women had never been raised with the same work expectations as men, they were often less well equipped for work. In addition, because they tended to focus on establishing families first, they lacked the training and experience that men had gained in the interim.[7] Nevertheless women did gain a degree of choice previously denied to them. Smaller families and the availability of labour saving devices in domestic appliances helped to give women more time for productive work outside the home. Indeed, so did the industries responsible for reducing the labour required for housework. The technologies that lay behind the consumer boom produced light industries that required unskilled labour. The shift to service oriented economy similarly provided women with new work opportunities.[8] A new symbiosis emerged: Women were attracted to work that emphasised social and communication skills, employers wished to utilize the comparative advantage women enjoyed in those skills.

At the end of the twentieth century, prospects for women in industrial societies were decidedly better than the women in the third world nations. The position of women in areas of Asia, Africa and Latin America are no better than that of wretched labour. Women in advanced industrial nations did not leave home in their early teens. They no longer produced four to six children. They no longer died at the age of 55. In fact, they were raised in smaller families. They continued their education through their teens in secondary schools, women made up half of the university population. Fewer women now married; and if they did it was in late 20's or early 30's. They bore one or two children after which they re-entered the work force. Women had won 40 per cent of seats in the European parliament in1999.[9] New Zealand entered the new century with a female prime minister, a female leader of the opposition, a female chief justice, a female attorney general, a female cabinet secretary and a female head of state.

But despite the above-mentioned healthier side of Gender gains, there is larger part of the world where scenario is as gloomier as ever, and in some cases perceptible reversals. In Eastern Europe the collapse of communism reduced female parliamentary participation in the Czech Republic from 30 percent to 6 per cent during the 1990s. In East Africa women comprised 80 per cent of the food producing workforce but received only 1 percent of agricultural loans. In West Africa their economic activities were often better recognised, but women still experienced extremely high death rates from childbirth: 980 deaths per 10,000 births compared with a first world average of 2.3.[10] With the decline in male employment and real wages brought about by neo-liberal restructuring, women's importance has grown. The reorganisation of production on a global scale is feminising[11] the labour force and changing the previous gender demarcation of domestic and wage labour. Gender inequality is reproduced in the work force and at the same time it continues in the household. The systematic subordination of women in the reproduction sphere is coupled with the systematic inequality of women in the reproduction sphere. It is clear that under globalisation there is sexual divison of labour. New forms of labour market segmentation between men and women and wage differential in the formal sector converse with unpaid domestic labour, and hardship imposed in the sphere of gendered social reproduction resulting in a deterioration of the status and social condition of most women from the mining and construction areas of India, maquilas of Mexico, Central American and the Carribean, to the new transnational agro-business plantations in Chile and Colombia, and the new industrial complexes in Brazil's north-east. Women in Latin America disproportionately and in some cases exclusively—engage in unskilled labour-intensive phases of globalised production.

The decline in wages and work conditions associated with new capital-labour relations at the production site takes place at a time when women increasingly make up the ranks of the workforce. The cost of restructuring by the capitalist production is especially borne by the women. Since the states have increasingly rolled down the state security sector, hence in an atmosphere of commodification and urbanisation, the women bear the brunt. These twin processes i.e; the deterioration of wages and social wages, have had a devastating impact on women and children (*Cornai, 1987;*

*Beneria and Feldman, 1992*). Women have disproportionately borne the burden of neo-liberal restructuring.

Today global poverty is feminized. 70 per cent of the world poor are women (*Veltmeyer, 1997, 224*). Thus teenage pregnancies afflict one in sixteen girls over 15 in India and Pakistan. Women in Latin America have a 34 per cent probability of belonging to the bottom 20 per cent of the income distribution as compared to 15 per cent probability for men (*World Bank, 1997: 48*). As women have entered the formal labour force the data indicates that they encounter a gender segmented labour market in which women are disproportionately concentrated in low wage employment and excluded from high wage employment. In the United States women still earn only 76 per cent of the male wage, up from 59 per cent at the start of the 1970s. In the top 500 US companies only 10 per cent of corporate officers are women. Australia is slightly better, women earn 85 per cent of the male wage, up from 65 per cent in the 1970s. But only 8.3 per cent of its corporate directors are women, 1.3 per cent of senior management. This inequality in labour force participation aggravates other gender based social inequalities (*World Bank, 1997: 197-202*).

As women enter the labour force they are also disproportionately relegated to the informal economy as part time domestic laundresses, street vendors, industrial home workers and so on. Women account for fully 70 percent of all new jobs in the informal sector (*Veltmeyer, 1997: 220*). The transformation in the status of women, and particularly women's increasing centrality in production and reproduction along with the 'double burden' has galvanised poor and working women. The Fig. (4.1) shows the share of women in wage employment in non-agricultural sector, by regional group of countries, 1999-2000.

The process of globalisation have unleashed a set of productive forces which has facilitated the incorporation of

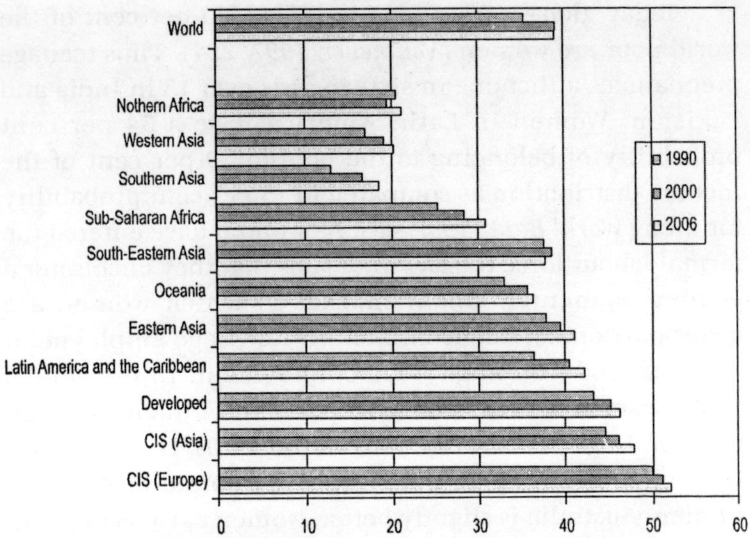


**Fig. 4.1. Female percentage share of wage employment in non agriculture sector (MDG 3.2), by regional group of countries, 1990–2000**

*Source:* ILO.

women in the productive chain. But most of the women workers are positioned in the peripheral side of production, with meager salaries. Due to the pre-ponderance of women workers in the casual and informal side of production chain, they are caught in a relationship of uneasy symbiosis. While the women's in advanced societies have fared better than their counterparts in third world, the scenario underscores the dramatic growth under globalisation of group and class inequalities and opportunities that cut across the gender divide to the extent that gains in formal equality and opportunity improve the condition of women as women, gender inequality is increasingly fused with class and group inequality under globalisation. This explains the mass participation and leadership role of women at every level in the struggle on popular issues, pertaining to local resources, diversity or environment protection, as they are the most affected.

## Social Movements

A common feature of both globalisation and westernisation are reactions against it. Groups and movements organising themselves using new technology and new ways of connecting across borders—described by some as a new 'global civil society'. More modestly what is new is the extent to which territorial location, territorial distance and territorial borders have lost their determining influence. Modern technology means that people can connect in a space unbounded by territory. Distance can be conquered and covered in no time. As a result, transnationally organised groups can identify in a new way, forming around a premise of supra-territorial solidarity instead of within national bounds whether it be around class, gender, religious faith, or profession.[12]

In particular neo-liberal states no longer truly serve the interests of the majority. Popular social forces have a much greater need to mobilise and organise in order to serve their own needs. They cannot rely on the state or on political parties. Elites that have been co-opted into neo-liberal globalisation no longer put the interests of their own people first, but rather attempt to discipline their people into accepting of Neo-liberalism. This situation changes the nature of national politics, because focus on the state to provide popular welfare no longer necessarily works. So people and movement have to create a new space for their struggle for popular rights, social rights and substantive democracy.

Most of the new global grassroots movements largely originate from the South. This is mainly due to failure of neo-liberal projects in the South. It is now an established fact that last two decades of globalisation have largely benefitted the North and people in the South have largely borne the brunt of negative effects of globalisation. The various data from ILO and the World Bank report point to the deleterious, and unequal economic fallout on the economy of the south. The inglorious and infamous effects of globalisation have largely impacted the environment, women, labour, farmers, indigenous people, children and migrants in differing proportions. Networking among these diverse groups has now become one of the distinctive characteristics of the global movement against neo-liberalism. The advent of electronic communications media and easier global transportation has facilitated new types of transnational organising. These new transnational movement pursue forms of social action that are becoming participatory as well as direct. Thus world Social Forum is one body comprising people from diverse background (writers, playrights, intellectuals, NGOs, leftists, media and cinema) which organizes protest against neo-liberal project. These bodies harp upon the theme that a better world without multinational corporations can be constructed that fully acknowledges respect for diversity and rights of the indigenous populations.

The recent marches in USA by the people against the ramshackle impact of neo-liberal project by denouncing New York stock exchanges in Feb. 2012 also struck the same tone. The protestors wanted to remind the Obama administration of its social responsibilities. The recent upsurge in Egypt, Tunisia, Syria by the people is also indicative of the people's power, able to overthrow regimes that enjoyed a long duration of power.

In India Medha Patekar's movement against Sardar Sarovar Project (Narmada Bachao Andolan), which entails the eviction of tribals from their homelands is also one of its similar kind. These movements emphasise the importance of ecology-essential for the survival of indigenous population. The height of the dam is the point of controversy. Greater height can submerge a larger catchment area thereby threatening the livelihoods of sizeable population.

The recent Lokpal movement (Anti corruption charter) led by Anna Hazare in India evoked popular response from all over India. The rampant corruption in government departments with a series of disclosures involving bureaucrats and politicians, mustered mass support in most of the cities in India. The government of India had to hurriedly convene the session of parliament to seize itself of the situation to arrest people's anger.

In Latin America women have also played a major role in the struggle against the incursion of capitalism and its disruption of community and autonomy, as epitomised in the mass participation and leadership roles of women in the Zapatista and other revolutionary movements or in the peasant-based landless movement (MST) of Brazil.

The nature of the grassroot social movement is largely adhoc and spontaneous, and therefore in the initial stages they appear to be somewhat erratic and disorganised. The movement themselves have a broad understanding that the situation that warrants, they are ill-equipped to truly unify all the movements under a single ideology, organisation or even a federation. They are primarily interested in creating a political space at regional and global level, where diverse movements can meet together to share each others experience and learn from each other – open up channels of communication between the ideologically diverse protest movements, and bring together at one place the vast masses of people whom globalisation has marginalised, and whom each of these movements is separately organizing.[13] They hope that this will eventually lead over a period of a more substantial unity, (*Asian Social Forum 2003*).

The international council of the world social forum, at its meeting in Porto Alegre on 21-22 January, 2003, adopted a set of resolution which emphasised their desire to continue promoting a process that is 'open and plural' and that works with the diversity of resistances, organisations and proposals (WSF, 2003). The statement entitled 'Call of the world social movements' issued at Porto Alegre in 2003, reflects the extremely broad agenda of the new global social movements of resistance.

> "We are social movements that are fighting all around the world against neo-liberal globalisation, war, racism, casteism, poverty, patriarchy, and all the forms of economical, ethnical, social, political, cultural, sexual and gender discriminations and exclusion, we are fighting for social justice, citizenship, participatory democracy, universal rights and for the rights of people to decide their own future" (*WSF 2003*).

One can identify three trends as part of strategy of the social grassroot movements against neo-liberal globalisation. These are protests, teach-ins and networking.

Protests constitute a popular form, wherein a series of large scale protests have been organised —Washington DC (April 2000); Prague (September 2000); Davos (January 2001); Porto Alegre (January 2001); Quebec city (April 2001); Genoa (August 2001); Florence (2002); Mumbai (2004) and Gleneagles (2005). These global protests have been organised in and around the bodies of neo-liberal projects such as IMF, World Bank,WTO and G-8 summits, the protest organised during the meetings of these bodies have drawn the attention of the media, people and civil society. Very often these institutions have caved in to the pressure of protestors. These bodies have undertaken the social programmes in third world with greater urgency encompassing areas such as nutrition, education and health. The deliberations in the IMF, World Bank, WTO and G-8 summit, which were clouded in secrecy, have now been brought into open, resulting in transparency and accountability.

The scale of the protests[14] by and large has been impressive, involving people from diverse regions and occupations. The numbers have ranged from tens of thousands to hundreds of thousands. For example, the World Social Forum (WSF) 2003, the third such forum held in Porto Alegre, Brazil in parallel with the World Economic Forum held in Davos, Switzerland, brought together 100,000 activists drawn from all continents. The meeting commenced with a march of the movements against neo-liberal globalisation, under the slogan of 'Another world is possible', by some 70,000 people and concluded with a march against war in Iraq. The European Social Forum held in late 2002 in Florence had 50,000 participants and culminated in a gigantic anti-war march of a million people.

The second purpose of the movements has been the organisation of international meetings among grassroot movements and activists in order to conduct teach-ins.[15] The largest of these to date was the Third World Social Forum in Porto Alegre in January 2003. The WSF international council identified five thematic areas to guide the discussions and exchange of information (*Dong-Sook S. Gills, 2005*). They are:

- Democratic sustainable Development;
- Principles and values, human rights, diversity and Equality;
- Media culture and counter-hegemony;
- Political power, civil society and democracy;

- Democratic world order, fight against-militarism and promoting peace;

Conferences based on these themes were organised with an aim to 'socialise' intellectuals and disseminate the information into masses, regarding the deleterious effects of neo-liberal economies and globalisation. Thousands of seminars and workshops have been conducted. The papers presented in these seminars have been translated in different languages.

Many grassroot groups have employed networking using web-based contacts, to conduct physical meetings in international gatherings—a successful example of effective global networking between different social movements and grassroot resistance groups is the people's Global Action (PGA). The Zapatistas in Mexico organised a global meeting of resistance to neo-liberal globalisation in Chiapas in 1996 and in Spain in 1997. Out of these meetings there emerged a network between ten social movements (*Dong-Sook S. Gills*), including movements Sem Terra (the landless peasant's) of Brazil, the Ogoni people of Nigeria, peasant movement in the Phillipines, the Karnataka street farmer's movement in India. In the meetings the delegates were of the opinion that despite the differences of politics, economy and geography, the fights are similar everywhere at the global level. This enabled the way for new launch pad, with strengthened Commitments, and solidarity (PGA 2001). This has resulted in the formation of different networks, such as North America-Direct Action Network (DAN); Montreal Anti-capitalist Convergence (CLAC), YABASTA- ITALY, and Reclaim the streets (UK), while many other associated groups all over the world.

Critics of these social grassroot movements claim that these groups lack coherency, and they are not clear in terms of strategy and goal. These groups are quiet porous, and do not have much in common except that they are against the neo-liberal economic globalisation.

## Multiculturalism

The last decades of the twentieth century, has for many reasons been a watershed, pertaining to diverse combination of state, ethnic, economic and political underpinnings which have considerably altered the shape and complexion of Global interchange of people and trade. Political and economic analysts have been left mesmerised by the sheer pace and speed of events that have unfolded during this period. One suddenly awoke in the morning to the reality of Russian dismemberment. No one thought it would come about so easily, as Western nations had spent considerable energy, money and time for the fortuitous moment in the past, without much of success. Similarly the East European countries threw the mantle of communist ideology, with relative ease, one apparently was left murmuring, about the Karl Marx's strength in social theory and scientific prediction. Under the guise of colour revolution one state or the other in East Europe bundled the Red Flag. The end of the cold war was declared. Socialist capitulation was decisive, with the exception of China. The triumph of capitalism was announced, with the end of the history thesis.

Third world nations were a worried lot the unipolarity of the world was a fact. The neo-liberal international institutions such as IMF, World Bank, WTO and G-8 acquired a new respect and orientation: Even China to whom these institutions were loathsome, joined in 2001 to these bodies. Over the past few decades, in ever more countries, national and ethnic communities with distinct language, histories and traditions have demanded recognition and support for their cultural identity. They demand group differentiated rights, power, status or immunities that go beyond the common rights of citizenship. These claims encompass demands for territorial autonomy ranging in its form from federalism to devolution and to the acquisition of the status of 'autonomous' region in either symmetrical or asymmetrical arrangements; for self government in certain key matters such as education, health, or family law; for guaranteed representation in the political institutions of the larger society on the basis of quota systems favoaurable to the group and guaranteed veto powers over legislation and policies that centrally affect the respective minorities; and for group specific legal exemptions (*Axtmann*). These demands are premised upon the belief that only by possessing and exercising these rights, powers, and immunities will it be possible for these communities to ensure the full and free development of their culture. A policy of assimilation which aims to incorporate (or melt) the "minority" into the dominant 'majority' culture, is therefore not an option (*Barry, 2000; Tully, 2001; Kelly, 2002; Kukathas, 2003; Parekh, 2000*).

These demands raise the question of the very nature, authority and permanence of the 'multicultural', state, of which these various cultural communities are part within Europe, pressure to increase the legislative powers of regional institutions also intensified. Germany and Belgium provided early models, soon taken up by movements for change in Spain and Italy. In Britain parliamentary assemblies were created for Scotland, Wales and Northern Ireland.

Sharing the power has never been on the agendas of nation states.[16] Now they have not only to share power among themselves through multilateral institutions and with transnational corporations, but also with their own people.[17] Through democratisation, globalisation has expanded the horizons of individual liberty". As nation state weakens, forgotten marginalised local cultures will re-emerge and display dynamic signs of life in the great concert of this globalised planet".[18] The much more fragmented decentralised institutional pattern emerging from this diversity would have to confront the questions of common, citizenship, common identity – the notions of political cohesion and social homogeneity are going to be under stress.

The political communities due to migration, will have to address the issues–first, democratic, communal self-government; second, a public debate on the matters communities have in common, third, protection of legitimate power to uphold autonomy; and fourth, the political coordination of the communities that keeps them part of one large community (*Cohen, 1996*), succinctly captures the essence of forth coming challenge. "Given that many of these communities have 'transnational' political, economic and cultural links with their 'home country' and retain a sense of loyalty to, and possibly derive even their identity from, their 'place of origin' the state will find it difficult to facilitate or, even more ambitiously, steer their interactions within the state territory". The net effect would appear to be a state that is limited to act as a coordinator of these political and cultural networks that are formed by a plethora of 'cultural' communities.

Samuel Huntington's thesis of 'clash of civilisation', has evoked profound responses varying from subtle denunciations to reinterpretations. To accept Huntington's thesis is to acknowledge that the framework for addressing global issues is cultural rather than universal nation states. Wave after wave of immigration encouraged at first, then viewed with diffidence soon turning into open hostility have altered dramatically the ethnic and social compositions of cities and whole countries. Diversity has become a dominating feature of modern life, whether it is valued for its contribution to a truly supranational society or opposed for its undermining effects on national identity.

The issue of multiculturalism reflects the most urgent necessity for the states, as this issue seems to have boiled up the social horizons of states with decisive presence of minorities. During much of the nineteenth and early twentieth centuries, states constructed their own histories and propagated them through mass education systems and the media to demonstrate ancestral rights of possession.[19] In the drive for 'totalism' their 'one size fits all' mentality ignored local traditions.[20] It had the US congress to declare after the first world war that the American identity would be white, Anglo Saxon, and preferably protestant (WASP). Salman Rushdie notes, "the idea of pure cultures, in urgent need of being kept free of alien contamination leads us inexorably towards apartheid towards ethnic cleansing towards the gas chamber".[21]

Robbie Robertson, 2003, in his book, 'Three waves of Globalisation' mentions:

> "The purpose of identity inventions is exclusion, sometimes exclusion involves disenfranchisement through the expansion of executive and corporate power, and through the disdain that policy making elites express for ordinary people. Some Americans feel this passionately and believe that the more predatory the forces that threaten local identities, the more pathological they become. This is certainly the case whenever exclusion assumes coercive forms, such as the Magyarisation of Slav minorities during the nineteenth century. Franco's repression of regional autonomy in Spain, the Bulgarisation of Turkish minorities, or the Bhutanisation of Nepalese minorities. It is equally the case where ethnic cleansing becomes the method of exclusion, as Jews, Germans, Gypsies, and Americans experienced during the last century. One Turkish politician declared, "If we had not cleansed eastern Anatolia of the Armenian Militia (*in*

> *1915 and 1916*), the founding of our national Republic would not have been possible. We took the risk of being thought of as murderers, another asserted to save the fatherland."

In some countries, ethnic cleansing depicts the end product of long process of Ghettoisation. In the 1990s Croatia reduced its Serb population from 12 per cent to 2 per cent. Slovenia halved its Serb population, while Croats similarly drove Serbs and Muslims from Croatia and Herzegovina, Muslims drove Serbs and Croats from Sarajevo, and Serbs drove Muslims and Croats from Kosovo. In all this ethnic cleansing two million were displaced. Ten years after the fall of the Berlin wall, Czechs erected a street wall in Ustin to separate Gypsies from their neighbourhood. In many parts of Europe, Gypsies are still treated differently. Ten thousand Gypsies fled from Kosovo after its NATO liberation. In Germany, citizenship is still based on blood lines. German citizenship is conferred on 'ethnic Germans' many of whom do not speak German and whose forefathers had migrated to Eastern Europe several generations ago. Citizenship as a prerogative has been denied to many Turks and other immigrants born in Germany and who speak German as their first language.

International migration caused due to globalisation is building multiracial societies who are beset with several socio-economic problems. Immigrant population maintain their residential and cultural enclaves in Europe and are not integrated into the social-welfare measures. Many of the offsprings of the immigrants find it next to impossible to avail status oriented education systems, and avenues of employment. Thus Britain's young blacks and France's young Arabs feel they are treated like outsiders, even if they are nationals of the countries in which they reside. Muslims constitute one third of all immigrants in western Europe, and, allowing for international flows, two thirds of non-EU nationals. The prospect of Islamic resurgence especially after 9/11 has caused deep suspicions, and distrust in the minds of Europeans. One of long standing issues is the problem of political participation of the Muslims, as Islamic tradition differs from a secular democratic society with its representative bodies. Furthermore European Union's five million Muslims include different strands of Islam (Shite, Sunni, and others) and several nationalities (e.g., Algerians, Bangladeshis, Moroccons, Pakistanis, Tunisians and Turks) (*Commission of the European communities 1990, 34; 1991, 25*). Attack on the immigrants in EU countries are increasingly becoming frequent. The xenophobic forces increasingly employ and appeal to nativist sentiment, economic insecurities, and threats to national identity. There is an alarm that 'invasion' of immigrants is in the offing.

The impact of new minorities has been profound for many nations. By 2000, ethnic minorities composed 7 per cent of the British population, and 34 per cent of inner London's and were growing at a rate fifteen times that of the non-migrant population. In Germany the migrants comprise around 12 per cent of the population, France has 8 per cent and Spain 2 per cent.

Above all, the challenge of diversity, and multi-ethnic character is going to fundamentally alter the terrain of demography in many nations. The earlier xenophobic nationalisms, with its emphasis on homogenisation and singularity has proved counterproductive, as ethnic groups have relentlessly stuck to their cultural core and language. Hence a new cohesive civil force has to replace narrow state nationalisms of the past and thereby promote common bonds of interest and affection, and a collective sense of belonging.[22] The example of European Union, of permitting non-national residents to vote in local elections, is a step forward in this direction. The election of President Barak Obama, signifies victory of cosmopolitan forces, who have been encouraged that the most powerful state on the earth has the heart to take into stride a so called 'other' to the most important office.

## Innocence Lost: View from Children

The labour of children, and their working conditions has drawn considerable attention of scholars and bodies like ILO. The project of globalisation without doubt has unfolded the process of low-paid child labour. According to the report released by the international labour office in November 1996,[23] about 205 million children between the ages of 5 and 14 were working for pay in developing countries of which 120 million were working full time. These estimates base on an improved methodology–and counting children aged 5-10 years for the first time - doubled previous estimates. Some 153 million of these child workers were in Asia, 80 million in Africa, and 17.5 million in Latin America. Africa constitutes the highest incidence of child labour, at around 40 per cent of children aged 5-14. A 1995 survey (ILO) of child labour in Ghana, India, Indonesia and Senegal found that 25 per cent of all children between 5 and 14 years of age had engaged in economic activity, and that around 33 per cent did not attend schools.

The ILO report also suggests that significant growth in child labour has also occurred in East European and Asian countries, which are on a transition path to capitalist growth under neo-liberal globalisation. The ILO data indicate that while there has been an overwhelming increase in the child labour in developing countries the developed nations have also registered an increase in child labour, particularly in U.S.A. where fast food outlets prosper on the basis of teenage work, and other business. In 1992, the US department of labour registered 19,443 offences against child labour laws, twice the level of 1980. Most of the cases pertained to the child labour, working in the fast food chain. Other cases pertained to children working in the garment factories in Manhattan, in construction works in Bronx, or in farms in California, Texas and Florida.

According to the National Safe Work Place Institute every year 300 children are killed and 70,000 injured in America due to the deteriorating working conditions in work places. Similar trends have been corroborated by Lavallette pertaining to child labour in Britain. His citation of study shows, that for school children aged 13-16 years, 80 per cent of girls and 69 per cent of boys had some form of employment. In Birmingham, a survey of 1827 school students aged 10-16 found that 43.7 per cent were working in some way, or had a job in the recent past.[24] Lavallette opines that "the existing studies of children part-time jobs in advanced economies, though limited in number, all suggest that child employment is an extensive activity carried out for little reward and performed in poor working conditions." One infers that a large scale employment to children, is also for the purpose of criminal economy particularly in drug traffic, petty thefts, and organised begging (*Hallinan,1994; Pedrazzini and Sanchez, 1996*). Much of the proliferation of street children is linked to these activities. Thus studies in Brazil, whose cities and particularly Rio-De-Janneiro, have been highlighted as the most striking examples of thousands of children living in the street, show that, in fact, most of them return to their poor homes at the end of the day, bringing their meagre gains to the family. A 1989 survey (*Manuel Castells, End of Millennium, p. 154*) of street children in Rio found that those living by themselves on the streets, without their families, accounted for only 14.6 per cent of street children, among whom 80 per cent shared street life with their families, 21.4 per cent were in the family home and worked in the streets under the control of their family.

The majority (50.5) per cent had contact with their families, but worked in the streets independently, and occasionally slept there. All of them shared a high risk of violence and death often at the hands of 'vigilantes' and policemen.

Besides, the above-mentioned employment of child labour, they are even employed in a whole array of hazardous activities, such as carpet weaving, brick kiln industries, brassware industry (India), Muro-ami fishing (involving deep-sea diving) in South-East Asia, in the pesticidepoisoned plantations in Sri Lanka, in toxic fume-filled repairshops and woodwork shops in Egypt, the Phillipines and Turkey, in small scale mines in Africa, Asia and Latin America and in millions of homes as domestic workers, frequently exposed to abuse. According to (ILO, 1996) around 5 million children are employed as domestic workers in Indonesia, and 5 million in Sri Lanka. In Venezuela, 60 per cent of the girls working between 10 and 14 years of age are in domestic work. A substantial proportion of child domestic workers are very young; 24 per cent in Bangladesh and 26 per cent in Venezuela, were less than 10 years old. ILO reports out that children are made to work under unhygienic conditions for 10-15 hours a day, and there is alarming evidence of physical, mental and sexual abuse of adolescents and women working as domestics.

Black (*1995*) reports that the rapid rise of tourism industry, which employs 7 per cent of the total global work force is a major contributor to the child labour around the world. Due to the seasonal character of the industry, it becomes convenient for employers to tap cheap labour in the form of child labour. The types of jobs in this sector encompasses bell boys, waittresses, maids, collector of fares in public taxis, massages, receptionists, 'hospitality' workers, boll boys, messengers etc. Payment to these child labours is very miniscule, and at times they have to survive on tips and commissions provided by the tourists.

Some child labour activities in gruesome form involve the practice of bonded labour. This is a form of slavery, as admitted by ILO in several of its report. Among all forms of child labour, this one is particularly most perilous, as child labourers are treated in the most pathetic fashion, the story of their exploitation has become a part of many literary novels, reminding Uncle Tom's Cabin.

Thus 1994 study of the US Department of Labor cites:

> "In India, where conservative estimates of adult and child bonded labourers start at 3 million, debt-bondage occurs when person needing a loan and having no security to offer, pledges his/her labour, or that of someone under his/her control, as a security for the loan... There are increasing reports of child bonded laborers in both the service and manufacturing sectors in India—In some countries, recruiters comb the country side paying parents to recruit their children for work in factories. For example, in Thailand many child workers come from poverty stricken parts of the north-east regions, having been sold by their parents, or made part of a debt bondage arrangements unscrupulous 'employment agencies' often negotiate the transaction and deliver children to industries like shrimp peeling, or prostitution. In the Phillipines, two separate raids on a Sardine canning factory found children as young as 11, filling cans with sliced fish to repay the debt to the labour recruiter."

US department of labour simply cites many other examples of child bondage, involved in commercial agriculture and carpet weaving cases in Bhadohi from India. The recent surge in child labour is due to the increasing poverty, and forces of globalisation; who make it contingent for the supply of cheap labour to gain competitive advantage in the market. The impoverishment of sizable populations in developing countries forces the family to divest of small children in gainful employment to sustain their meager resources. The families are not in a position to afford education for their children, with dwindling social commitments of the states under liberalisation, they are perforce constrained to afford the luxury of not sending children in money making activity.

Another reason for employing child labour is that the children are less aware of their rights, less troublesome and more willing to take orders and to do monotonous work without complaining, most trustworthy, less likely to steal, and less likely to be absent from work. Children's lower absentee rate is especially valuable for employers in informal sector industries, where workers are employed on a daily, casual basis and a full contingent of workers must be found each day (*ILO, 1996*).

Thus children as ready to use, disposable labour, have become the defining features of over-exploitation under network global capitalism.

Apart from the above mentioned sources and typology of exploitation (manufacturing, mining, construction, agriculture and hospitality) a new form of child exploitation is increasingly manifested in sex trade. By taking advantage of the globalisation of tourism and images, they are vehemently being utilised as sexual commodities. In Thailand, the hot spot of the global sex industry, it is estimated that as many as 800,000 children are in postitution.[25] A 1991 survey of India today puts the number of child prostitutes in India somewhere between 400,000 and 500,000. In Sri Lanka estimates range around 20,000. In the tiny Dominican Republic over 25,000 minors were in prostitution. One of the fastest growing markets for child prostitution is in the United States and Canada, where in

1996, estimates varied widely between 1,00,000 and 300,000 child prostitutes (*Clayton, 1996; Flores, 1996*). Child pornography has become a new menace on the internet creating a fast buck for those who control child pornography. The reasons for increase in this trend which abuses the children, encompasses the prize value, and commodification in the globalised market. The element of anonymity brought about by the use of internet, technology and hotel industry makes law enforcement impossible. Even if there is possibility of penal punishment, the touts and pimps often succeed in bribing their way through. Such large scale incidence of sex trade among minors cannot flourish without the complicity of enforcement machinery and politicians.

Thus the network society devours itself as it destroys and abuses its own future seeds, necessary for the continuation of species. The large scale disintegration of traditional societies throughout the world, has exposed children to the vagaries of the market, and 'mega cities' slums. The weakening of institutions of support for children rights, such as labour unions or the politics of social reform, has further aggravated the plight of children. At the roots of children exploitation are the mechanisms generating poverty and social exclusion throughout the world extending from Sub-Saharan Africa to the United States of America. A 1996 report from the US department of Health and Human Services estimated that child abuse and neglect in the United States doubled between 1986 and 1993, growing from 1.4 million children affected to over 2.8 million in 1993. Children from the lowest income families were 18 times more likely to be sexually abused, almost 56 times more likely to be educationally neglected and 22 times more likely to be seriously injured from maltreatment (*Sedlak and Broadhurst, 1996*).

## GATED Communities

Gated communities are ostentatiously provided with security measures – the fences and gates that represent closeness, exclusivity and security. The sales of devices and a physical expression of what *Reich (2001)* called the 'Secession of the rich' is rampant in many countries, such as USA, Britain, Germany, Singapore, India and France. The contemporary idea of protecting private residences through technological devices, formerly a possibility only for the very rich is defended as a modern, middle class emanation of that urge to self-defence.

In the new sub-urban housing developments in megacities such as San Diego, Mumbai, Delhi, Dubai, London and New York all new apartment buildings in the densely populated downtown area are secured with gates and cameras. In these kinds of housing developments Real Estate developers use these defining features as premium exclusive and sign of status. These kind of housing patterns emphasise exclusivity, closeness and security. Do the gated communities provide security against crimes committed by neighbours. One might surmise that the "community" character of living under like conditions and being members of the same association would create a cooperative spirit that would act to lower the level of customary conflict. In the literature about gated communities significantly in Blakely and Snyder's (1997) ethnographic descriptions of a large number of developments, it is pointed out that while inhabitants do feel closer to each other than to people "outside the community" designation does not necessarily reflect strong social integration or a close knit community feeling in gated communities. Quite frequently the often very detailed lifestyle regulations of homeowner associations engender conflict and suspicion among neighbours (*Mckenzie, 1994*).

Gated communities, which are one of the spatial reflections of the dynamics of globalisation, is the most debated one among these new housing trends. While gated communities are debated within the context of the global economic and social actors and factors of gated lifestyles, they have also been subjected to several examinations by real estate developers, local authorities and users. In the context of globalisation it has come under increasing criticism for privatisation of the public sphere due to the social and spatial segregation it has created. In advertisements, there are numerous references to certain lifestyles, that connote high status and to the absence of unpleasantly different neighbours.[26] Physical security is stressed less than social and economic predictability. Furthermore, these "middle-class" neighborhoods tend to be racially exclusive. Very few people of African descent can be found living inside the gates (*Blakely and Snyder, 1997*). A subtle language of social and racial exclusivity is employed to classify those who are not welcome (*Low, 2001*). Fences are there to define a space in which life is lived in a certain way, allowing inhabitants to overlook and neglect unpredictability, immorality and insecurity.

Thirty years ago and even earlier the residences of the rich if they were in the city center were separate buildings, that included luxury services.

Marcuse and Kempen (*2000*) make clear that while this pattern continues, in addition a new pattern seems to be developing. And this pattern includes a spatial concentration within cities of a new urban poverty on the one hand and of specialised 'high level' internationally connected business activities on the other, with increasing spatial divisions between each of them. As a result of this development, boundaries between divisions, reflected in social or physical world among them, are increasing and the divisions are assumed to be 'indicators' of what is happening to cities under the influence of globalisation.

With their natural beauty and high quality of life, gated communities which are walled and gated residential neighbourhoods, represent a form of urbanism where public spaces are privatised. Gated communities have become a magnet for growing number of Americans (*Mcmohan, 2003*) and depending on this, they represent a substantial part of the new housing market, especially in the recently urbanised areas (*LeGoix, 2005*). This phenomenon of housing patterns is increasingly becoming popular in other parts of the world, such as South America, South Africa, the Middle East and South-East Asia. The cities of Southern China are full of the security guarded estates of modestly sized Mediterranean-style villas, in some African cities it would appear that most new private residential developments are walled and guarded (*Webster, 2001*). In the case of South American (such as Brazil and Chile), enclaves are not located in remote suburban areas but rather in city centers (*Salcedo and Torres, 2004*). In addition, the expansion of gated communities has become an increasingly important element in the changing Indian mega cities such as Mumbai, Delhi and Bangalore. They have become a symbol of metropolitan fragmentation. They are an expression of the increasingly diverging lifestyles of urban society under the influence of globalisation and have been criticized as being sources of segregation, social inequality and disintegration of society and as an enclave characterised by walling and the attempt of self-sufficiency.

Most of the mega cities in the world have witnessed migratory pressures due to globalisation development. The builders and real estate developers have taken advantage of the growing market for housing. Since most of the mega cities lack the mechanism for affordable housing, the real estate companies have made a fast buck in this market. The companies have colluded with local authorities, bought land at pittance. Using advertisements purveying single roof facilities such as swimming pool, jogging tracks, parks, Golf courses, recreation centers, schools and hospitals, they have appealed successfully to the rising middle class, who have obliged to avail of better and world class lifestyle in a fenced wall. While this is the successful side of global communities, this exhibition of island of prosperity has not been without its cost of urban sustainability. Gated communities have the potential to negatively impact the goal of urban sustainability relating to sustainable urban economy, urban society, urban life and urban democracy.

## SEX Trade

The development of international capitalism and globalisation has brought sex trade to the central position and is increasingly taking the form, as natural part of the economy. The processes of globalisation have generated, for a section of people huge bounties in terms of income and power of instrumentalities.[27] Sex trade has created market of billions of dollars, as woman and children have been converted into sexual commodities.[28] The issues pertaining to sexual trade, have opened a plethora of debate which extends across processes such as economic exploitation, sexual oppression, patriarchy, capital accumulations, international migration and unequal development and such related conditions as racism and poverty. The sexual trade has involved the mass production of sexual goods and services structured around a regional and international divison of labour. These 'goods' are human beings who sell sexual services. The international market in these 'goods' simultaneously encompasses local and regional levels, making its economic imperatives impossible to avoid, such as prostitution and related sexual industries—bars, dancing clubs, massage parlours, pornography producers etc. The whole structure of sex trade covers a massive subterranean economy controlled by pimps and local police complicity giving it a character of organised crime. In the hindsight, connected business such as international hotel chains, airline companies, and the tourist industry benefit greatly from the sex industry. In Thailand, trafficking is a 500 billion Bahts annual business (equivalent to approximately 124 million US dollars), which represents a value equal to around 60 percent of the government budget.[29] In 1998 the International Labour Organisation (ILO) estimated that prostitution represented between 2 and 14 per cent of the economic activities of Thailand, Indonesia, Malaysia and Phillipines (*Jeffreys*).

According to a study conducted by Ryan Bishop and Lilian Robinson, the tourist industry brings four billion dollars a year to Thailand. It is not without reason, then, that in 1987 the Thai government promising sexual tourism through advertising "The one fruit of Thailand more delicious than Durian [a local fruit], its young women" (*Hechler*).

The scale and magnitude of sex trade under globalisation has led to a series of debate among the intellectuals and feminist scholars. Some claim that just as all sex work in not linked to trafficking, all trafficking is also not linked to sex work. While it is certainly true that many women (and children) enter sex work under violent and exploitative conditions, this is no different from other livelihood occupations such as agricultural and domestic work, construction and industrial labour. Ironically, those who demand the abolition of sex work to stop trafficking do not make the same argument for domestic work despite the fact that conditions, wages, working hours, levels of exhaustion are far worse for domestic workers. Feminist scholars point out that the invasion of the human body by another person whether empowered by many or violence or authority—is dehumanising in itself. There are many other jobs in which people are exploited, but prostitution is the only one that by definition crosses boundary of our skin and invades our most central sense of self.[30] There is another opinion gaining ground, especially led by sex worker's rights movement that has tirelessly argued that trafficking (that is induction in the trade through force, coercion or deception) is a crime whereas the exchange of sexual services between two consenting adults is not. That's especially striking given the profound difference in their lives, from Manhattan call girls to women in the brothel lineups of Sonagachi (India), from women in the countries around Las Vegas, the only place in the US where prostitution is legal, to the bar girls from the villages of Ghana and the scheduled castes in Bihar (India) where women are consigned to prostitution by birth.

The industrialisation of the sex trade and its globalisation are fundamental factors that make contemporary prostitution qualitatively different from the prostitution of yesterday. 'Consumers' in the economic north now have access to 'exotic' and young, very young bodies worldwide, notably in Brazil, Cuba, Russia, Kenya, Sri Lanka, Phillipines, Vietnam, Nicaragua. The sex industry is diversified, sophisticated and specialised, it can cater to all kinds of demands. Notable alteration in the character of trade is that prostitution has acquired a development strategy for some countries under obligations of debt-repayments. Numerous Asian, Latin American and African states were encouraged by international organisations such as the International Monetary Fund (IMF) and the World Bank to develop their tourism and entertainment industries. In each case, the development of these sectors inspired the development of the sex trade.[31] In some cases such as Nepal, women and children were deployed directly on the regional or international markets, without it experiencing any notable increase in local market flesh trade. In other cases, such as Thailand, local, regional and international markets developed simultaneously.[32] The above trend is an increasing pointer, that 'goods' in this market move transcontinental and transnationally from regions with weak concentrations of capital towards region with stronger concentrations.

For instance, over ten years, 200, 000 Bangladeshi women and girls were the object of traffick into Pakistan (CATW) and it is found that between 20,000 to 30,000 Thai prostitutes are from Burma (CATW). A good part of the migratory trend is way towards industrialised countries. A political-economic analysis of prostitution and trafficking in women and children is an eye opener—hierarchical relationship between imperialist and dependent countries. In recent years (post-1990) many countries of the third world as well as in the ex-USSR and Eastern Europe, women and children have become 'new raw resources' within the framework of national and international business development. The collapse of communism in Russia and East European countries, virtually eliminated the social security mechanisms of families (food, pension, health and education). The switch over to capitalism in these countries brought dreaded inflation to apocalyptic levels, thereby threatening many families to compromise, and women proved to be a great reliever, thereby prompting many girls from Russia to join the international markets in Hong Kong, Bangkok and Melbourne. Capitalist globalisation is more and more characterised by a feminisation of migration (*Santos*). Women of ethnic minorities and other relatively powerless groups are particularly exploited. The internal traffic of Thai females consists mostly of 12-16 year olds from hill tribes of the North and the North- East. In Taiwan, 40 per cent of young prostitutes in the main red light districts are aboriginal girls.[33] At the world level the customer of the North abuse women of the south and of the East as well as local women from disadvantaged groups.

Kidnapping, rape and violence continue to act as lubricants of this industry. These abuses are not only fundamental for the development of markets, but also for, the "manufacturing" of these 'good's as they contribute to making them 'functional' for an industry that requires a constant supply of bodies. Research have shown that between 75 and 50 per cent of prostitutes were sexually abused in their childhood.[34] More than 90 per cent of prostitutes are controlled by pimps.[35] A study of street prostitutes in England established that 87 per cent had been victims of violence during the last 12 months and 43 per cent suffered from grave physical consequences of abuse (*Raymond*). An American study showed that 78 per cent of prostitutes had been victims of rape by pimps and customers, on average 49 times a year; the average age of entrance into prostitution in the United states is 14 years (*Silbert and Pines, 1981*).

According to Feidholdt only 15 percent of the prostitutes in the United States have never contracted a venereal disease. Fifty eight percent of the prostitution of Burkina Faso have AIDS, as have 52 per cent in Kenya, about 50 per cent in Cambodia and 34 per cent in the North of Thailand. In Italy, in 1980, two per cent of the prostitutes had AIDS, compared to 16 percent 10 years later. In Cambodia it is estimated that there are 50,000 to 70,000 prostitutes out of this a third comprises less than 18 years old and 50 per cent of these are HIV positive (Veran). Given such a horrific picture a claim by some researchers, that 'Sex work' as a predominantly a freely chosen occupation/activity is hard to understand.

Since the last three decades (when the process of globalisation has intensified) most of the countries of the Southern Hemisphere have witnessed a profound growth in prostitution. Two million women prostitutes are active in Thailand,[36] 400,000 to 500,000 in the Phillipines,[37] 650,000 in Indonesia,[38] about ten million in India (of whom 200,000 are

Nepalese),[39] 142,000 in Malaysia (CATW), between 60,000 and 70,000 in Vietnam (CATW), one million in the United States, between 50,000 and 70,000 in Italy (of whom half are foreighners notably from Nigeria), 30,000 in Netherlands (CATW), 200,000 in Poland[40] and between 60,000[41] and may be even more in Germany. German prostitutes sell sexual services to 1.2 million "customers" per day (*Opperman, Ackerman and Filter*).

According to the UNICEF, around 1 million children are brought into the sex industry every year. The industry of child prostitution exploits 400,000 children in India (*UNICEF*, 2003), 10,0000 and 30,0000 in Thailand (*Oppermann*). 10,0000 in Taiwan (UNICEF, 2001). According to some studies during a period of one year the prostituted "sexual services" of one children are sold to 2,000 men (*Robinson*).

The migratory trends in sex trade, shows that sexual workers migrate from rural areas to urban areas, due to veil of anonymity. Similarly prostitutes from the South move to international centers in Japan,Western Europe and North America, due to higher values for services. The studies reveal that migratory trends of sexual workers and prostitutes is intensifying and shows no sign of abatement, despite the attempts by national governments, international agencies (UNICEF, CATW) and NGOs.

The women and children of South and South-East Asia constitute the most important group-400,000 persons a year are objects of the aforementioned traffic. Russia and independent states from the ex-USSR constitute the second most important group (175,000 persons a year)[42] followed by Latin America and the Carribean (about 10,000 persons) and Africa (50,000 persons).

Prostitutes from the Phillipines, Taiwan, Thailand and Russia installed in Japan is estimated at 1,50,000 (CATW). In Netherlands the Dominican prostitutes nearly comprised

70 per cent of the occupants of 400 Amsterdam sex-shop 'windows'.[43] About 500,000 women of Eastern Europe and between 150,000 of ex-USSR states, such as Georgia, Ukraine, Belarus prostitute themselves in Western Europe. Of these it is estimated that 150,000 are in the red light districts of Germany—a country where 75 per cent of the prostitutes are foreighners (*Oppermann*). About 40 per cent of the Zurich's prostitutes are from a third world country (*Oppermann*), and 50,000 foreigners arrive each year in the United States to supply the prostitution networks (*O' Neill*).

The attempt by many NGOs, to seek legalisation of the prostitution has not helped the situation. In Australia and the Netherlands where prostitution has been legalised, for instance, trafficking and the harms that come with prostitution have not decreased but increased. In Victoria (Australia) it not only allowed legal brothels to proliferate, but illegal brothels increased by 300 per cent in one year. A hospitable environment for sex tourists and other buyers drove up demand, local women and girls had too many alternatives to becoming the supply and women and girls were trafficked from South-East Asia. The same is true of Amsterdam where trafficked Eastern European and North African girls outnumber Dutch citizens in brothels. The mayor of Amsterdam reports that the red light district has become a centre for illegal immigration and money laundering. In Germany and in an area near Las Vegas in the US where prostitution has been legalised, government agencies tried to make applicants for unemployment benefits, show that they had attempted to find 'work' in the so called 'hospitality industry' of prostitution in order to become eligible for such benefits.[44]

If one looks at the international circuit of prostitution, sex tourists do not limit themselves to poor countries. In countries that have legalised prostitution, or where it is tolerated, prostitution has become an important tourist draw. In Thailand women and children are brought from Burma, Yunnan province in China, Laos and Cambodia for a price varying between 6,000 and 10,000 US dollars (CATW). In Canada, the intermediaries pay 8,000 dollars for a young Asiatic from the Phillipines, Thailand or Malaysia whom they resell for 15,000 dollars to a pimp (CATW). In Western Europe, the current price of a European women from the former 'socialist' countries is between 15,000 and 30,000 US Dollars (CATW).

The informational capitalism made up of mob of pimps and child abusers, has hastened the commodification of humans. The consumerist culture, with the crumbling of social institutions, behind the facade of repetitive formulas on the virtues of a traditional family that, by and large, has ceased to exist, leaves individuals and particularly men, alone with their desires of transgression with their power surges, with their endless search for consumption characterised by an immediate gratification pattern has opened avenues to prey on the most defenceless member of society (women and children). Over the last 30 years the world has seen an extremely profitable 'sexualisation' of many societies based on social domination. The world has witnessed the industrialisation of prostitution of the traffic in women and children, of pornography, and of sexual tourism. A marginal market once, has become the central aspect of current capitalist globalisation. Sex multinationals have become independent economic forces (Barry) quoted on the stock exchange. The 'leisure industry' underscores the systematic violation of human rights, for it requires a market in commodified human beings, and preys upon the hapless women and children, who have been emptied by the economic forces to the marginalised cauldron.

## Social Exclusion

One of the key issues of debate over the impact of globalisation has been the issue of exclusion. It is contended that globalisation has left many a population, rather has even succeeded in creating a dual world. One which is networked, and has succeeded in cornering the chunk of gains (materially, socially, politically), while a great majority of people have been left pauperised. The politics of exclusion takes many forms. One can see this in shooting of street children in Brazil and Columbia, and in the anti-immigration laws and the policing of the Mediterranean waters around 'fortress Europe'. We witnessed it in the policy of mass incarceration in the US where over two million people (disproportionately black, young and unemployed) languish in Jail at any one time. We see it happen in the politics of AIDS research where 90 percent of research and investment is spent on the development of drugs for the treatment of the 8 per cent of people who have AIDS in the developed countries while snuffing out the funds and the research agendas for cheap vaccines to prevent the further spread of AIDS in the third world (*Ankie Hoogvelt, 1997*).

Similarly in America at the turn of the millennium, inner city ghettos, particularly black ghettos, but also some Latin Ghettos, such as the one in East Los Angeles, concentrate the worst expressions of inequality discrimination, human misery and social crisis precisely at the time of the rise of informationalism in America.[45] We also observe the politics of exclusion in more subtle forms. For example, the privatisation of mass public space and the gradual replacement of public by private forms of security guards patrol private shopping centers, recreational parks and offices than there are policemen on the beat. Privatisation of mass public space entails a diminution of citizen rights. In India the government abandoned the pension, in state run institutions in 2004. The government also encouraged the employees to undertake voluntary retirement scheme to make government bodies, lean and thin. This was undertaken under the neo-liberal agenda of cutting the non-plan expenditures. In many of the cities known for their textiles (Kanpur, Ahmedabad), the industries were closed, since they could not compete with the latest technology, which had cost advantage labour in these areas were retrenched and left high and dry. In USA the proportion of the private work force covered by pensions fell from 50 per cent in 1979 to 43 per cent in 1989. By 1992, 83 per cent of people under 65 had no health insurance, and all attempts to introduce a national health scheme had been defeated by insurance and pharmaceutical companies. Unemployment insurance covered only half the unemployed.[46] The weight of democracy's collapse in the US fell heaviest on Afro-Americans.

By 1975 there were 38,000 prison twenty years later there were 1.6 million prisons, or 645 prisons for every 100,000 citizens, between six and ten times the incarceration levels in the European Union. If one includes individuals on parole or probation, the total US prison population stood at 5.4 million people. This growth invariably can be attributed to the fall in the outlay of health, education and social welfare budgets. It also came at the expense of the black community. Racial profiling, police discrimination and the practice of the court, all combined to constitute the Afro-Americans 50 per cent of prison population.[47]

Irwin, Austin, Toury among others, have carefully established the profile of the prison population, reasons for this incarceration and the social consequences of their imprisonment. In their survey, Irwin and Austin found that most crimes were "much pettier than the popular images promoted by those who sensationalise the crime issue—our inner cities actually contain a growing number of young men, mostly non-white, who become involved in unskilled, petty crime because of no avenues to a viable, satisfying conventional life (*Irwin and Austin: 1994: 59-60*). They cite that 64 per cent of inmates lack a formal high school education, and most of them are 'uneducated, unskilled and highly disorganised persons'. One third of state prison inmates participate in drug treatment programmes and almost 3 percent of state prison inmates are HIV positive or sick with AIDS. The incidence of tuberculosis is four times higher than for the population at large, and about one quarter of inmates have some types of clinical psychiatric problems (*Mergenhagen, 1996*).

China acquired the title of second biggest economy leaving behind Japan in 2012. Yet it brought few chxeers to the government in Bejing amid fears of discontent over domestic inequalities. China's Per Capita income is over 10 times lower than Japan's and its population 10 times bigger. In 2009 China's rural-urban income divide widened to its highest since 1978, when Beijing began economic reforms to lift millions out of poverty.[48] On chat forums, netizens from underdeveloped provinces have reacted with comments about rising costs and deteriorating living standards. A man from eastern Jiangsu province wrote that the number two encouraged him to 'fight for his life'. At the gateway of Liangshanzuang village a farmer had arranged a transport for Reshma Patil (correspondent). As the cart jostled past the village hill, the locals said would be developed into a Ski resort with artificial snow. Inside his one storey home overlooking the future Ski resort, the farmer has stocked one tonnes coal cakes cheaper in summer to stay warm in winter. The families will burn 4 tonnes in winter. Thirty minutes away in Riviera, foreigners and the wealthy Chinese live in centrally heated villas that some Beijing planners describe as ghettos.

Such stories of marginality and exclusion abounds in most of the countries of South-East Asia and South Asia. A train travel to New Delhi; across the river Yamuna, gives one nightmares of scenes of poverty. Children around Yamuna slums, dive into the river, which is loathsome to many, due to innumerable drains dropping the industrial affluents. In Calcutta, so much for the informational society, one can see men in the role of horses plying the cart, to earn a living. A chunk of central India is reverberating with red colour flags, who have lost their faith in Indian democracy, resorted to their own brand of governance. This huge chunk of humanity has been by-passed by the globalisation project. The government of India is constrained to find the reasons for the revolt, which is gathering storm. The Maoist guerillas have taken a heavy toll of Indian security forces, who are out on patrols.

In his book, 'The State We're In', Will Hutton outlines an emerging 30/30/40 society in Britain. He argues that development in the labour market home led to new categorisation of British society. There is a bottom 30 per cent of unemployed and economically inactive who are a marginalised disadvantaged group (a better term of this social segment is 'excluded'. Another 30 per cent is constituted by those who, while in work, are in forms of employment that are structurally insecure. Finally, there are only 40 per cent who can count themselves as holding tenured jobs which allow them to regard their income prospects with any certainty.

Hutton's key concern is with the middle layer. They are the very people who make the growing army of part time, casualised contract workers, workers sacked and then retired as temporary, part time, self employed and agency workers. These people are insecure in their job prospects, but they have to also confront an uncertain future, with social security provisions such as pension, health and education continue to roll down by the state. Similar three tier structures are also growing in other parts of the world encompassing developed and underdeveloped countries. The difference between developed and underdeveloped countries is solely on the size of the various segments, with the excluded sector in the third world often approaching 50 per cent or more with the better part between 20 and 30 per cent.

Johannesburg, in South Africa affords another example of social polarisations due to capitalist production and changes in employment. The rise in importance of the service sector, have begun to erode the entrenched correspondence between racial and class divisions that characterised racial economic development and employment pattern during much of the apartheid era. The new socially excluded residents of Johannesburg are not only black but those, belonging to white population who are superfluous to the requirements of the global economy and Johannesberg place in it. They include former mining and manufacturing workers as well as door-to-door salesmen. Broadly speaking, the majority of this declining working class live to the South of the city, while the upwardly mobile working in communications and information technology live and work to the North. Thus changing patterns of residential polarisation are increasingly associated with shifting trajectories of economic development in the city, resulting in new geographies of exclusion (*Dr. JoBeal, 2002*).

Ahmedabad (India) presents a picture not different from Johannesberg. The city in its heydays was known for its cotton textile manufacturing. An estimated 85,000 workers with regular contracts were dismissed during the last two decades of the 20th century. The closure of 50 corporate textile mills has created a class of new poor, who can be seen in the fringes of Ahmedabad. The casualisation and contract form of working labour has undermined the conditions of the workers (*Jan Breman, 2004*). Any visitor to Ahmedabad can not fail to observe the sprawling slums on the East bank of the river, which have spread rapidly over the past few decades. A large segment of the city's population is cramped together in these deprived quarters, exposed to environmental degradation and excluded from the most elementary civic amenities. There is close link between living in slum and working in the informal sector of the economy. Fall in the standards of living of the former mill worker undermined their self-confidence. After the shock of being expelled from the mill came the discouraging experience of looking for a new job, accompanied as it was by the loss of skill and a much lower wage. The workers would not take and refuse to take food. Husband and wives quarreled, often leading to violence by the man, and sometimes even vice-versa. Tensions also increased between parents and childrens. Many sociologists point out the connection in Ahmedabad riots (*Hindu vs Muslim*) to the large-scale retrenchment of labourers, who constituted the fodder, in large scale brutalisation and subsequent violence. In yester-years Gujaratis constituted the most pacifist community with hardly any record of violence. The conversion of increasing sections of the community as a brute, indisciplined mass of blood seekers against the members of their own neighborhood, is a pointer to capital's tyranny, which changes societal mindsets. Competition for work has led to much tension and conflict, both in residential areas and at the work place. The process of levelling down to the bottom has become manifest in the spread of squalor and has helped to create an atmosphere of undiluted depression.

The crisis which hit the economies of South-east Asia in 1997-98 and affected Indonesia in particular gave rise to instantaneous and fierce debates. In the initial stages an alarming increase in impoverishment and unemployment was predicted. The minister of manpower in office went on record as saying that 22 per cent of Indonesians total work force would be unemployed by the end of 1998. The ILO Regional office for Asia and the Pacific estimated that the combination of wage stagnation and high inflation might cause 37 per cent of the population to fall below the poverty line by mid-1998, with a further spurt to 48 per cent before the end of that year.[49] In comparison with the all-time low of 10.1 per cent reported for the period before the start of the monetary crisis in mid-1997, this implied a three to fourfold jump in the incidence of poverty.[50]

This was an acceleration that threatened to undo much that had been achieved in raising the standard of living of all and sundry since the mid 1970s. The ILO further argued that the lack of improvement in household incomes and the likelihood of more price rises might even result in two-thirds of the population dropping below the poverty line in 1999. In February 1998, the World Bank conceded that dissolute poverty might eventually rise to 17 per cent. During this mayhem, the state could not rectify the wrongs done by the market, and people had to undergo through a period of misery, threatened livelihood and homelessness, thereby leading people towards Islamic Fundamentalism, which was on the rise in this period.

The territorial confinement of systemically worthless populations, disconnected from networks of valuable functions and people, is indeed a major characteristic of the spatial logic of the network society. The marginalisation of peoples and communities in the broader part of the world, is increasingly reflective of the neo-liberal capitalism, which selects few and marginalises many to the peripheral areas. Thus (*Manuel Castells*) points out that social exclusion is manifest in American inner-city ghettos, Spanish enclaves of mass youth unemployment, French Banlieues warehousing North

Africans, Japanese Yoseba quarters, and Asian mega cities shanty towns. It is populated by millions of homeless, incarcerated, prostituted, criminalised, brutalised, stigmatised, sick and illiterate persons. They are majority in some areas, the minority in others, and a tiny minority in a few privileged contexts. But everywhere, they are growing in number, and increasing in visibility, due to informational capitalism, and the political break down of the welfare state has intensified social exclusion.[51]

## References

1. For any analysis of how scientific and technological achievement becomes a measure of the value of civilisation in the eighteenth century, justifying the right to 'civilize' inferior races and to dominate the world, see Adas, 1989.
2. For a study of law this continues today in the Amazon, see Lewis, 1988.
3. Keith Griffin, 'Global Futures Shaping Globalisation (2001), Zed Books, London, p.196.
4. *Ibid,* p.196.
5. Shannon Peters Talbott, "Analysis of Corporate Culture in the Global Market Place: Case Study of Mcdonald's in Moscow," paper presented at International Institute of Sociology conference, Trieste, 1995.
6. James H. Mittleman, "Globalisation Syndrome, Transformation and Resistance, "Princeton University Press, (2000), New Jersey, p. 76.
7. Luke Anderson, "Genetic Engineering Foods and the Environment," Australian, 22 February, 2000, p.15.
8. Guardian Weekly 1-7 June, 2000, p. 8.
9. Graeme Donald Snooks, "The Dynamic Society : Explaining the Sources of Global Change, London and New York, Routledge, 1996, pp. 427-29.
10. Anthony Giddens, Runaway World, p. 34.
11. IF female labour initially is (or is perceived to be ) more easy to control, it is the result of gender socialisation combined with

real relations of patriarchy and gender inequality and pre-existing sexual divisons of labour that render female workers less powerful than their male counterparts.

12. Ngaire Woods, "Good Governance in International Organisation", Global Governance, 5 (1999), 39-61 at p. 56.
13. Dong-Sook S. Gills, ed. (Anthony Mcgrew and Nana K. Poku) in "Globalisation Development and Human Security, 2007, polity, Cambridge, p. 200.
14. The protests have been led by people belonging to the civil society organisations. Many of the NGOs working in diverse and disparate regions pertaining to certain functions such as education, health, water, livelihood etc. have been in the fore front of the protests.
15. This is a process of socialising and preparing the people for definitive actions in the future. Such exercises are meant to provide the fertile ground for agitation and mass action.
16. Centralisation of power was a key feature of Nation States encompassing social, political and economic terrain.
17. KeithSuter, 'Little to be Gained by Returning to a Mythical Nationalist Era, 'Australian, 1 May, 2001, p. 9.
18. Mario Vargas Llosa, "The culture of Liberty," catedre sigle XXI Lectures to the Inter-American Development Bank, Washington, 20 September, 2000, Background Briefing' abc. net, au, 8 April, 2001.
19. Anne-Marie Thiesse, 'Inventing a National Identity', Le monde Diplomatique, June 1999, pp. 6-7.
20. James C. Scott, Seeking Like a State: How Certain Schemes to Improve the Human Condition Have Failed, New Haven, Yale University Press, 1999.
21. Salman Rushdie, "A culture of Easy criticism", Age, 10 march, 1999, p. 7.
22. Thiesse, "Inventing a National Identity", Runnymede Trust, p.11
23. ILO (1996).
24. Lavolette (1994, 29-31).
25. This figure was estimated by "The Center for Protection of Children's Rights," a well established non-governmental organisation.
26. The advertisements studied were in the real state section of the San Diego Union Tribune, the major newspaper for the whole region, over four sundays in March-April, 2002.

27. Truong, T.D, "Sex, Money and Morality: Prostitution and Tourism in South-east Asia, London 1990, Zed Books.
28. Oppermann, M., Introduction to Sex Tourism and Prostitution Aspects of Leisure Recreation and Work, ed. M. Oppermann, New York, 1998, Cognizant Communication Corporation, pp. 6-19.
29. CATW, 2001 [Cited March 2, 2003] Available online: http// catwinternational.org/fb/.
30. Shohini Ghosh, The Hindu, April 6, 2012, p. 9.
31. David Hechler, Child Sex Tourism [online], New York, Don't buy Thai, 1995 [cited May 6, 2001], p.27.
32. Kathleen Barry; 'The Prostitution of Sexuality, New York University Press, 1995, New York.
33. *Ibid.* p.139.
34. S.B. Satterfield, "Clinical Aspects of Juvenile Prostitution", Medical Aspects of Human Sexuality 15 (9), 1981, p.126.
35. M. Silbert and A.M. Pines, "Entrance into Prostitutions", Youth and Society, 13 (4) 1982, pp. 471-500.
36. Kathleen Barry, "The Prostitution of Sexuality, New York University Press, 1995, New York, p. 132.
37. CATW, 2001 [cited March 2, 2003] Available online htttp// catwinternational.org/fb/.
38. *Ibid.*
39. *Ibid.*
40. Oppermann M. "Introduction to Sex Tourism and Prostitution: Aspects of Leisure, Recreation and work, ed. M. Oppermann, New York, Cognizant Communications Corporation, 1998, pp. 1-19.
41. Pascale Guericolas, "Geographic de I" incacceptable", Gazatte des femmes 22 (1), May-June, 2000, pp.27-31.
42. UUSC, The Modern International Slave Trade, Cambridge, MA, UUSC, 2001. [cited May14,2001] online http//www.uusc.org/ programs/index.
43. Pascale Guericolas, "Geographie de I' Inacceptable", Gazette des femmes 22 (1), May-June 2000, p. 31.
44. The Hindu, April 6, 2012, p.9.
45. Manuel Castells, "End of Millennium", Blackwell Publishers, 1998, USA, p.141.

46. Australian, 25-26 November, 1995, p. 29.
47. This analysis draws heavily on the research of Wacquant in 'Imprisoning the American poor', pp. 88-9.
48. Hindu, "Tale of Chinas Two Economies", February 17, 2012, p. 9.
49. Jan Breman, "Social Exclusion in the context of Globalisation, working No. 18, ILO, 2004, Geneva, p.12.
50. *Ibid,* p.12
51. Manuel Castells "End of Millennium", Blackwell, Publisher 2000, Oxford, U.K.

# 5

# Globalisation and Environment : Passport to Destruction

The absoluteness of truth cannot be discounted, the natural world, in intrinsic terms and for human life is fundamental, without it no one can survive. The revolutionary set of policies with pinpointed acclaim of rationality-efficiency and comparative cost advantage, seems to be wrecking the ship, we are sailing in. In reality the environment is the greatest casuality of economic globalisation. The states monopoly in erstwhile communist countries and South Asia led to frenzied exploitation of natural resources. Growth soon became synonymous with expanded extraction from nature. Oil in the Soviet Union, Nigeria or Mexico, coal in India and China, wood in the Ivory Coast and Indonesia, minerals in Zaire. Alternatively, the use of resources in former communist countries was much higher than in the west, for natural resources were seen as a cost effective means of fuelling industrial development. Creating an increasingly global unfettered markets for trade and investment has significantly increased the destructive impact of economic activity upon the earth, exhausting the world's natural resource endowment and ecological carrying capacity at such a voracious rate as to jeopardise the planet's ability to support future generations.

The ecological picture appears more horrowing, as the new rules and dynamics of economic globalisation have simultaneously led to the holding back or removal of regulations and taxes designed to protect the natural environment, just when they are needed most. The presence of multinationals as an important determinant in world production and trade, makes the situation all the more critical as these corporations have no compunction for environmental responsibility— the sole aim is to maximise profits and increase the shareholders value. They are free to bribe the governments, to take hold of global stock of natural resources. The way multinationals have gone for shopping, for the natural resources with bagful of cash in the South makes the picture murky and dreadful. The rush for iron ores, manganese, zinc, bauxite, oil and gas has made economic accountability and democratically achieved environment protection virtually a farce. As a result, the world faces uncontrolled global crises in deforestation, bio-diversity loss, climate change, fisheries depletion, soil loss, land degradation and freshwater depletion. The combined effect of all this is that the earth is being pushed to the fringe of its tolerance. Despite the outcry of environmental health, reported in newspaper, the situation is not turning out to be better. The global pattern of resource use remained the same since the UN's spectacular conference on the environment and development was held in Rio De Janeiro in 1992. The most affluent 20 per cent of countries use up 85 per cent of the world's timber, 75 per cent of the processed metals, and 70 per cent of energy (*Hans-Peter Martin and Harold and Schumann, Zed Books, 1996, The Global Trap, p.29*). These data constitute the inherent potential of division between North and South over the issue of environmental responsibility. The biggest threats as pointed by environmentalists, is going to be in the South, with rapid economic growth and burgeoning population. The countries of the South on the other hand, accuse the North countries of being the prime villian—therefore should bear the onus of responsibility, while the North underlines the collective responsibility, shorn of spatial vindictiveness.[1]

The environmental concerns in the South have caught the attention of many NGOs, who have urged the developed nations to cast aside a percentage of their fortunes, for responsible environmental practices. Such calls, however, have gone unheeded.[2] In an increasingly urbanised world, disparities between rural and urban population remain substantial. Rural areas account for three in every four people living on less than US $1 a day and a similar share of the world population suffering from malnutrition.[3] Increase in urbanisation can not be attributed, as growth in human progress, as urban slum growth is outpacing urban growth by a wide margin (*World Development Report, 2007–08*).

The state of the world's environment is a direct corollary of human needs and consumption habits. In the South, entrenched poverty and critical dependence of population on environment, for livelihood, can increase pressures on the ecosystem. Thus flash and burn activities, in tropical areas, mining activities, overgrazing, fishing practices, excessive forest felling all can combine to push ecosystem to its limits. In 2005, the United Nations (UN) millennium Ecosystem Assessment drew attention to the global deterioration of vital ecosystems, including mangrove swamps, wetlands and forests.[4] These ecosystems are highly vulnerable to climate change as are the people who depend on the service they provide. Peoples capacities to manage pitfalls of climate change vary according to specificities and spatial distribution. The differences in their capacities to confront climate change, can in fact fuel inequalities in opportunity—thereby creating schism among nations, undermining the collective efforts to combat the Ecological deterioration.

## Dynamics of Environmental Damage

The boom in world trade and investment that has resulted from economic globalisation has contributed to a number of very specific ecological problems for trade to take place, it requires transportation. As transportation is driven by fossil fuels whose combustibility release various harmful gases into the air including green house gases. With exhaust fumes already beyond control, a billion cars—are expected to contribute to a global seize-up by the year 2020. Citizens of the European Union today waste the equivalent of roughly 1.5 per cent of GNP in traffic jams, in Bangkok the figure is 2.1 per cent. Journey through Thailand's paralysed capital, the erstwhile Venice of the East, takes so long that drivers carry portable toilets as a precaution. Companies in Japan routinely send three lorries to clients, by different routes, to make sure they keep their delivery deadlines (*Hans-Peter Martin and Harold Schumann, The Global Trap, 1996*). The inhabitants of Shanghai awake nearly every working day beneath a deep orange cover of smog. Near Chengdu, unfiltered black-and white smoke streams for tens of miles from thousands of lime kilns and brick factories. These are but a few examples, the story is the same in most of the megacities.

Given the marauding nature of globalisation with its incessant emphasis on consumption, and hedonism, there has been an all round conversion of raw-material into finished products. Metals must be mined from the ground to be converted into cars, trees must be felled to be converted into papers, packaging and furniture, oil and coal must be mined to be converted into electricity, fisheries are exploited for fish products, and soils are exploited for cash crops. With the removal of barriers to exports and imports; these natural resources, many of which are non-renewable, are now accessible on a scale that they never were before (*Edward*

*Goldsmith and Gerry Mander, 2001*). The primary commodities are made available to meet corporate production needs and this trend shows an eighteen fold increase in global consumption of materials since 1900 (*Gardner and Sampat in State of the World, 1999, pp. 43-49*).

The consequences of rapid exploitation of resources has left an indelible imprint of destruction in the forms of tracts of land, and vast quantities of earth's surface each year, than natural erosion by rivers (cited in *Gardner and Sampat in State of the World, 1999, pp. 43-49*). The excessive fishing has led to the depletion of fish stocks, so much so that traditional centers of fishing have been relegated to devastating levels. The exploitations of wood products, threaten more than 70 percent of the world's large virgin forests (*Bryant et al, 1997*). The large scale production of cash crops for global food chain is causing severe and unsustainable ecological damage, including soil erosion, land degradation, desertification, water depletion, salination, chemical contamination, bio-diversity loss, and deforestation.

With the growing inter-linkages in the world trade due to reduction in trade barriers, the local symbiotic food habits have been destroyed. The traditional agricultural practices which have sustained populations over centuries, are made to understand the benefits of cash crops, on the simplistic logic of economic figures. Thus in 1990, 99 per cent of the coffee produced in Burundi, 93 per cent of bananas grown in Costa Rica, 83 per cent of the cotton cultivated in Burkina Faso, 71 per cent of the tobacco produced in Malavi, half the trees felled for timber in Malaysia; and half of Icelands fish catch—were all for exports (*cited by French in costly trade offs, Reconciling Trade and the Environment, 1993, p.12*).

The trend of pollution and waste has reached a level of gargantuam proportions, due to the maneuverability and freedom to exercise the choices, by multinational corporations. The increasing reach and the width of multinational corporations has enabled them to tap resources, by employing capital, technology and expertise, in the four corners of the world in the manner that is appropriate to them. When the resources of one area have been thoroughly depleted the corporations move on to another place. This results in often permanent ecological damage.

This damage does not end with the extraction of primary commodities, rather by processing them into more and more manufactured goods is also highly polluting. It requires large quantities of energy mostly in the form of fossil fuels, contributing to air pollution and climate change. In US for example, material processing and manufacturing alone claimed 14 percent of the country's energy use in 1994 (*Gardner and Sampat in State of the World, 1999, p.48*). Manufacturing also partakes use of large quantities of chemicals. As there has been an exponential growth in the manufactured products, made worldwide, the annual world production of synthetic organic chemicals has increased enormously. From 7 million tonnes in 1950, chemical production has grown to nearly a billion tonnes today and is generating huge amount of hazardous waste in the process (*Karliner, The Corporate Planet, 1997, p.16*). The outcome of this is consequential decrease in bio-diversity and exponential growth in cancer patients. A white male in the US today, for example, is twice as likely to get cancer as his grandfather (*Davis et, al, 1994; cited in Rachels Hazardous Waste News, 14 April, 1994*).

The threat of bio-diversity loss though is real but according to few experts, certainly exaggerated. Most early estimates used simple island models that linked a loss in habitat with a loss of biodiversity. As a rule of thumb, a loss of 90% forest meant a 50 per cent loss of species. As rain forests seemed to be cut at alarming rates, estimates of annual species loss of 20,000-100,000 abounded. Many people expected the number of species to fall by half globally within a generation or two. However, the data simply do not correspond to these predictions. In the eastern United States, forests were reduced over two centuries to fragments totaling just 1-2 per cent of their original area, yet this resulted in the extinction of only one forest bird. In Puerto Rico, the primary forest area has been reduced over the past 400 years by 99 per cent, yet 'only' seven of 60 species of bird have become extinct. All but 12 per cent of the Brazilian Atlantic rainforests were cleared in the 19th century, leaving only scattered fragments. According to the rule of thumb half of all its species should have become extinct, yet, when the world conservation union and the Brazilian society of zoology analysed all 291 known Atlantic forest animals, none could be declared extinct. Species therefore seem more resilient than expected. And tropical forests are not lost at annual rates of 2-4 per cent, as many environmentalists have claimed: the latest UN figures indicate a loss of less than 0.5 per cent. Thus the opinion on bio-diversity extinction seems to be divided. Environmentalist concerns are pooh-poohed by the economists, but there is no denying the fact that species extinction is a fact, however less may be the speed. That forest cover is under threat due to excessive exploitation, and the fish stocks are seeing a pressure due to large scale fishing and containerisation.

Trade and production liberalisation has also created a asymmetrical shift of spatial products on processes. Thus Northern based multinational corporations who dealt in hazardous production activities, containing ecological risks, have gradually moved their operation in the South, having lenient environment regimes, and where costs of financial cleanups, pertaining to unhealthy environment practices are not particularly severe. There are numerous instances, in which hazardous production processes have been relocated from the North to escape strict and costly environmental standards. They include produces of asbestos, benzidine dyes, ozone destroying CFCs, certain pesticides, such as DDT, as well as lead and copper smelters, and some mineral processors (*Leonard, 1988*). Similarly, the practices undertaken worldwide for the disposal of the wastes such as incineration and landfill pollutes water supplies, leaches more mercury, generates more methane, and fills the air we breathe with more cancer-causing dioxins.

Thus tearing down of barriers to trade and investment around the world clearly contributes to all of these problems by providing growth-oriented corporations with unprecedented access to consumers and raw materials, and by maintaining the unsustainable industrialised way of life beyond its natural limits while extending it to the rest of the world (*Edward Goldsmith and Jerry Mander, The Case Against Global Economy, p. 193*).

## Framing Policy Framework for Environment Management

As most environment issues are of global concern, they have increasingly occupied the central focus, of international deliberations since the early 1970s within the institutions of the United Nations.[5] The UN Conference on Environment and Development (UNCED)- the 'Earth Summit' held in Rio De Janeiro Brazil, in 1992, is generally regarded as the climax of international environment activities to date. It was there that the 178 participating countries decided that 'sustainable development' would become their joint political principle for all future discussions on environment and development, both globally and nationally. The 'above' line of action was accented by all the participating nations as a common goal, to increase the chances of survival for today's generations. Sustainable development would henceforth constitute the central philosophy within the interactive processes of social, ecological and economic development, encompassing divergences in poverty and development and seek way towards global solution (*Theodor Quendler and Tobias Reichert, the WTO, Agriculture and Sustainable Development, 2002, p. 235*).

The climate framework convention and the convention on biological diversity (both binding on international law) as well as the Forest Declaration, The Rio Declaration and Agenda 21 (none of these is binding on international law) were all adopted at the Earth summit in Rio. These constitute the comprehensive action programme for the 21st century. At the same time the Commission for Sustainable Development (CSP) was established to monitor and support implementation of the decisions taken in Rio. The Global Environment Facility (GEF) was set up to finance the programme, the costs of which are estimated at US$ 600 billion per annum. The fund is affiliated with the World Bank and is also controlled by the UN Environment Programme (UNEP) and The UN Development Programme (UNDP).

Five years after the Rio conference in 1997, the discussions on the environment took a turn around with assessment, pertaining to implementation. In June 1997 an extraordinary meeting of the UN General Assembly was held in New York in which 115 nations participated. The conference took stock of the progress made, after the Rio summit. It also laid down the environment and development priorities for the future. An important analysis in this context was provided by UNEP's first report on the Global Environment Outlook 1997 (GEO), and the UN Secretary General's high-level Advisory Board on Sustainable Development (HLABSD 1997, a report for a special session of the General Assembly to review and appraise progress in the implementation of Agenda 21, particularly regarding the critical issues of energy, water and transport).

The majority of reports, presented, painted a gloomier side of environmental responsibility, undertaken either globally or nationally and blamed vested interests, whether they be political, or economic extending across corporations, governments or sectoral interests. The provision of finances for environmental protection, was also severely constrained. A perusal of the reports brought following facts (*Fischer Taschenbuch, 1997, column, 1175*):

- The 1990s have brought no improvement in the disparity between rich and poor, which is still increasing at unchecked speed. The gap between the richest and the poorest fifth of the world population has doubled over the past 30 years. Today 1.3 billion people earn less than US $1 a day, 60% of the world population earns less than US $2 a day.[6]
- Air pollution has become a serious health risk. It threatens 1.5 billion people. A further 1 billion people do not have clean water, and 2 billion people live without sanitary facilities.
- Less than one-quarter of all humankind is consuming three-quarter of the world's resources and is producing three quarter of all solid waste.
- The population of 13 of the 15 primary varieties of edible saltwater fish are being depleted rapidly.
- Emissions of carbon dioxide ($CO_2$), the major 'green house', gas have increased by 10 per cent, 40 percent in many developing countries. $CO_2$ emissions have shown an all round increase globally.
- Approximately 4.6 million hectares of rain forests are still disappearing each year. Between 150 and 250 species are becoming extinct everyday.

A number of important conventions, all of binding in international law, came into force in the wake of the Rio conference subject to national ratification. These included the climate convention, signed in Rio (March, 1994), the convention on biological diversity (December, 1993), the convention to combat desertification (December, 1996) and the convention on the law of the sea (CLOS, November, 1994).

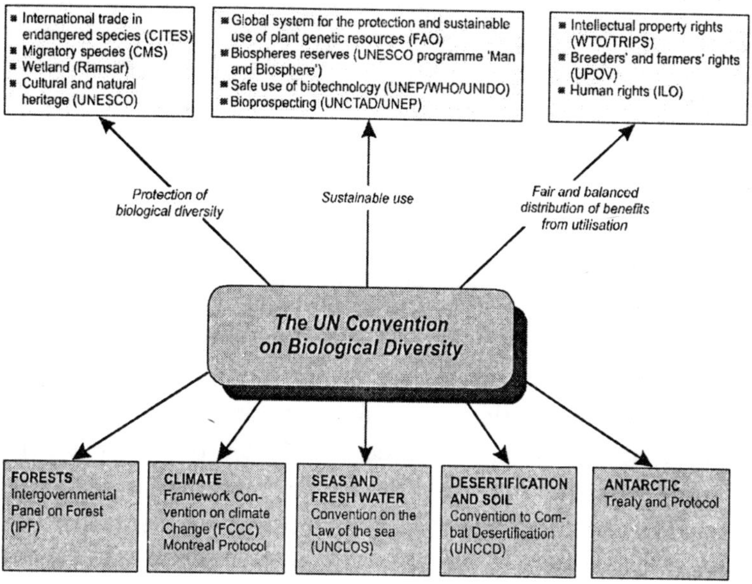


**Fig. 5.1. The Convention on biological diversity: its interactions with other international agreements.**

***Source:*** Fischer Taschenbuch 1997: columns 1203f.

The fig. (5.1) gives an overview of the available instruments regarding different components of the biosphere, and the complexity of variables involved in this connection. The various aspects pertaining to biological diversity underline the responsibility of governments, environment friendly practices, sustainability and peoples awareness—key to bio-diversity preservation. The role of Non-governmental agencies, business groups, politicians and campaign for global awareness regarding sustainable use of resources will help the cause of environment protection.

In order to understand the important aspects of environmental challenge and sustainability the following selected areas provide the key to unfold the intricacies and available options to preserve the ecological soundness:

1. Soil,
2. Water
3. Biological Diversity and
4. Climate Change.

## Soil: Basis of Agriculture and Food

Soils constitute the most important basis for human existence. Yet the fatal level of soil deterioration due to manmade exploitation seems to be eroding the very basis of human sustainance. The food supply chain is constantly under pressure due to increase in population pressure especially in the South. The degree of Soil deterioration, its nature and its causes vary from place to place with regard to arable land, the percentage of land that is damaged is 75 per cent in the Americas (North America and Latin America), 25 per cent in Europe and 16 per cent in Oceania with regard to permanent grassland, the percentage of damaged land is 31 per cent in Africa and 11 per cent in North America. With regard to forests and Savannahs, the damaged percentages are 38 per cent in central America and 1 per cent in North America (Fischer Taschenbuch 1996: Column 1131).

**Table 5.2 Amount and Kinds of Soil Degradation in Different continents**

| | *Total area* | *Share of degraded area (%)* | *Share of degraded area (%)* | | | | *Share of degradation type (%)* | | |
|---|---|---|---|---|---|---|---|---|---|
| | | | *Arable Land* | *Parmanent grassland* | *Forests & savannahs* | *Water erosion* | *Wind erosion* | *Physical degrad-ation* | *Chemical degrad-ation* |
| Europe | 9.50 | 23 | 25 | 35 | 26 | 52 | 19 | 17 | 17 |
| North America | 18.85 | 5 | 26 | 11 | 1 | 63 | 36 | 1 | < 1 |
| Latin America | 21.91 | 14 | 51 | 14 | 14 | 55 | 15 | 4 | 25 |
| Africa | 29.66 | 17 | 65 | 31 | 19 | 46 | 38 | 4 | 12 |
| Asia | 42.56 | 18 | 38 | 20 | 27 | 58 | 30 | 2 | 10 |
| Oceania | 8.82 | 12 | 16 | 19 | 8 | 81 | 16 | 2 | 2 |
| World | 130.13 | 15 | 38 | 21 | 18 | 56 | 28 | 4 | 4 |

* Million of square kilometres

***Source:*** Fischer Taschenbuch 1997: Columbus 1189f; WBGU 1994

The causes of soil degradations may vary from area to area. The degradation of soil is due to a number of factors operating simultaneously, such as deforestation, overgrazing and farming. The only comprehensive overview on this issue is the Global Assessment of Soil Degradation (GLASOD) co-ordinated by the International Soil Reference and Information Centre (ISRIC), published in 1990 (*Olderman 1997: 24; WRI 1992:112*). The densely populated continents such as Asia and Europe show higher rates of soil degradation than the more sparsely populated Americas and Oceania. An important exception is Africa, where 29.8% of all used area is degraded, the highest share of any continent in spite of a comparatively low population density. The regional distribution of degraded areas can be obtained from table 5.3.

## Table 5.3 Soil Erosion in Different Continents

| Land Mass | Total utility | Share of degraded | | Share modrately and highly degraded | |
|---|---|---|---|---|---|
| | Area | millions ha | % | million ha | % |
| Europe | 741.0 | 218.9 | 29.5 | 158.3 | 21.4 |
| North America | 1,188.0 | 95.5 | 8.0 | 78.7 | 6.6 |
| Latin America | 1,763 | 297.2 | 16.9 | 199.4 | 11.3 |
| Africa | 1,661.4 | 494.2 | 29.8 | 320.6 | 19.3 |
| Asia | 2,681.0 | 747.0 | 28.9 | 452.5 | 16.9 |
| Oceania | 688.0 | 102.9 | 15.0 | 62 | 0.9 |
| World | 8,722.4 | 1,955.7 | 22.4 | 1,215.7 | 13.9 |

*Source:* Oldeman 1997:24; WRI 1992: 112-17.

GLASOD: identifies five different causes of soil degradation:

- Overgrasing by livestock, 35 per cent of all degraded land, occurring mainly in arid and semiarid areas.
- Deforestation, which exposes soil to wind and water erosion through the removal of tree coverage includes logging and the conversion of land to agricultural or industrial area. This accounts for 30 per cent of all degraded areas.
- Agricultural activities such as cultivation with too short a fallow period lead to a loss of nutrients, and subsequently to loss of fertility. The application of an overdose of fertiliser or manure leads to soil acidification and water pollution. Poor irrigation management leads to salinisation.[7] Family agricultural practices are responsible for 28 per cent of global soil degradation.
- Over exploitation of fuel wood strips the land of vegetation and exposes it to wind and water erosion, causing 7 per cent of global soil degradation, with the highest prevalence in dry areas.

- Industrialisation with the resulting accumulation of industrial waste and acidification of soils by airborne pollutants (acid rain), account for only 1 per cent of global soil degradation but it is more in Europe (9 per cent).

Table 5.4 show the causes of soil degradation on various continents.

**Table 5.4 Causes of soil degradation in the various continents**

| | Share (%) | | | | |
|---|---|---|---|---|---|
| *Land Mass* | *Agricultural activities* | *Overgrazing* | *Deforestation* | *Over-exploitation of fuelwood* | *Industrialization* |
| Europe | 29 | 23 | 38 | <1 | 9 |
| North America | 66 | 31 | 4 | - | <1 |
| Central America | 45 | 14 | 23 | 18 | <1 |
| South America | 26 | 28 | 41 | 5 | <1 |
| Africa | 24 | 49 | 14 | 13 | <1 |
| Asia | 27 | 26 | 40 | 6 | <1 |
| Oceania | 8 | 80 | 12 | - | <1 |
| World | 28 | 34 | 30 | 7 | 1 |

*Source:* Fischer Taschenbuch 1997: Columbus 1189f; WBGU 1994.

Increasing intensification of farming is recognised as one of the main cause for soil degradation in many industrial countries. Globalisation induced industrial agriculture is characterised by an increasing use of heavy machinery, consolidation of farm land, monocultivation of plants with a high yield, excessive use of fertilisers and pesticides and intensive irrigation.[8] Agriculture activities account for about 25 per cent of total degradation in most parts of the world, with the important exceptions of Oceania (8 per cent) and North America where 66 per cent of the degradation is caused by agricultural activity.

Overgrasing is the most important cause in the arid and semi-arid areas of Oceania and Africa. Overgrasing by cattle is the cause of desertification of large areas, particularly in the arid regions of Africa in turn destroying the soil and vegetation in this part of the world. Large scale growing of cash crops and monocultures has been having a telling effect. The rapid increase in population has caused additional pressure, thereby destroying the fragile ecosystem.

In Latin America, Asia and Europe, deforestation has lead to soil degradation. Deforestation, for commercial logging,[9] particularly in tropical regions, has caused irreversible damage to the soil and entire ecosystem. Extensive washout of nutrients and soil compaction have made regeneration and reforestation impossible. Thus in Tibet, 45 per cent of forest cover has been lost since 1965, which is going to have its repercussions on the water balance. With seven rivers originating in Tibet, half the world population is dependent on the water from Tibet.

## Water: Ticking Time Bomb

Fresh water is the single most important food for human and the basic ingredient for the production of all other foodstuffs. The growing scarcity of the world's fresh water resources is seriously damaging ecosystems. It is setting limits on food production, putting people's health at risk and giving rise to various regional conflicts over the distribution of water. Pollution of ground water is also affecting the water resources.

97 per cent of all water is sea water, which accounts for the 7 per cent of the earth's surface. The remaining 67 per cent of the 3 per cent freshwater is stored as ice, either in glaciers or in the polar regions. Of the 33 per cent left, the greater part occurs as ground humidity or water at depth, and as such, in inaccessible to humans. Less than 0.4 per cent of all water is found is rivers, lakes and ground water reservoirs to be utilised by humans (*Fischer Taschebuch, 1996:* column 1145).

The exploitation of water resources by humans has increased dramatically since the beginning of the 20th century. Between 1900 and 1995 global water consumption grew more than sixfold, the rapid growth in consumption is attributable to the increase in use of irrigation in agriculture as well as an increase in industrial and private use. Agriculture by far the largest consumer, accounting for 70 per cent of all water used. Irrigated agricultural land already supplies 40 per cent of the world's growing demand for food on a surface area of only 17 per cent of all agricultural land (*Fischer Taschenbuch*). The recent increase in food production, is generally seen as a direct consequence of increased irrigation. Water consumption in agriculture has seen an increase of 60% since 1960. The challenge here is reflected in more and more usage of ground water resources, which are renewed at a slow pace in the water cycle, and its implication, as the most important source of drinking water.

Empirical studies as claimed by (*Quendler and Reichert*, 2002) shows that a country's water supply starts to become sparse when the extraction of fresh water exceeds the water supply annually by precipitation and from other countries by 10 per cent. Extraction of 20 per cent-40 per cent over the renewable supply is considered to indicate moderate scarcity of water. Approximately 460 million people (more than 8 per cent of the world's population) live in countries with server scarcity of water and 25 per cent live in countries with moderate scarcity of water. Together these make up one-thirds of world population. Around 80 per cent of this group lives in countries with a low per capita income. In other words, water scarcity, primarily effects the poorer regions of the world.

The demand for water in future will show an upward increase, at alarming rates. Today, 28 countries with a total population of more than 300 million people are being regarded as under 'water stress'. This figure could increase to 50 countries, with a total population of about 3 billion people (*Pinstrup-Anderson, 1997:23*). The demand for water is expected to shift from agriculture to industrial use, which accounts for 80 per cent of the additional withdrawal of water in developed countries, and such use will grow faster than agricultural use in developing countries. Many of the countries in the world have witnessed falling water table levels, due to over exploitation for irrigation purpose. The lower amounts of water in downstream rivers, due to large usage for commercial activities, may threaten the ecosystems, thereby hampering aquatic life and fisheries. Northern areas of Mexico, Southern areas of USA, have seen a remarkable decrease in water table levels due to diversion of ground water for commercial farming such as fruits and vegetables on large scale. Similar trends could also be noticeable in China and India, with the introduction of capital and technology in future years to come, the race to water security, point experts, could well be the cause of wars among nations in the 21st century.[10]

## Bio-diversity: Lost for ever

'Bio-diversity' as a term encompasses the entire range of fauna and flora, diversity of ecosystems as well as the diversity of individual species. In connections with biological diversity three different facts are recognised, namely the diversity of ecosystems, the diversity of species and the genetic diversity or variability within a species. The 'humid' warm rainforests cover only 7 per cent of the land surface yet accommodate 90 per cent of the different terrestrial species. The economic exploitation and intervention in these areas, has subjected the habitat under intense pressure, thereby undermining the survival of many species, micro-organisms, birds and insects. The conversion of tropical areas into pastureland, agricultural land, settlements, roads and railways, industrial land or land for tourist infrastructure has reduced the habitat, and the very survival of numerous species are at stake.

Individual surveys, clearly indicate the damaging influence attributable to humans. According to some surveys, more than 50 per cent of natural ecosystems worldwide have been impaired by moderate to extensive human intervention. The greater part of these activities have taken place in Europe, where only 10 per cent of all natural habitat remains untouched. Other causes of the loss of species include—

- Pollution from industry,
- Over exploitation of wild animals and plant population as source of raw material or food,
- Unintentional killing of sea animals in commercial fishing nets,
- Accidental or deliberate import of exotic species of pathogens, and
- Tracking and deliberate extermination of pest species, with often unanticipated consequences for ecosystem.

The growing importance of international tourist activities is also a serious risk, as ecosystems responsible for maintaining bio-diversity, such as coasts, small islands, coral reefs, dunes, freshwater ecosystems are threatened, due to tourists, as they are offered variety of adventure sports, that hamper and disturb the surroundings. Another notable feature is that the expansion of modern-day commercial agriculture and the introduction of new varieties of plants have also caused a loss of genetic diversity among commercial plant species. On account of new breeding methods and the forceful penetration of new, high performing varieties of cultivated crop, there has been a major decline in agricultural biodiversity. In the USA, for example, 95 per cent of the cabbage varieties, 91 per cent of the corn varieties, 94 per cent of the pea varieties and 81 per cent of the tomato varieties have been lost during the past 100 years. Of the 10, 000 types of wheat cultivated in China in 1949, only 1,000 had survived by the 1970s. In India, the number of rice varieties grown went down from 30,000 in the 1950s to only 50 today (*Fischer Taschenbuch, 1999*). A startling 90 per cent of world food production is based on less than 100 different plants. The reasons behind this are agricultural policy that puts too much emphasis on production ownerships. The continued genetic erosion and monoculture in connection with cultivated crops is major issue in bio-diversity discussions. Experts point out that this development will lead to increased food security risks, since the loss of genetic diversity constrains the potential to adopt cultivated plants to changing conditions, including those of anthropogenic origin such as climate change (*Fischer Taschenbuch, 1997: columns: 1142*).

Though several measures have been undertaken to preserve bio-diversity such as 1992 convention on bio-diversity for sustainable use of genetic resources, the expansion of world trade, and neo-liberalism does, not promise much, as profits have always been leveraged at the cost of environment. Countries with powerful lobby groups, pertaining to agricultural commodities, tourism, land development, colonisation etc. have succeeded in furthering their agenda at the cost of nature.

## Climate Change

Climate change, it is widely believed, will be one of the strongest forces in the 21st century, that is going to have its impact on wide ranging issues of human survival and security. Through its impact on ecology, rainfall, temperature and weather systems, global warming will widely affect all countries. Nobody will be immune to its consequences. However, some countries and people are more vulnerable than others. In the long run, the whole of humanity faces risks but more immediately, the downtrodden and the marginalised are particularly at greater risk.

While uncertainties prevail among experts on climate, about the timing, nature and scale of future impacts, the forces unleashed by global warming can be expected to magnify existing disadvantages. Concentrated in fragile ecological areas, drought prone arid lands, flood prone coastal areas, and precarious urban slums, the poor are highly exposed to climate change risks— and they lack the resource to manage these risks (*Human Development Report, 2007-2008*).

The impact of climate change invariably would depend upon a combination of factors, such as differences in social and economic coping capacities, by public policy choices, employment and livelihood questions among the many. All these aspects would be weighed in the back drop of human security available to population.

As Human Development Report, 2007-2008, suggests that the back drop does show a few silver linings as international agencies and governments have shown the promptness and urgency to raise the multitude of humanity in Africa and Asia (where most of the poor reside) to minimum threshold of human survival (nutrition, health, education). Thus the share of the population living in developing countries on less than US $ 1 a day has fallen from 29 percent in 1990 to 18 percent in 2004. Over the same period child mortality rates have fallen from 106 deaths per thousand live births to 83 and life expectancy has increased by 3 years. Progress in education has gathered pace. Globally the primary school completion rate rose from 83 percent to 88 percent between 1999 and 2005 (*Human Development Report, 2007-2008, p. 24*).

Due to improvement in the economic growth, poverty reduction has undergone pace in Asia. Based on strong growth, numbers living in extreme poverty fell by 135 million between 1999 and 2004. The darker side of the story connotes the deep division between have and have-nots, wherein disparity in incomes are ever on the increase. This situation is particularly manifest in India, Pakistan, Bangladesh and countries of Africa. Most of the countries are way behind, in terms of achieving millennium development goals by 2015. What agitates the experts on human security is, that emerging risks will fall disproportionately on countries already characterized by high levels of poverty and vulnerabilities.

- ***Income poverty:*** There are still around 1 billion people living at the margins of survival on less than US $ 1 a day with 2.6 billion—40 percent of the world's population living on less than US $ 2 a day unless efforts are made to accelerate poverty reduction, it is anticipated that MDG target would be missed by around 380 million people.
- ***Nutrition:*** 28 per cent of all children in developing countries are estimated to be underweight or stunted, Two important regions, South Asia and Sub-Saharan Africa appear to be off track in terms of achieving MDG target of halving under nutrition by 2015. In India one half of all rural children are underweight for their age roughly the same proportion as in 1992.
- ***Child Mortality:*** Progress on child mortality lags behind progress in other areas. Around 10 million children die each year before the age of 5. Only around 32 countries out of 147 monitored by the World Bank are on track to achieve the MDG of a two thirds reduction in child mortality by 2015. South Asia and Sub-Saharan Africa are comprehensively off track. On current trends the MDG target will be missed by a margin that will represent 4.4 million additional deaths in 2015.
- ***Health:*** An estimated 40 million people are living with HIV/AIDS, with 3 million deaths in 2004. Every year there are 350-500 million cases of malaria, with 1 million fatalities: Africa accounts for 90 per cent of malarial

deaths and African children account for over 80 percent of malaria victims worldwide.

The above mentioned contrasts (*Human Development Report, 2007-2008*) hold a dismal picture of the growth and poverty. Clearly such human deficit gaps present in the global system, would undeniably increase the challenge of climate impact on those communities, who are yet to achieve a respectable degree of human security choices. The impact of climate change would hold differing prospects for rich and the poor, with poor largely at the receiving end.

Increasing temperatures of the earth is a major cause of concern, as this would unfold a chain of event which could prove fatal to human populations. It is believed that the world is warming and that the average global temperature has increased by around 0.7 degree centigrade since the advent of the industrial era. It is also known that the trend is accelerating, average mean temperature is rising at 0.2 degree centigrade every decade. With the global rise in temperatures local rainfall patterns are changing, ecological zones are shifting, the seas are warming and ice caps are melting. The abrupt changes, in various climate zones can be witnessed (*Human Development Report, 2007-2008*). One can witness the ice tipped peaks in the deserts of Oman. Flash floods can be seen in new areas in India, such as Punjab and Bombay. Erratic rains play havoc with the farmers in India, China and Bangladesh, undermining crops. Since the passing of the UN Framework Convention on Climate Change (UNFCC), enough conferences, and guidelines have agitated the minds of environmentalists, international agencies and national governments to undertake everything that stabilises the green house gas concentrations in the atmosphere that would prevent dangerous anthropogenic interference with the climate system. The impending danger of green house gases to ecological stability, perforce commits global community to cut green house gases in a stipulated time period, so that the food systems for the survival of humanity are not threatened.

Average global surface temperature is the most fundamental measure of climate change. Temperatures in the past half centuries have probably been the highest of any 50-year period for the past 1300 years. The world is now at near the warmest level on record in the current inter-glacial period, which began around 12,000 years ago. There is a strong evidence that the process is accelerating. Eleven of the twelve warmest years since 1850 occurred between 1995 and 2006. On a decade by decade basis, the linear warming trend for the past 50 years is nearly twice that for the past 100 years See fig. 5.5.

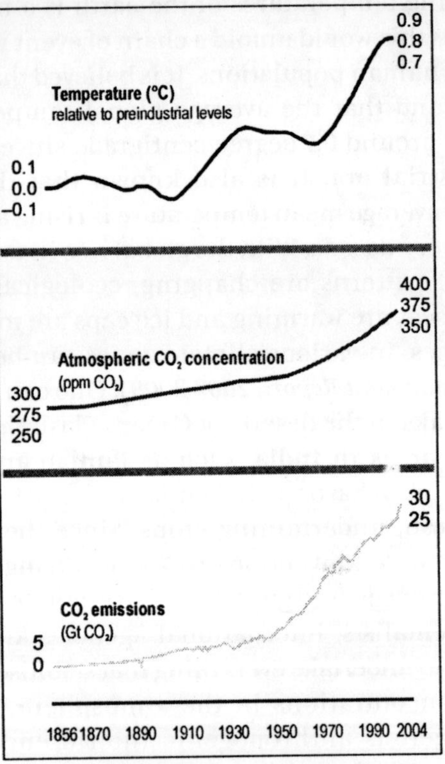


**Fig. 5.5. Rising $CO_2$ emissions are punished up stocks and increasing temperature.**

*Source:* CDIAC 2007; IPCC 2007a.

The scientific evidences gathered by experts, link rising temperatures to increased concentration of $CO_2$ and green house gases, that are emitted due to industrial and transport uses. It is pointed out by scientists that the earth would have been cooler by 30 °C, had it not been the presence of these gases in the atmosphere. These gases absorb outgoing solar radiation and thereby keep the planet warm, which in turn sustains various life forms. Throughout the Earth's four previous glacial and warming cycles, there has been a high correlation between atmosphere concentration of $CO_2$ and temperature.[11] The current warming cycle is not unique in terms of temperature change but it is the first time that humanity has decisively changed a cycle. The atmospheric concentration of $CO_2$ are rising sharply, so are the other green house gases such as methane and nitrous dioxide. By 2030 green house gas emissions are set to increase by between 50 and 100 percent above 2000 levels.[12] At the same time the earth's capacity to absorb this, may dwindle, largely because of feedback between the climate and the carbon cycle may be weakening the absorptive capacity of the World's oceans and forests. For example, warmer oceans absorb less $CO_2$ and rainforests could shrink with higher temperatures and reduced rainfall.

The various hypotheses suggested by agencies project a gloomier side of earths warming. If emissions continue to rise following the current trends then stocks will be increasing at 4.5 parts per million a year by 2035, almost double of current rate. Accumulated stocks will have risen to 550 parts per million. Even without further increases in the rate of emissions, stocks of green house gases would reach over 600 ppm by 2050 and 800 ppm by the end of the 21st century.[13] The IPCC which has hypothesised six possible scenarios, as possible emission pathways do not project a stabilization below 600 ppm, rather in three scenarios its figures shoot to 850 ppm or above. The above projection by

IPCC regarding greenhouse concentration ranges the temperature increase between 2.3°C and 44.5°C (factoring in the 0.5°C increase from the start of the industrial era to 1990). None of the future scenarios point to a below 20°C temperature increase, as given by IPCC. Illustrative probability range identified in modelling work includes the following (*Human development Report, 2007-2008.*)

- Stabilisation at 550 ppm, which is below the lowest point on the IPCC scenarios, would carry an 80 percent probability of overshooting the 2°C dangerous climate change threshold (*Meinshausen, 2005*).
- Stabilisation at 650 ppm carries a probability of between 60 and 95 percent of exceeding 3°C. Some studies predict a 35-98 per cent likelihood of overshooting at round 883 ppm, well within the IPCC non-mitigation scenario range, there would be a 50 percent change of exceeding a 50°C temperature increase.

The above modeling based on probability ranges are of great significance in understanding the possible impact on climate change. It is held that an excess of 2-3°C increase in temperatures, can cause damaging consequences on ecology, with concomitant effects on social and economic sector.[14] The chances of heightened risks, pertaining to ecological reversals, and catastrophic weather conditions, may lead to growth reversals, undermining human security.

The continued unchecked industrialisation with continued release of green house gases, could spell doom, with ocean levels rising, due to warming. The oceans absorb 80 percent of the carbon, and therefore act as a major source of sink.[15] The looming danger world over of climate change threatens to cause massive human displacement and the collapse of livelihood on a vast scale. Associated outcomes, can encompass to include movement of displaced people across national borders to the potential collapse of fragile states.

## Carbon Accounting

The global pool of green house gas emissions are measured by the carbon contribution in the atmosphere.[16] This accounting helps in the relative comparison of nations responsibilities and the sectoral divisions in releasing the carbon. All activities, all countries and all people register in the global carbon account but some register far more heavily than others.[17] This accounting can help in the mitigation of the green house effects by underlining the issue of equity and distribution. The figure 5.6 shows the country wise contribution regarding $CO_2$ emission.

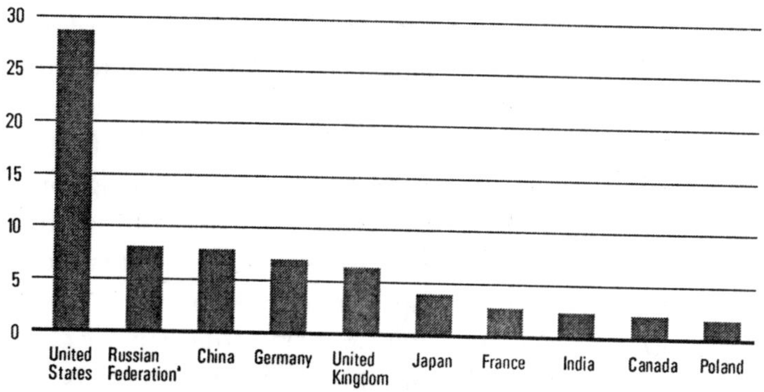


**Fig. 5.6. Rich countries dominate the cumulative emissions account**
**Share of Global $CO_2$ emissions, 1840–2004 (%).**

a. Includes a share of USSR emissions proportional to the Russian Federation's current of CIS emissions.
*Source:* CDIAC 2007.

The figures are an increasing pointer, that rich countries relative share in $CO_2$ emissions are far more as compared to third world countries. It indicates that only serious efforts to address the problem of green house gases, will have to be directed more towards developed nations.[18]

Most human activities fossil fuel, combustion for power generation, transport, land use changes and industrial processes generate emissions of green house gases— this makes the mitigation of green house gases a daunting task. The figure shows that half of emission comes from burning of fossils fuels. Land use change also plays an important role. Deforestation is by far the largest source of $CO_2$ emissions in this context, releasing sequestered carbon into the atmosphere as a result of burning and loss of biomass. One of the conclusions to emerge from the sectoral analysis of carbon footprints is that mitigation aimed at reducing $CO_2$ emissions from power generation, transport and deforestation is likely to generate high returns.[19]

Rich countries dominate the overall emissions account. Collectively they account for about 7 out of every 10 tonnes of $CO_2$ that have been emitted since the start of the industrial era. Historic emissions amount to around 1,100 tonnes of $CO_2$ per Capita for Britain and America, compared with 6 tonnes per capita for China and 23 tonnes per capita for India. The United States is the largest emitter, accounting for one fifth of the total, collectively the top five— China, India, Japan, the Russian Federation and the United States account for more than half; the top ten over 60 percent (*Human Development Report, 2007-2008, p. 41*). While climate change constitutes a global problem, the actions of relatively small group of countries and groupings such as, G-8, the European Union (EU), China and India, would encompass a large share of the total flow of emissions. In 2004, the developing countries accounted for 42 per cent of energy related $CO_2$ emissions, compared to around 20 per cent in 1990. China may be about to overtake the United States as the world's largest emitter and India is now the world's fourth largest emitter. By 2030 developing countries are projected to account for just over half of total emissions.[20] With just 15 percent of the world population, rich countries account for 45 per cent of $CO_2$ emissions. Sub-Saharan Africa also accounts for around 11 per cent of the world population, but represent 2 per cent of global emissions. Low income countries as a group account for one-third of the world's population but for just 7 per cent of emissions (*Human Development Report 2007-2008*).

## Inequalities in Carbon Emissions

The world picture of carbon additions, named as carbon foot printing, denotes increasing carbon debts, accumulated by rich countries over years. People in the rich world increasingly voice concern over carbon emissions by the developing nations, but they tend to be less aware of their own place in the global distribution of $CO_2$. Consider the following examples–

- The United Kingdom (population 60 million) emits more $CO_2$ than Egypt, Nigeria, Pakistan and Vietnam combined (total population 472 million).
- The Netherlands emits more $CO_2$ than Bolivia, Colombia, Peru, Uruguay and the seven countries of Central America combined.
- The state of Texas (population 23 million) in the United States register $CO_2$ emissions of around 700 mt $CO_2$ or 12 percent of the United States total emissions That figure is greater than the total $CO_2$ footprint left by Sub-Saharan Africa a region of 720 million people.
- The 19 million people living in New York State have a higher carbon footprint than the 146 mt $CO_2$ left by the 766 million people living in the 50 least developed countries.
- The state of New South Wales in Australia (population 6.9 million) has a carbon footprint of 116 mt $CO_2$. This figure is comparable to the combined total for Bangladesh, Cambodia, Ethiopia, Kenya, Morocco, Nepal and Sri Lanka.

Per capita emissions of carbon in developing countries indicates that its per capita carbon footprint is less than one-tenth of that in high income countries. In Ethiopia, the average per capita carbon footprint is 0.1 tonnes, compared with 20 tonnes in Canada. The per capita increase in emissions since 1990 for the United States (1.6 tonnes) is higher than the total per capita emissions for India in 2004 (1.2 tonnes). The per capita increase for Canada since 1990 (5 tonnes) is higher than per capita emissions for China in 2004 (3.8 tonnes) (*Human Development Report, 2007-2008*). The distribution of current emissions points that carbon footprint of the poorest 1 billion people on the planet are at 3 per cent of the world's total footprint. These are the people who are living on the margins, such as rural areas, urban slums and periphery. These people have not had much role in Carbon emissions, yet the catastrophic consequences of carbon emissions, are going to impact these people in larger ways. The effort to mitigate the climate change will have to address these issues, to really make it sustainable.

## Kyoto Protocol: Efforts at Mitigation

The Kyoto protocol was the first step in the multilateral response to climate change. It set targets for cutting green house gases, emissions against 1990 levels by 2010-2012 with governments embarking on negotiations for the post-2012 multilateral framework that will build on the current commitment period, it is important that lessons are learnt. The lessons learnt so far have not been encouraging. Firstly there is huge gap between ambition and actual deliverance. Targets adopted under the first commitment period were modest, averaging around 5 per cent for developed countries. The second is binding the targets. Two important countries USA and Australia did not ratify the protocol. The countries who ratified have been considerably off the work, from even the modest level of 5 per cent. The developing countries further have no quantitative targets.

The progress under the Kyoto protocol does not hold much promise as 68 countries are off track. The emission growth had shown further increase. The following outcomes can be deciphered:

- The European Union made average emission reduction commitments of 8 per cent under Kyoto. Actual cuts have amounted to around 2 per cent and European environment agencies projections suggest that current policies will leave this picture unchanged by 2010. Emissions from the transport sector increased by one-quarter. Emissions from electricity and heat generation increased by 6 per cent. Large increases in renewable energy supply will be required to meet the Kyoto targets but the European Union is falling short of investments needed to meet its own target of 20 per cent provision by 2020.
- The United Kingdom has surpassed its Kyoto target of a 12 percent emissions reduction, but is off track to meet a national target to reduce emissions by 20 per cent against 1990 levels. Most of the reduction was achieved before 2000 as a result of industrial restructuring and market liberalisation measures that led to a switch from carbon-intensive coal to natural gas.
- Germany's emissions were 17 per cent lower in 2004 than in 1990. Reductions reflect deep cuts from 1990 to 1995 following reunification and industrial restructuring.
- Italy and Spain are off track of their targets. In Spain emissions have increased by almost— 50 per cent since 1990, with strong economic growth and increased use of coal power following droughts. In Italy the primary driver of increase emissions has been the transport sector.
- Canada agreed under the Kyoto Protocol to target a 6 percent cut in emissions. In the event emissions have

increased by 27 per cent and the country is now around 35 percent above its Kyoto target range. While green house gas intensity has fallen, efficiency gains have been swamped by an increase in emission from an expansion in oil and gas production. Net emissions associated with oil and gas exports have more than doubled since 1990.

- Japan's emission in 2005 were 8 per cent above 1990 levels. The Kyoto target was for a 6 per cent reduction. On current trend Japan will miss its target by 14 percent. Most of the emission increase in Japan has been due to transportation (50 per cent).
- The United States is a signatory to the Kyoto protocol but it has not ratified the treaty. If it had, it would have been required to reduce its emissions to 7 per cent below 1990 levels by 2010. Overall emissions have increased by 16 percent.
- Like the United States, Australia did not ratify the Kyoto protocol. Overall emissions have grown at around twice the rate that would have been required had the country participated, with emissions rising by 21 per cent since 1990. High levels of dependence on coal fired power generation contributed to large increases in the energy sector, with $CO_2$ emissions rising by over 40 per cent.

The above facts remind that any arrangement at global level to reduce emission norms, will have to undertake long time framework, along with genuine requirements, specific to country's development goals. Mere ambitions in the framework would not help in mitigating the seriousness of climate change. To achieve a game changing configuration, the developed countries will have to include emission

***Source:*** (*Human Development Report, 2007-08*): citings from EEA 2006; EIA 2006; Government of Canada 2006; IEA 2006c; Government of the United kingdom 2007c; IKKATAE 2007; Pembina Institute 2007a.

reductions of around 30 percent by 2020 and at least 80 percent by 2050, in order to achieve sustainable emissions pathway. Reductions by developing countries will have to be facilitated by financial and technology transfers, so that the burden of shift becomes less painful.

The energy security background is important for climate change mitigation strategies. As experts point that coal is perhaps the biggest contributor of $CO_2$ compared to oil and natural gas. For each unit of every generated, coal generates around 40 per cent more $CO_2$ than oil and almost 100 percent more than natural gas. Coal is the world's cheapest and most widely dispersed and most $CO_2$ intensive fossil fuel. Using just half of the world's known coal reserves during the 21st century would add around 400 ppm to atmosphere stocks of green house gases guaranteeing dangerous climate change in the process.[21] Moreover, coal figures very prominently in the current and future energy profiles of major $CO_2$ emitters such as China, Germany, India and the United States.

The threats from climate changes, have seised the academic and international agencies. Due to emissions and global warming it is likely that tropical cyclone, typhoons, hurricanes will become more intense, as the energy level of oceans rise. Drought and flood will become more frequent and widespread across the world. The population living in coastal belts, deltaic regions, wetlands and urban slums will face increasing threats. The landslides as reported from different parts of the world are becoming more and more frequent. The world will have to address the issue of climate change more responsibly, if it wants to preserve the gains due to industrialisation and expansion of trade. Threatening climate change scenarios in the future calls for reigning the globalisation project, as multinational corporations increasingly bet on the altruistic gains sans environmental responsibility.

## References


1. Human Development Report, 2007-2008, p. 28.
2. It is alleged by the South, who have been late entrants in the process of industrialisation, that nations of the North have been the chief villians of environmental pollution, hence they should bear the cost of environmental cleanup. The South also accuses the North of not enabling the technologies for environment clean up, The North states that technologies for environment clean up are owned by multinationals hence they cannot be forced to part with it, as the rules of corporate behaviour do not permit the same.
3. The North comprising of European union and USA have not been particularly forthcoming, to part with their GDP, for taking greater responsibility to clean up environmental mess.
4. In 1993, 32% of the 130 million kmz of ice free landmass covered by forests, 11% was farmland and 26% was pasture. The remaining 31% was largely made up of uncultivated grasslands or wetlands or was apportioned to human settlements and transport infrastructure (*Fischer Taschenbuch 1996: column 1130*). According to the only worldwide survey of soil to date, in 1990 15% of all ice free land was observed to have been severely damaged by human activities. In other words, 38% farmland, 21% of permanent grasslands and 18% of all forests and savannahs were affected of this damage, 56% was caused by water erosion and another 28% of damage was caused by wind erosion.
5. In 1972 the following were established, the conference on Human environment, Stockholm; the headquarters of the UN Environment Programme (UNEP), Nairobi, Kenya.
6. World Development Report, 2007-2008.
7. Guardian Weekly, 6-12 April, 2000, p. 26; Age, 10 August, 1998, p. 11.
8. Bjorn Lombarg, The Skeptical Environmentalist, Cambridge University Press, 2001.
9. A large part of logged wood is used in construction industry, from Malaysia, Phillipines and Indonesia.
10. Water disputes among countries is on increase, as countries look for water resources to manage the burgeoning population. Thus water disputes have surfaced between India and Pakistan over

Indus; between Nepal and India over Kali river, and India and Bangladesh over Hoogly river. Recent Chinese activities on the Brahmaputra river has soured relations between India and China.

11. This correlation highlights carbon cycle feed backs, with the biosphere losing carbon to the atmosphere in response to higher temperature which in turn drives temperatures upwards.
12. IPCC, 2007.
13. Stern, 2006.
14. The rise in Sea level can threaten the fragile communities along the sea coast, due to flooding by sea water. Livelihoods of millions of people can be threatened.
15. The carbon released is mainly absorbed by the oceans. Oceans are becoming warmer and increasingly acidic, rising acidity attacks carbonate, one of the essential building blocs for corals and microorganisms which are part of food chains.
16. The carbon contribution, Provides the scale of greenhouse effects caused due to industrialisation and developmental changes. Experts have accepted this as, a measure of greenhouse variations.
17. The increase in the carbon release is an increasing determinant of transformation and developmental activities, resorted by respective countries.
18. The world manufacturing is increasingly dominated by developed nations, hence their requirement of fossil led energy is more, thereby increasing the carbon release.
19. Since most of the Carbon emissions are accounted by energy requirements, shift from fossil fuels to alternate energy systems can produce impact on carbon emission.
20. IEA 2006C.
21. Hansen, 2007C.

# Bibliography


Acuna, R.L., "A Culture of peace", Le Mode Diplomatique.

Adam, H., Siabbert, F. and Moodley, K. (1997), Comrades in Business: Post-Liberation Politics in South Africa, Cape Town: Tafelberg Publishers.

Adler, Emmanuel and Michael Barnett (eds.), Security Communities, Cambridge, UK: CUP.

African Development Bank (1993), Economic Integration in Southern Africa, Abidjan: Ivory Coast, (Three volumes).

Ahmed, E., Hill, C., Sen, A.K. and Dreze, J. (eds.) (1999), Social Security in Developing Countries (2nd ed), New Delhi/ London: Oxford University Press.

Albrow, M. (1990), "Introduction in Globalisation", Knowledge and society: Readings from International Sociology, Sage, London.

Alston, P. (1994), 'International Law and the Right to Food' in B. Harriss-White and R. Hoffenberg (eds.), Food: Multi-disciplinary Perspectives, Oxford: Blackwell, pp. 205-16.

Amin, Samir (1972), 'Underdevelopment and Dependence in Black Africa: origins and contemporary forms'. Journal of Modern African Studies 10 (4), December, 503-524.

Anderson, L., 'Genetic Engineering Foods and our Environment', Australian, 22 Feb., 2000.

Anderson, S., Cavanagh, J. and Lee, T. (2000), Field Guide to the Global Economy, NY, The New Press.

Anderson, Sarah and John Cavanagh, 1996, CEOs Win, Workes lose: How wall street Rewards Job destroyers, Washington DC, Institute for Policy studies.

Armstrong, J. (1995), 'Uganda's AIDS Crisis and its Implications for Development', World Bank Discussion Paper 059-21OX, Washington, World Bank.

Arnott, Richard, Bruce Greenwald, and Joseph E. Stiglitz. 1994, "Information and Economic Efficiency," Information Economics and Policy 6 (1): 77-88.

Arrighi, G., "The three Hagemonies', Review, Fernand Brandel centre, XXII (3: 1999).

Aulakh, Preet S. and Michael G. Schechter (eds.) (2000), Rethinking Globalisation(s): from corporate transnationalism to local interventions, London, Macmillan.

Axtmann, R., (ed.) 1998, Globalisation and Europe : Theoretical and Empirical Investigations, London, Pinter.

Bach, D. (ed.) (1999), Regionalisation in Africa: Integration and Disintegration, Oxford, James Currey.

Bacon, D. (2000), 'Can Global Workers beat Globalisation?', Sodalist Register Discussion Pages (sodalist-register@yorku.ca).

Baldwin, R. and Forslid, R. (1996), "Trade Liberalisation Endogenous Growth: A q-theory approach', NBER Working Paper No. 5549, April, 1996.

Banco de Mexico, Informe Anual 1998, april, 1999.

Bardhan, P. (1997), 'Method in the Madness? A Political Economy Analysis of the Ethnic Conflict in Less Developed Countries', World Development, 25, 9, 1381-98.

Barnard, D. (1998), PRODDER: The South African Development Directory, 1998-09, Braam Fontein: HSRC.

Barnet, R. and Cavanagh, J. (1994), Global Dreams: Imperial Corporations and the New World Order, NY, Simon and Schuster.

Barnet, R.J., The Alliance, America-Europe-Japan: Makers of the post war world, New York, Simon and Schuster.

Baudrillard, J. (1993), 'Simulacra and Simulations: Disneyland', In C. Lemert (ed.) Social Theory: The Multicultural and Classic Readings, Boulder, Co, Westview Press, 524-529.

Bauman, Z., Globalisation: The Human Consequences: Cambridge, Polity Press, 1998.

Bayart, J.F., Ellis, S. and Hilson B. (1999), The Criminalisation of the State in Africa, London, Institute of African Affairs/James Currey.

Baylis, J. and Smith, S. (eds.) (1997), The Globalisation of World Politics: an introduction to international relations, Oxford, oup.

Beccatini, G. (1979), 'Dal "settore" industriale al "distretto industriale": alcune considerasioni sull' unita de indagine dell' economia industriale', Rivista di Economia e Politica Industriale, 1, pp. 35-48.

Bello, W., 1998, "Globalisation and the Asian Financial Crisis", Paper Presented at the Toda Conference on Globalisation, Employment and the Quality of life, University of Sydney.

Bergsten, E. (1996), 'Globalising free trade', Foreign Affairs 75 (3),105-120.

Bernstein, H. (1994), 'Agrarian Classes in Capitalist Development', in L. Sklair (ed.), Capitalism and Development, London, Routledge, pp. 40-71.

Bernstein, P. (1996), Against the Gods: the Remarkable Story of Risk, New York, Wiley.

Bidwai, P. and Vanaik A. (1999), South Asia on a Short Fuse: Nuclear Politics in the Subcontinent, New Delhi, Oxford University Press.

Bienfield, Manfred, 1989, Financial Deregulation: Disarming the nation State, studies in political Economy, Volume 37.

Blakely J. Edward and Mary G. Snyder, 1997, Fortress America: Gated communities in the United States, Brooking Institutions Press.

Blownfield, A.I. 1959, Monetary Policy under the International Gold Standard, New York.

Boas, M., Marchand, M. and Shaw, T. (1999), 'The Weave-world-Regionalisms in the South in the New Millennium', Third World Quarterly 20(5), October, 1061-1070.

Boas, M., Marchand, M. and Shaw, T. (eds.) (1999), Special Issue: New Regionalisms in the New Millennium, Third World Quarterly 20(5), October, 987-1070.

Boutwell, Jeffrey and Michael T. Klare (eds.) (1999), Light Weapons and Civil Conflict Controlling the Tools of Violence, Lanham: Rowman and Littlefield for AAAS and Carnegie Commission.

Boyce, J. (1992), 'The Revolving Door? External Debt and Capital Flight: a Philip pino Case Study', World Development, 20, 3, pp. 335-49.

Braathen, Einer et. al. (eds.) (2000), Ethnicity Kills? The politics of war, peace and ethnicity in Sub-Saharan Africa, London, Macmillan.

Bray, F. (1994), 'Agriculture for Developing Nations', Scientific American July, 33-35.

Brecher, Jeremy and Tim costello, 1994, The Race to the Bottom, South End press, Cambridge.

Breman, J. (1996), Footloose Labour: Working in India's Informal Economy, Cambridge, Cambridge University Press.

Breman, Jan, 2004, 'Social Exclusion in the context of Globalisation' working No. 18, ILO, Geneva.

Brodhead, L. (1996), 'Commissioning consent: globalisation and global governance'. International Journal 51, 651-668.

Brown, L.R., Kane, H. and Ayres, E. (1993), Vital Signs 1993, NY, W.W. Norton.

Bryan, L. and Farrell, D. (1996), Market Unbound: Unleashing Global Capitalism, NY, John Wiley.

Bryans, Michael et. al. (1999), 'Mean Tunes: humanitarian action in complex emergencies - stark choices, cruel dilemmas', Coming to Terms, Toronto, University of Toronto, 1(3), January.

Bryant, D, 1997, Last Frontier Forests: Ecosystems and Economies on the Edge, World Resource Institute, Washington.

Buffie, R. (1992), 'On the conditions of export-led growth', Canadian Journal of Economics 211-225.

Burawoy, M. (1999), 'The Great Involution: Russia's Response to the Market', Dept. of Sodology, Berkeley, University of California.

Burnside, Craig, and David Dollar, 1997, "Aid, Policies, and Growth." Policy Research Working Paper 1777, World Bank, Policy Research Department, Washington DC.

Buzan, Barry, 1991, The Idea of the State and National Security in N. Glazer and D.P Moynihan (eds.), Perspectives on world politics, 2nd Edition London, Routledge.

Cable, V. (1995), 'The Diminished Nation-State: A Study in the Loss of Economic Power', Daedalus 124 (2), Spring, 23-53.

Cadene, P. and Holmstrom M. (eds.) (1998), Decentralised Production in India: Industrial Districts, Flexible Specialisation and Employment, New Delhi, London, Sage.

Caroline Thomas, 2007, sociologies of Disability and Illness, Contested Ideas in Disability studies and Medical Sociology, Palgrave; Macmillan.

Castells, M. (2000), The Rise of the Network Society, Blackwell, Oxford.

Castells, M., 1998, End of Millennium, Oxford, Blackwell.

Castells, M. (1989), The Informational City, Oxford, Blackwell.

Cecchi, C. (2001), 'Rural Development and Local Systems: the Case of Maremma Rural District', Ph.D. Thesis, University of Wales, Cardiff.

Chabal, P. and Daloz, J. (1999), Africa Works: disorder as political instrument, Oxford, James Currey for IAI.

Chen, E. and Kwan, C. (eds.) (1997), Asia's Borderless Economy: the emergence of sub regional zones, St Leonards, NSW, Allen and Unwin.

Cilliers, J. (1999), 'Regional African Peacekeeping Capacity: mythical construct or essential tool?', African Security Review 8(4), 20-33.

Cilliers, J. and Mason, P. (eds.) (1999), Peace, Profit or Plunder? The privatization of security in war-torn African societies, Halfway House, ISS.

Clapham, C. (1996), Africa and the International System: the politics of state survival, Cambridge, UK, Cambridge University Press.

Clapham, C. (ed.) (1998), African Guerillas, Oxford, James Currey.

Clemens, Walter C. (1998), Dynamics of International Relations: conflict and mutual gain in an era of global interdependence, Lanham, Rowman and Littlefield.

Cliffe, L. (ed.) (1999), Special Issue: Complex Political Emergencies, Third World Quarterly 20(1), March, I-256.

Cobus de Swardt Kraus, 2000, Globalisation for Sale: An Analysis of the Interdynamics of Globalisation, valorisation and Marginalisation. Kagan International.

Cohen, David, 1998, 'The wealth of the world and the poverty of Nations, Cambridge. MIT Press.

Collier, Paul, Anke Hoeffler, Catherine Pattillo, 2001, Flight Capital as a Portfolio choice, The world Bank Economic Review, Vol. 15, No. I.

Connor, W. (1994), Ethnonationalism: The Quest for Understanding, Princeton, NJ: Princeton University Press.

Correa, G. and Medina, A. (1999), 'Los grandes perdedores del TLC: campo, salariosy emple'. Proceso Mexico, 29 Agosto.

Court, Julius (1999), 'Development Research: Directions for a New Century', UNU Work in Progress 16 (1), Winter, 1-20.

Cox, Robert W. (1999), 'Civil Society at the Turn of the Millennium: prospects for an alternative world order'. Review of International Studies 25 (1), January, 3-28.

Crawford, Darryl (2000), 'Chinese Capitalism: cultures, the Southeast Asian region and economic globalisation', Third World Quarterly 21 (1), February, 69-86.

Crawford, N. and Audie, K. (eds.) (1999) How Sanctions Work: Lessons from South Africa. London, Macmillan.

Dam, K.W., 1982, 'The Rules of Game, Reform and Evaluation in the International Monetary System Chicago.

Daves, D.W., and L.R. Christensen, 1980, "The Relative Efficiency of Public and Private Firms in a Competitive Environment: The Case of Canadian Railroads," Journal of Political Economy 88 (4): 958-76.

Davis R. Donald and David E Weinstein, Bones, Bombs, and Break Points: The Geography of Economic activity, The American Economic Review.

Dhagamwar, V. (1992), 'The Disadvantaged and the Law', in B. Harris, S. Guhan and R Cassen (eds.), Paverty in India: Research and Policy, New Delhi, Oxford University Press.

Dicklitch, S. (1998), The Elusive Promise of NGOs in Africa: lessons from Uganda, London, Macmillan.

Dickson, A.K. (1997), Development and International Relations: A Critical Introduction Cambridge, UK, Polity.

Dornbusch, R. (1992), 'The case for trade liberalisation in developing countries', Journal of Economic Perspectives Winter, 69-85.

Douglas S. Massey, 2002, Patterns and Processes of International Migration in the 21st Century, Johannesburg, South Africa.

Dreze, Jean, Amartya Sen, and Athar Hussain, eds. 1995. The Political Economy of Hunger: Selected Essays, New York, Oxford University Press.

Duffield, M. (1999), 'Globalisation and War Economies: Promoting order or the Return of History?', Fletcher Forum of World Affairs 23(2), Fall, 21-36.

Dunn, J. (ed.) (1995), Contemporary Crisis of the Nation State? Oxford, England, Blackwell.

Dunn, K. and Shaw, T. (eds.) (2001), Africa's Challenge to International Relations Theory, London, Macmillan.

Dunning, J. (1998), 'Globalisation and the New Geography of Foreign Direct Investment', in N. Woods (ed.), Globalisation, Special Issue, Oxford Development Studies, 26, 1, pp. 47-70.

Economic and Political Weekly, India.

Eichengreen, B., 1998, Globalising Capital : A History of the International Monetary system, Princeton, Princeton University Press.

Esping-Andersen, G. and van Kersbergen, K. (1992), 'Contemporary Research on Social Democracy', Annual Review of Sociology 18, 187-208.

Esposito, John, 1984, Islam and Politics, Syracruse University Press, New York.

Falk, R., 1993, "The making of Global Citizenship", In Global visions: Beyond the New world order, eds. J. Brecher, J. Childs and J. Cutler, Boston, South End Press.

FAO, 1997.

Feenstra, R.C. and Rose, A.K. (1997), 'Putting things in Order: Patterns of Trade Dynamics and Growth', NBER Working Paper No. 5975, March.

Ferguson, C. (1999), Global Social Policy Principles: Human Rights and Social Justice, Social Development Department, Department for International Development, London.

Feyzioglu, Tarhan, Vinaya Swaroop, and Min Zhu, 1997, "Foreign Aid's Impact on Public Spending," Policy Research Working Paper 1610. World Bank, Policy Research Department, Public Economics Division, Washington DC.

Fischer Taschenbuch (1996), Der Fishcher Weltalmanch, 1997 (Frankfurt: Fischer Taschenbuch).

FitzGerald, E.V.K. and Stewart F. (eds.) (1997) War, Economy and Society, Special Issue, Oxford Development Studies, 25, 1.

Foucault, M. (1990), The History of Sexuality, NY, Vintage Books.

Fowler, C. and Mooney, P.R. (1990), The threatened gene: food, politics and the loss of genetic diversity, Cambridge, Lutterworth.

French, R. (2000), 'Coping with Ecological Globalisation', In L.R. Brown (ed.) State of the World 2000, NY, W.W. Norton, 184-202

Friedman, Milton, 2002, Capitalism and Freedom, University of Chicago Press.

Gardner, G. (1996), 'Die Erhaltung Landwirtschafttlicher Ressourcen', in Worldwatch Institute Report: Zur Lage der Welt, 1996 (Frankfurt: Worldwatch Institute) : IO4-132.

Gardner, G. and Halweil, B. (2000), 'Nourishing the Underfed and Overfed'. In L.R. Brown (ed.) State of the World, NY, W.W. Norton, 59-78.

Gazcón, F. (1999), 'La inversión Extranjera Fortalece el empleo, asegura la Secofi', El Financiero, 26 agosto.

Gelb, S. (1997), 'SouthAfrica's Post-Apartheid Political Economy', In L.A. Swatuk and D.R. Black (eds.) Bridging the Rift: The New South Africa in Africa, Boulder, Westview Press.

Gelb, S. and Manning, C. (1998), 'Spatial Development Initiatives: unlocking economic potential', Development Southern Africa 15(5), Summer, 717-942.

Gellner, E., 1992. 'From the ruins of the Great contest: Civil Society, Nationalism and Islam, Times Literary supplement.

George, S. (forthcoming) 'Globalising Rights', in M.J. Gibney (ed.), Globalising Rights: the Oxford Annesty Lectures, Oxford, Oxford University Press.

Germain, R. (ed.) (2000), Globalisation and its Critics: perspectives from political economy, London, Macmillan.

Gibb, R. (1998), 'Southern Africa in Transition: Prospects and Possibilities Facing Regional integration'. Journal of Modern African Studies 36 (2) June, 287-306.

Gidden, A., 2000, Runway World : How Globalisation is reshaphing our Lives, London, Profile Books, 2001.

Giddens, A. (1998), The Third Way: the renewal of social democracy, Cambridge, Polity.

Gilbert, Milton, 1980, Quest for Monetary order, The Gold Dollar system and its Aftermath, New York, John Wiley.

Gill, S. (1996), 'Globalisation, Democratisation and the Politics of Indifference', In J.H. Mittelman (ed.) Globalisation: Critical Reflections. Boulder and London, Lynne Rienner Publishers, 205-228.

Gills, S. Dong-sook 2007 ed. (Authony Mcgrew and Nana, K. Poku) in Globalisation Development and Human Security, Polity, Cambridge.

Gills, B. (ed.) (1997), Special Issue: Globalisation and the Politics of Resistance. New Political Economy 2(1), March, 5-200.

Godson, R. and P. Williams (1997) 'Strenthening Co-operation Against Transsoverign Crime', ch. 5 in R. Godson, R Schultz and G Quester (eds), Security Studies for the Twenty-first Century, Washington/ London, Brassey's.

Goldin, Claudia, 1994, The Regulated Economy, A Historical Approach to Political Economy, University of Chicago Press.

Goldsmith, E. (1997) 'Development as Colonialism', The Ecologist 27, 69-76.

Goldsmith, E. (1997) 'Can the Environment Survive the Global Economy?', The Ecologist 27, 242-248.

Goodman, D. and Watts M. (1994), 'Reconfiguring the Rural or Fording the Divide: Capitalist Restructuring and the Global Agro-Food System', Journal of Peasant Studies, 22, 1, pp. 1-49.

Goodman, R., White G. and Kwon H. (1998), The East Asian Welfare Model: Welfare Orientalism and the State, London, Routledge.

Gourevitch, Philip (1999), We wish to inform you that tomorrow we will be killed with our families: stories from Rwanda, NY, Picador.

Gray, J. (1998), False Dawn: the Delusions of Global Capitalism, London, Granta.

Gray, J., 1998, False Dawn: The Delusion of Global capitalism London, Granta.

Greenwald, Bruce, and Joseph, E. Stiglitz, 1986, "Eternalities in Economies with Imperfect Information and Incomplete Markets," Quarterly Journal of Economics 101 (3): 229-64.

Greenwald, Bruce, and Joseph, E. Stiglitz, 1988, "Pareto Inefficiency of Market Economies: Search and Efficiency Wage Models," American Economic Association Papers and Proceedings 78: 351-5.

Griffin, Keith, 2001, Global futures shaping Globalisation Zed Books, London.

Griffith, B., 2001, The Gardens of their Dreams : Desertification and culture in World History, Nova Scotia, London and New York, Fernwood Publishing and Zed Books.

Grugel, J. and Hout, W. (eds.) (1999), Regionalism Across the North-South Divide: State strategies and globalisation. London, Routledge.

Guehenno, J. (1995), The End of the Nation State, Translated by Victoria Elliot, Minneapolis, MN.

Guhan, S. (1994) 'Social Security Options for Developing Countries', International Labour Review, 133, 1, pp. 35-53.

Hale, A. (ed.) (1999), Trade Myths and Gender Reality: Trade Liberalisation and Women's Lives, Uppsala, Global Publications Foundation.

Hampton, M. (1996), 'Where Currents Meet: the Offshore Interface between Corruption, Offshore Financial Centres and Economic Development', in B. Harriss-wpite and G. White (eds.).

Harrison, A. (1996), 'Openness and growth: A time-series, cross-country analysis for developing countries', NBER Working Paper No. 5221, May.

Harriss-White, B. and Hoffenberg R. (eds.) (1994), Food: Multidisciplinary Perspectives, Oxford/London, Blackwell.

Harriss-White, B. and White G. (eds.) (1996), Liberalisation and the New Corruption, Special Issue, Bulletin of the Institute of Development Studies, 27, 2.

Harvey, D. (1989), The Condition of Postmodernity, Cambridge, MA.: Basil Blackwell.

Hashim, Y., and Meagher, K. (1999), 'Cross Border Trade and the Parallel Currency Market-Trade and Finance in the Context of Structural Adjustment', Research Report 113, Uppsala, Nordiska Africa Institutet.

Haynes, S., 1999, Religion, Globalisation and Political culture in the Third World, New York, St. Martins Press.

Held, D. and A. Mcgrew, 1993 "Globalisation and the Liberal Democratic State," Government and opposition.

Held, D., McGrew, A., Goldblatt D. and Perraton J. (1999), Global Transformations: Politics, Economics and Culture, Stanford, Stanford University Press.

Helena, Hodge, Merrifield, Gorelick, 2000, Bringing the food economy Home, The Social, ecological and economic benefits of local food, International society for Ecology and culture.

Hellman, Thomas, Kevin Murdock, and Joseph Stiglitz, 1997, "Financial Restraint: Towards a New Paradigm." Stanford Graduate School of Business Research Paper, Stanford, California.

Helmich, H. and Smillie, I. (eds.) (1999), Stakeholders: Government-NGG partnerships for international development, London, Earthscan.

Hensman, R. (1999), 'How to Support the Rights of Women Workers in the Context of Trade Liberalisation in India', in A. Hale (ed.), Trade Myths and Gehder Reality, Uppsala, Global Publications Foundation, pp. 71-88.

Hettne, B. and Soderbaum, F. (eds.) (1998), Special Issue: the New Regionalism, Politeia, 17 (3), 1-142.

Hettne, B., Inotai, A. and Sunkel, O. (eds.) (1999) Globalism and the New Regionalism, London, Macmillan for UNUIWIDER.

Higgott, R. (2000), 'Global Governance and the Anti-Politics of the Post-Washington Consensus', ESRC Centre for Globalisation and Regulation, Warwick University.

Hirst, P. and Thompson, G. (1996), Globalisation in Question. Cambridge, England, Polity Press.

HLABSD (High-Level Advisory Board on Sustainable Development, of the United Nations Secretary General) (1997), Critical Issues and Policies, for Sustainable Development: Energy, Water and Transport (New York, HLABSD).

Holden, B. (ed.) (2000), Global Democracy: Key debates. London, Routledge.

Holton, R., 1998, Globalisation and the Nation state, London, Macmillan.

Hoogvelt, A., 1997, Globalisation and the post colonial world: The New political Economy of Development, London, Macmillan.

Horseman, M. and Marshall, A. (1994), After the Nation State, London, Harper Collins.

Howe, H. (1998), 'Private Security Forces and African Stability: the case of Executive Outcomes', Journal of Modern African Studies 36(2), June, 307-331.

Hulme, D. and Edwards, M. (eds.) (1997), NGOs, States and Donors: too close for comfort? London, Macmillan for SCF.

Huntington, S. (1996), 'The West unique, not universal', Foreign Affairs 75 (6), 28-46.

Huntington, S., 1997, The clash of civilisation and the Remaking of world order, London, Simon and Schuster.

ILO Reports, 1995-98.

ILO, 1994.

IMF Survey, 1990-2000.

International Labour Office (1999), Decent Work, International Labour Conference, 87th Session: Report of the Director-General, Geneva, ILO.

Jackson, C. and Pearson R. (eds.) (1999), Feminist Visions of Development: Gender Analysis and Policy, London, Routledge.

Jackson, K.T. (1985), Crabgrass Frontier: The Suburbanisation of the United States, NY, Oxford University Press.

Jencks, C. (1996), What is Post-Modernism?, London, Academy Group.

Johnson, Harry G. (1968), 'Economic development and international trade', In R.E. Caves and H.G. Johnson (eds.) Readings in International Economics, NY, R.D. Irwin, 281-299.

Juárez Sánchez, L. (1999) 'Neoliberalismo y salario', Trabajadores, Universidad Obrera de México, Julio-Agosto.

Juárez Sánchez, L. (1999) Los trabajadores de México: entre los más pobres del mundo, Universidad Obrera de México, mimeo, septiembre.

Jung, C. and Shapiro, I. (1995), 'South Africa's Negotiated Transition: Democracy, Opposition and the New Constitutional Order', Politics and Society 23 (3), September, 269-308.

Kamat, S. (1999), 'NGOs as a New State Formation in the Global Economy', Exchanges, 27, December, pp. 3-12.

Kaplan, R. (1994), 'The Coming Anarchy', Atlantic Monthly 273(2), February, 44-75.

Kapstein, E. (1991/92), 'We are US: the myth of the multinational', The National Interest 26, 55-62.

Karliner, J. (1997), The Corporate Planet: Ecology and Politics in the Age of Globalisation. San Franscisco, Sierra Club Books.

Kasfir, N. (ed.) (1998), 'Special Issue on Civil Society and Democracy in Africa: critical perspectives', Commonwealth and Comparative Politics 36(2), July, 1-149.

Keck, M., Sikkink, K. (1998), Activists beyond Borders: advocacy networks in international politics. Ithaca, NY, Cornell University Press.

Kennedy, P. (1993), Preparing for the Twenty-First Century, NY, Random House.

Kennedy, P. (1999), 'Sub-Saharan Africa's Current Plight and the Threat or Promise of Globalisation?', Global Society 13(4), October, 441-466.

Kenny, C. and Moss, T. (1998), 'Stock Markets in Africa: emerging lions or white elephants?', World Development 26(5), May, 829-843.

Kepel, G, 1984, The War of Muslim minds: Islam and the West, Bel knop Press, London.

Kimbrell, A. (1998), 'Why Biotechnology and High-Tech Agriculture Cannot Feed the World', The Ecologist 28 (5), 294-298.

Kingma, K. (ed.) (2000), The Impact of Demobilisation in Sub-Saharan Africa. London, Macmillan for BICC.

Kleinberg, R. and Clark, J. (eds.) (2000), Economic Liberalisation. Democratisation and Civil Society in the Developing World, London, Macmillan.

Kohler, Miles, 1990, 'Orthodoxy and its Alternatives Explaining Approaches to Stabilisation and adjustment, in Joan Nelson (ed.). Economic crisis and policy choices: The Politics of adjustment in the Third World, Princeton University Press.

Korten, David, 1995, 'When corporations rule the world, Berret-Koehler Publishers, Cambridge.

Kotthoff, Jost and Detlev, Gabel, 2008, 'Outsourcing' Munich.

Kuemmerale, Walter, 1999, 'The Drivers of FDI into Research and Development : An empirical Investigation, Journal of International Business studies, Vol. 30, No.1 (1st Quarter, 1999).

Kumar, A. (1999), The Black Economy in India, New Delhi, Penguin.

Kumar, Rajendra, Failure of the Doha Round -Looking back to look ahead, South, Asian Politics, January, No. 9.

Kurien V. Mathew, AOA, Trips and the Third world Agriculture Mainstream, Dec., 22-28.

Lamberton, Donald, 2002, Managing Global I.B Tauris Publishers, New York.

Lasch, S. and Urry, J. (1999), Economies of Signs and Space, 2nd edn.. London, Sage.

Latham, P. (2001), The Captive Local State, Nottingham, Spokesman Books.

Lawrence, R., 1993, 'Futures for the world Trading system: Implications for Developing countries, in M. Agosin and D. Tussie (eds.), Trade and Growth New Dilemmas in trade policy, London, Macmillan.

Lawson, R and J. Gwartney, 1999, Economic Freedom of the world, Interim Report Vancouver, Fraser Institute.

Lechner, F. and Boli, J. (ed.) (2000), The Globalisation Reader, Oxford, UK, Blackwell.

Leftwich, A., 1993, 'Governance, Democracy and Development in the Third World, Third world Quarterly, 14 (3).

Lograin, P. (2000), 'Against Globophobia', Prospect, 52, pp. 30-5.

Lehman, K. and Krebs, A. (1996), 'Control of World's Food Supply', In J. Mander and E. Goldsmith (eds.) The Case Against the Global Economy, San Francisco, Sierra Club Books, 122-130.

Lewis, T. (1997), Divided Highways, NY, Penguin Putnam.

Leys, (ed.) Barbara Harris White, 2002, Globalisation and Insecurity, Palgrave.

Leys, C. (2001), Market Driven Politics: Global Economic Forces, National politics and Public Services in Britain, London, Verso.

Lindberg, S. and Sverrisson, A. (eds.) (1997), Social Movements in Development: the challenge of globalisation and democratisation. London, Macmillan.

Lindert H. Peter and Geoffrey G. Williamson, 2001, Does Globalisation Make the world more unequal?, Chicago, University of Chicago Press.

Lipschutz, R. and Mayer, J. (1996), Global Civil Society and Global Environmental Governance, Albany, NT, SUNY Press.

Llosa, M.V., 2000, 'The Culture of Liberty', single XXI Lecture to the Inter American Development Bank, Washington.

Logan, Ikbolajeh, 2002, Globalisation and the Third world State, London, Ashgate.

Lombarg, Bjorn, 2001, 'The Sckeptical Environmentalist, Cambridge University Press.

Low, L. Andra, 2001 A study of Two-step Spinoffs.

Luttwalk, E. (1998), Turbo Capitalism: Winners and Losers in the Global Economy, NY, Harper Collins.

Luttwalk, E., 'Why Slavery Persists," Times Literary supplement, 26 Nov. 1999.

MacFarlane, S. Neil (1999), 'Doing Good, Doing Wrong', International Journal LIV(4), Autumn, 537-561.

McLean, S. and Shaw, T. (1996), 'Civil Society and Political Economy in Contemporary Africa: what prospects for sustainable democracy?'. Journal of Contemporary African Studies,14 (2), 247-264.

Maddison, A., 2001, 'Growth and Interaction in the world Economy, The AEI Press, Washington DC.

Mander, J. and Goldsmith, E. (ed.) (1996), The Case Against the Global Economy, San Francisco, Sierra Club Books.

Marchand, M., Boas, M. and Shaw, T. (1999), 'The Political Economy of New Regionalisms', Third World Quarterly 20(5), October, 897-910.

Marcuse, P and Van Kempen, 2000 ed. Globalising cities: A new spatial order, Blackwell Publishers.

Martin-Sala, Xavier, 2002, The Disturbing rise of Global Income Inequality, Discussion Papers, 0102-44, Columbia University, Dept. of Economics.

Marx, K. (1976), Genesis of Capital, Moscow, Progress Publishing House.

Mathews, J. (1997), 'Power Shift', Foreign Affairs 75, 50-66.

Mbeki, Moeletsi (1998), 'The African Renaissance', South African Yearbook of International Affairs 1998-09. Johannesburg, South African Institute of International Affairs, 209-217.

McCarthy, C. (1996), 'Regional Integration: part of the solution or part of the problem?', In S. Ellis (ed.) Africa Now: people. policies and institutions, London, James Currey, 211-231.

Meagher, K. (1995), 'Crisis, Informalisation and the Urban Informal Sector in Sub-Saharan Africa', Development and Change, 26, 2.

Meagher, K. (1999), 'Globalisation through the Back Door: Adjustment, Globalisation and Cross-Border Trade in West Africa', Paper at the Conference on Structural Adjustment and Social and Economic Change in Sub-Saharan Africa, Centre for

Development Studies, Copenhagen.

Meher, R. (1999), 'Interstate Disparities in Levels of Development', Review of Development and Change, 4, 2, pp. 198-224.

Mendelson, J. (1998), 'Roundup: The World's Biggest-Selling Herbicide', The Ecologist 28. (5), 270-275.

Menotti, V. (1998), 'Globalisation and the Acceleration of the Forest Destruction Since Rio', The Ecologist 28, 354-362.

Middendorf, G., Skladany, M., Ransom, E. and Busch, L. (1998), 'New Agricultural Biotechnologies: The Struggle for Democratic Choice', Monthly Review 50, 85-97.

Mittleman, J.H. (ed.) 1996, Globalisation: Critical Reflections, London, Lynne Rienner.

Monbiot, G. (2000), Captive State: the Corporate Takeover of Britain, Basingstoke, Palgrave Press.

Murphy, C. (ed.) (2000), Egalitarian Social Movements in Response to Globalisation, London, Macmillan.

Murphy, Craig N., 1994, International organisation and Industrial change: Global Governance since 1850, Cambridge: Polity.

Nayyar, Deepak, 2002, Governing Globalisation, Oxford University Press, New Delhi.

Nel, P. and McGowan, P. (eds.) (1999), Power, Wealth and Global Order: an international relations textbook for Africa, Cape Town, UCT Press for FGD.

Norberg-Hodge, Helena (1991) Ancient futures: Learning from Ladakh, San Francisco, Sierra Club Books.

Ohmae, K. (1990), The Borderless World: Power and Strategy in the Interlinked Economy NY, Harper Business.

Ohmae, K. (1995), The End of Nation States: the Rise of Regional Economies, New York, Free Press.

Ohmae, K. (1999), The Borderless World, NY, Harper Collins.

Oltersdorf and Weingartner, 1996, A Programme to end Hunger, Bonn.

O'Neill, O. (1994), 'Hunger, Needs and Rights', pp. 217-33 in Harriss-White and Hoffenberg (eds.).

Oppermann, M. 1998, 'Introduction to sex Tourism and prostitution, Aspects of Leisure Recreation and work, ed. M. Oppermann, New York, cognizant Communication Corporation.

Ottaway, M. (1999), 'Amca', Foreign Policy 114, Spring, 13-25.

Owusu, M. (1992), 'Democracy and Africa - A View from the Village', The Journal of Modern African Studies 30 (3), 369-96.

Pack, H., and J.R. Pack, 1990, "Is Foreign Aid Fungible? The Case of Indonesia, "Economic Journal 100 (March), 188-94.

Pack, H., and J.R. Pack, 1993, "Foreign Aid and the Question of Fungibility," Review of Economics and Statistics 75 (May), 258-65.

Paris, E., 2001, Long Shadows: Truth, Lies, and History, London, Bloomsbury.

Payne, A. (1998), 'The New Political Economy of Area Studies', Millennium 27(2), 253-273.

Payne, A. (1999), 'Reframing the Global Politics of Development', Journal of International Relations and Development 2(4), December, 369-379.

Porter, M. (1990), 'Dónde radica la ventaja competitiva de las naciones?', Harvard-Deusto Business Review 4' trimester, 3-26.

Prabhu, S. (1997), 'Promotional and Protective Social Security During Economic Reforms', Review of Development and Change, 11, 1, pp. 24-51.

Pretty, Jules, 1998, The Living Land : Agriculture, Food and community Regeneration in Rural Europe, London Earthscan.

Quadir, E, MacLean, S. and Shaw, T. (1999), Pluralisms and the Changing Global Political Economy: ethnicities in crises of governance in Asia and Africa, Halifax, Ford Project, Dalhousie University.

Rahnema, M. and Bawtree, V. (1997), The Post-Development Reader, London, Zed.

Reich, Robert, 1983, The Next American Frontier.

Reno, W. (1998), Warlord Politics and African States, Boulder, Co, Lynne Rienner.

Richards, P. (1999), Fighting for the Rain Forest: war, youth and resources in Sierra Leone, Oxford, James Currey for IAI.

Rifkin, J., (1996), 'New Technology and the End of Jobs', In E. Goldsmith and J. Mander (eds.) The Case Against the Global Economy, San Francisco, Sierra Club.

Rifkin, J., 1996, Unstable future for work, Arizona, Daily Sun.

Rinehart, J. (1995), 'The Ideology of Competitiveness', Monthly Review 47 (5), October, 14-23.

Ritzer, G. 1993, The Mcdonaldisation of society, London, Sage.

Robertson, R., 1992, Globalisation: Social Theory and Global Culture, London, Sage.

Robertson, R.T., 1986, The Making of the Modern World, London, Zed Books.

Rodrik, D. and Rodriquez, F. (1999), 'Trade policy and economic growth: A sceptics guide to the cross-national evidence', NBER Working Paper No. 7081, April.

Rodrik, Dani, 1999, 'The new Global Economy and Developing countries: Making openness work, Washington DC.

Roy, R.(1996), 'State Failure in India: Political-Fiscal Implications of the Black Economy', pp. 22-31 in Harriss-White and White (eds.).

Runnymede Trust., 2000, "The future of the Multi Ethnic Britain", Guardian Weekly, 19-25 October.

Rushdie. S, 1999, 'A Culture of Easy Criticism, Age, 10 March, 1999.

Sachs, J. and Warner, A. (1995), 'Economic Reform and the process of Global Integration', Brookings Paper on Economic Activity, 1-118.

Sachs, W (1992) For the Love of the Automobile: Looking Back into the History of Our Desires, Berkeley, University of California Press.

Sachs, W. (ed.) (1995), Development Dictionary: A Guide to Knowledge and Power, London, Zed.

Salcedo R. And A. Torres, 2004, Gated Communities in Santiago, International Journal of Urban and Regional Research 28 (1).

Sanchez, M and Y Pedrazzini; 1996, The Power of Identity: The Information Age, Economy society and culture.

Sappington, David, and Joseph E. Stiglitz, 1987. "Privatisation, Information, and Incentives," Journal of Policy Analysis and Management 6: 567-82.

Sartori, G. (1991), 'Rethinking Democracy: Bad Polity and Bad Politics', International Social Science Journal (August), 129.

Sassen, S. (1998), Globalisation and its Discontents: Essays on the

New Morality of People and Money, NY, New York Press.

Sassen, S., 1991, The Global city: New York, London, Tokyo, Princeton, Princeton University Press.

Sassen, S., 'Home Truths : Guardian Weekly, 27 April, 3 May, 2000.

Saxenien, A. L. (1994), Regional Advantage: Culture and Competition in Silicon Valley and Route 128, Cambridge, MA, Harvard University Press.

Schechter, M. (ed.) (1999), The Revival of Civil Society: Global and Comparative Perspectives, London, Macmillan.

Schmidt, V. (1995), 'The New World Order, Incorporated: The Rise of Business and Decline of the Nation-State', Daedalus 124 (2) Spring, 75-106.

Schmitter, P.C. (1995), 'Democracy's Future: More Liberal, Preliberal, or Postliberal?', Journal of Democracy 6 (1), 15-22.

Schmitz, H. and K. Nadvi (eds.) (1999), Industrial Clusters in Developing Countries, Special Issue, World Development, 27, 9.

Scholte, J. (2000) Globalisation: A Critical Introduction, London: Macmillan.

Schott, Jeffrey, 1989, Free Trade Areas and US Trade Policy, Peterson Institute.

Schuurman, F. (2000) 'Paradigms Lost, Paradigms Regained? Development Studies in the twenty-first century', Third World Quarterly 21(1), February, 7-20.

Scott. J.C., 1999, Seeing like a state: How certain Schemes to improve the Human Condition Have Failed, New Haven, Yale University Press.

Sedlak, J. Andrea and D. Broadhurst,1996,Third National Incidence study of Child abuse and Neglect.

Shaw, T,. MacLean, S. (1999), 'The Emergence of Regional Civil Society: contributions to a new human security agenda'. In Ho-Won Jeong, (ed.) The New Agenda for Peace Research. Aldershot, Ashgate, 289-308.

Shaw, T. (1998), 'African Renaissance/African Alliance: Towards new regionalisms and new realism in the Great Lakes at the start of the twenty-first century', Politeia 17(3), 60-74.

Shaw, T. (1999) 'Globalisations and Conflicts in Africa: prospects for human security and development in the new millennium',

ACCORD, Conflict Trends 3, 20-22.

Shaw, T. (2000) 'Overview: global/local- states, companies and civil societies', In K. Stiles (ed.) Global Institutions and Local Empowerment, 1-8.

Shaw, T. (2000) 'Conflicts in Africa at the Turn of the Century: more of the same?'. In Albert Legault (ed.) Conflicts in the World, 1999-2000, Quebec: IQHEI, Laval University.

Shaw, T. and Nyango'ro, J. (1999), 'Conclusion: African Foreign Policies and the Next Millennium: alternative perspectives, practices and possibilities', In S. Wright (ed.) African Foreign Policies. Boulder, CO, Westview Press, 237-248.

Shaw, T. and Nyango'ro, J. (2000), 'African Renaissance in the New Millennium? From Anarchy to Emerging Markets?', In R. Stubbs and G. Underhill (eds.) Political Economy and the Changing Global Order, 275-284.

Shaw, T. and Schnabel, A. (1999), 'Human (In) Security in Africa: prospects for good governance in the twenty-first century', UNU Work in Progress 15(3), Summer, 16-18.

Shaw, T. van der Westhuizen, J. (1999), 'Towards a Political Economy of Trade in Africa: states, companies and civil societies', In B. Hocking and S. McGuire (eds.) Trade Politics, London, Routledge,

Shearer, D. (1999), 'Outsourcing War', Foreign Policy 112, Fall: 68-81.

Shiva Vandana, 2005, Earth Democracy, Justice, Sustainability and Peace, South End press.

Shiva, V. (1991), The Violence of the Green Revolution: Third World Agriculture, Ecology and Politics, London, Zed Books.

Shiva, V. (1993), Monocultures of the Mind, London, Zed Press.

Shiva, Vandana (2000), Stolen Harvest: The Hijacking of the Global Food Supply, Cambridge, MA, South End Press.

Short, R. John, 2000, Global Dimensions Space, place and the contemporary World, Reaktion Books.

Silbert, M and A. Pines, 1981, Sexual Child Abuse as an antecedent to Prostitution child Abuse and Neglect, 5.

Silbert, M. and A.M Pines, 1982, Entrance into Prostitution, Youth and Society 13(4).

Silver, B. and Arrighi, G. (2000), 'Workers North and South', in L. Panitch and C. Leys (eds.), Working Classes: Global Realities,

Socialist Register 2001, London, Merlin Press.

Simai, M., 1994, The Future of Global Governance, Washington, DC, United States Institute of Peace.

Sinclair R. Mark, 1994, An objective cyclone climatology for the southern Hemisphere, National Institution Wellington, New Zealand.

Sjolander, C. (1996), 'The rhetoric of globalisation: what's in a wor(l)d?',. International Journal 51, 603-616.

Slovic, Paul, Mark Layman, and James H. Flynn, 1993, Perceived Risk, Trust, and Nuclear Waste: Lessons from Yucca Mountain. Durham, NC., Puke University Press.

Smillie, I., Lansan, G. and Hazelton, R. (2000), The Heart of the Matter: Sierra Leone, diamonds and human security, Ottawa, Partnership Africa Canada.

Snooks, G.D., 1996, The Dynamic Society, Exploring the source of Global change, London and New York, Routledge.

Soja, E.W. (1989), Postmodern Geographies: The Reassertion of Space in Critical Social Theory, NY, Verso.

Spears, I. (1999) 'Angola's Elusive Peace: the collapse of the Lusaka Accord', International Journal LIV(4), Autumn, 562-581.

Special Issue on Africa's Wars (1999), Current History 98(628), May, 195-241.

Srinivisan, T.N., 2011, Utilisation of labour in South Asia, working paper.

Stalker, Peter, 1994, 'The work for stranger: A survey of International Labour Migration, ILO, Geneva.

Steinbrecher, R.A. and Mooney, P.R. (1998), 'Terminator Technology: The Threat to World Food Security', The Ecologist 28 (5), 276-279.

Stiglitz, J. (2000), 'What I Learned at the East Asian Crisis', The New Republic, 17 April.

Stiglitz, Joseph E., 1990, "The Economic Role of the State: Efficiency and Effectiveness," In Thomas P. Hardiman and Michael Mulreany, eds., Efficiency and Effectiveness, Dublin, Institute of Public Administration.

Stiglitz, Joseph E. 1994, Whither Socialism. Cambridge, Mass., MIT Press.

Stiglitz, Joseph E., 1996, "Some Lessons from the East Asian Miracle.," The World Bank Research Observer 11 (2): 151-78.

Stiglitz, Joseph E., 1997, "An Agenda for Development for the Twenty-First Century.," In Pleskovic, Boris, and Joseph E. Stiglitz, eds. Annual Bank Conference on Development Economics, 1997, The World Bank, Washington DC.

Stiglitz, Joseph E., and Mamou Uy., 1996, "Financial Markets, Public Policy, and the East Asian Miracle.," The World Bank Research Observer 11 (2): 249-76.

Stiles, K. (ed.) (2000), Global Institutions and Local Empowerment: competing theoretical perspectives, London, Macmillan.

Stubbs, R. and Underhill, G. (eds.) (2000) Political Economy and the Changing Global Order, Toronto, OUP, Second edition.

Suter, K., Little to be gained by returning to a mythical Nationalist Era, Australian, 1 May, 2001.

Tabbarah. Afif, 1988, Spirit of Islam, International Book Centre.

Taylor, Ian (2000), Public-Private Partnerships: lessons form the Maputo Development Corridor toll road DPRU, University of Cape Town.

Taylor, Lance, 1979, Macro Models for Developing Countries, New York, McGraw-Hill.

Teunissen, Jan Joost (ed.) (1996), Regionalism and the Global Economy: The rise of Africa, The Hague, FONDAD.

Thiesse, A.M., Inventing a National Identity, Le Monde Diplomatique, June 1999.

Tomlin, Brian et al. (eds.) (1998). To Walk without Fear: the global movement to ban landmines, Toronto, OUP.

Tomlinson, J., 1999, " Globalisation and its limits: Reports of the death of the National Economy are Greatly Exaggerated: In National Diversity and Global Capitalism, eds. S. Berger and R. Dore, New York, Cornell University Press.

Ufford, P.Q. van (1999), Trade and Traders: the Making of the Cattle Market in Benin, Amsterdam, Thela.

UN 1988-89, The Worlds Women; Trends and Statistics, New York, UN.

UN environment Program 1991, Report of The Global Assembly Of Women and the Environment, Nairobi, UN Environment Programme.

UN Industrial Development Organisation 1993, Global Report, 1993-94,. Vienna, UN.

UNDP (1994), Human Development Report, 1994, NY, OUP.

UNDP (1999), Human Development Report, 1999, NY, OUP.

UNDP 1995-99, World Development Reports: New York, Oxford University Press.

UNDP, 1996.

United Nations (1999), World Survey on the Role of Women in Development: Globalisation, Gender and Work, UN Department of Economic and Social Affairs, New York.

US Department of Defence (1998), Foreign Military Sales, Foreign Military Construction Sales and Military Assistance, DSCA, Washington.

US Department of Justice (1999), Overview of International Criminal Organisations, Drugs Enforcement Agency, Washington.

USEPA (US Environmental Protection Agency), 1987, Unfinished Business: A Comparative Assessment of Environmental Problems. Washington, DC.

Uvin, P. (1998), Aiding Violence: the development enterprise in Rwanda, West Hartford, Kumarian.

Vale, P. and Maseko, S. (1998), 'South Africa and the African Renaissance', International Affairs 74(2), April, 271-287.

Vale, P., Swatuk, L. and Oden, B. (eds.) (2001), Theory, Change and Southern Africa's Future, London, Macmillan.

Van Rooy, A. (1999), 'Civil Society and Global Change', Canadian Development Report, 1999, Ottawa, North-South Institute.

Van Walraven, K. (1999), The Pretence of Peace-keeping: ECOMOG, West Africa and Liberia (1990-1998), The Hague, NIIR, November.

Veltmeyer, Henry, 1997, 'Class and Identity: The Dynamics of new social Movements in Latin America, The Journal of Peasant studies, Vol. 25 No. 1.

Venables J. Anthony, 2001, Geography and International Inequalities : The impact of New Technologies, CEP Discussion Papers, 0507, Centre for Economic Performance, LSE.

Wacquant, L., Imprisoning the American Poor, Le Monde Diplomatique, Sep. 1998.

Wade, Robert. 'National Power, coercive liberalism and Global finance, in Robert Art and Robert Jervis (ed.), International Politics; Enduring Concepts and contemporary Issues (New York, Wesley Longman).

Walters, M. 1995, Globalisation, New York, Routledge.

Watts, M. (1992), 'Peasants and Flexible Accumulation in the Third World', Economic and Political Weekly, 25 July, pp. 90-7.

Weiss, T. (1999), Military-Civilian Interactions: Intervention in humanitarian Crises, Lanham, Rowman and Littlefield.

White, G. (ed.) (1988), Developmental States in East Asia, London, IDS/ Macmillan.

White, G. (ed.) (1993), The Political Analysis of Markets, Special Issue, Bulletin of the Institute of Development Studies, 24, 3.

White, G., Howell J. and Xiaoyuan S. (1996), In Search of Civil Society: Market Reform and Social Change in Contemporary China, Oxford/ London, Oxford University Press.

Wilfred, D. 1985, The IMF Policy Paradigm, New York, Princeton.

Williams, P. (1994), 'Transnational Criminal Organisations and International Security', Survival, 36, 1, pp. 96-123.

Williams, P. (ed.) (1999), Illegal Immigration and Commercial Sex: the New Slave Trade, London, Frank Cass.

Winters, L.A., 2004, Trade liberalisation and povetry. The Evidence so far, Journal of economic Literature, Vol. XLII.

Wolfensohn, J. (1999), 'A Proposal for a Comprehensive Development Frame work', World Bank, Washington.

Woods, N. (1998), 'Globalisation: Definitions, Debates and Implications', in N. Woods (ed.), Globalisation, Special Issue, Oxford Development Studies, 26, 1, pp. 5-16.

Woods, N., 2004, 'Globalisation: Definitions Debates and Implications, in N. wood (ed.) Globalisation, special Issue, Oxford, Development Studies.

World Development Report, 1995-2004.

World Bank (1981), Accelerated Development in SubSaharan Africa: an Agenda for Action, World Bank, Washington.

World Bank. 1993, The East Asian Miracle: Economic Growth and Public Policy, A Policy Research Report, New York, Oxford University Press.

World Bank, 1994, Adjustment in Africa: Reforms, Results, and the Road Ahead, A Policy Research Report, New York, Oxford University Press.

World Bank, 1997, Global Development Finance 1997, Washington, DC.

World Bank, 1997, Global Economic Prospects and the Developing Countries, Washington DC.

World Bank, 1997, World Development Report 1997, The State in a Changing World, New York, Oxford University Press.

World Investment Report, 1996.

Wright, S. (ed.) (1999), African Foreign Policies, Boulder, CO, Westview Press.

Wulf, G. (1998), Conventional Arms Transfers, Surplus Weapons and Small Arms, Bonn, International Centre for Conversion.

Yapa, J. (1993), 'What Are Improved, Seeds? An Epistemology of the Green Revolution', Economic Geography 69, 254-273.

Yapa, J. (1996), 'What Causes Poverty? A Postmodern View', Annals of the Association of American Geographers 86, 707-728.

Young, Katherine., 1996, 'Loyal wives, Virtuous Mother' Russian Life 39 (3).

Zartman, W. (ed.) (1995), Collapsed States: The Disintegration and Restoration of Legitimate Authority, Boulder and London, Lynne Rienner Publishers.

# Index

U



V